Are We Winning Yet?

Are We Winning Yet?

HOW WOMEN ARE CHANGING SPORTS AND SPORTS ARE CHANGING WOMEN

Mariah Burton Nelson

 RANDOM HOUSE · *New York*

Grateful acknowledgment is made to Meg Christian for
permission to quote five lines from the song lyrics,
"Ode to a Gym Teacher" by Meg Christian,
Thumbelina Records, 1974.
Reprinted by permission of the author.

Library of Congress Cataloging-in-Publication Data

Nelson, Mariah Burton.
    Are we winning yet? : how women are changing sports and
sports are changing women / by Mariah Burton Nelson.
        p.   cm.
    Includes bibliographical references (p.   ) and index.
    1. Sports for women. 2. Sports for women—Social aspects.
3. Femininity (Psychology) 4. Sex discrimination in sports.
I. Title.
GV709.N44   1991
796'.0194—dc20   90-42698

Manufactured in the United States of America

9 8 7 6 5 4 3 2

First Edition

Book design by Debby Jay

To my first team:
Mom, Dad, Carol, and Peter

Competition

I like to swim naked
I like to swim fast
swimming next to you I swim faster
shed more layers of flesh
learn your rhythms as well as my own
Each time I breathe I see you
breathe
stroke
breathe
stroke
and see you again
You can tell by my stroke that I need you
you can tell by my stroke
by the way that I breathe
that I need your stroke, your breath
that to be my best I need you
swimming beside me

—MBN

Acknowledgments

I AM BLESSED with many friends and colleagues who nurtured me and helped shape my ideas throughout the writing of this book. First I want to thank the athletes who generously offered their time, their feelings, and their thoughts. The women and men quoted in the book graciously invited me to watch them, participate with them, and talk with them, usually for hours at a stretch.

Coaches and athletic administrators were helpful. Sports scholars, too, were generous. They sent me copies of articles, referred me to other professors, and stimulated my thinking through lectures and long personal discussions. To all these people quoted and cited in this book, I offer my heartfelt thanks, in particular Cheryl Cole, Katie Donovan, Pat Griffin, Don Sabo, Carole Oglesby, Mimi Murray, and Lisa Rubarth. The Women's Sports Foundation, the Melpomene Institute, and the sports information departments of several universities were also helpful.

Felicia Eth, my literary agent, "discovered" me from a *Ms.* article I'd written and expertly guided me through the process of planning the book, writing the proposal, and choosing the right publisher. Then, throughout the research and writing phases, Felicia provided encouragement and assistance beyond the call of duty.

Charlotte Mayerson, my editor, carefully read chapters as

ACKNOWLEDGMENTS

I drafted them, wrote long, thoughtful letters in response, and cared enough to contemplate my book during her own tennis matches, and during conversations with her friends. I am grateful to her for asking tough questions, for answering naive questions, and for her playfulness and wisdom.

Several friends read drafts of individual chapters. Thanks to Carol Galbraith, Carole Grunberg, and Kate Cudlipp for their attentive feedback, and especially to Sue Carrington and Pat Lenihan for reading a draft of the entire book and offering suggestions.

Other friends believed in the book, sent me references, invited me to stay with them while I traveled, or otherwise offered support: Nancy Kass, Sean Tunis, Meredith Maran, Shelly Felt, Tres Schnell, Catherine Clinger, Cherie Barkey, Elisavietta Ritchie, Martha Nelson, Hugh Delehanty, Barbara Graham, Rich James, Rive Nestor, Michael O' Loughlin, and Kimberly Carter. I also thank Cheri Huber, whose spiritual training guides my writing and my life.

Despite long hours at the computer and with the tape recorder, I somehow always managed to play, so I offer thanks to my swimming, water polo–playing, cycling, bowling, and golfing friends for sharing with me not only the joys and welcome distraction of sports but also their perspectives on the topics I was writing about. Thanks in particular to Katie Gekker, my rowing doubles partner and friend.

I can't write a book about women athletes without thanking some of the women who helped me shape my sporting ethic and sustain the courage to pursue my sports dreams, including my early gaggle of girlfriends—Barbara Logan, Janne White, Carol Stone, Debra Babcock, Mary Jo Spratt, Jean and Joan Spinelli, Charlotte Francis, and Chris Penn. Thanks also to all my college teammates, especially Stephanie Erickson and Sonia Jarvis, and to my pals in the pros, in particular Lin Marie, Heidi Wayment, and Nancy Nerenberg. And I want to thank some wise and caring coaches: Dottie Bunting, Sandy Haddock, Sandy Pippin, Gay Coburn, Ken Morgan, Dottie McCrea, and Sue Rojcewicz.

My parents and siblings, to whom this book is dedicated, have served as informal playmates, coaches, trainers, and fans throughout my life, supporting my passion for both sports and writing. I am immensely grateful to each of them for their myriad expressions of love.

Leslie Fink shared in the conception, development, and editing of the book. She listened earnestly to every doubt and quandary, let me know when my thinking or writing had gone astray, and offered advice on technical, philosophical, and political decisions. She also kept me laughing at life's daily absurdities and loved me even when I was busy and grumpy. To my surprise, the process of writing this book was mostly tremendous fun, and Leslie's daily humor and support, along with the support of family, friends, and colleagues, had a lot to do with that.

Contents

Are We Winning Yet?

Playing with the Boys: An Introduction

*M*Y friend Leslie surprises her male golf partners. Rather than accept the handicap of the "ladies'" tees, she drives from the "men's" tees, slightly farther from the hole. "You're supposed to play from the ladies' tees," men will sometimes instruct her when play begins. She graciously declines, then calmly drives the ball 230 yards. That's far for a weekend golfer. It is also far "for a girl," the men comment, amazed.

At thirty-five, Leslie is enjoying golf because for the first time in her life she's dedicating herself to a sport, "learning about mastery and discipline," she says. She also likes golf because her success is not associated with other players' failure. "You don't have to try to beat anyone," she notes. "You just hit the ball as close to the pin as you can."

The story of women's sports is a story about mastery, and discipline, and handicaps. It is also a story about men, since sports are increasingly coed. And it's a story about the *way* women play sports: how they feel about teamwork, competition, and victory.

. . .

Women athletes used to practice and play in the privacy of the "women's gym," abiding by a sports ethic that was deliberately different from the win-at-all-costs mentality so prevalent in men's sports. Female physical educators in the first half of this century deemphasized competition, instead promoting skill, friendship, fair play, "high moral conduct," and participation for all.

In the early seventies, as sexism became a household word, women began to resent the lack of college scholarships, the limited travel schedules, the bake sales. They began to seek greater challenges, wider arenas in which to stretch, move, and run.

"We want what the men have," they said.

While these women crouched at the starting blocks, ready to sprint toward equal opportunity, many female coaches feared that the values they had been teaching for decades would be destroyed by the influx of money, prestige, and cutthroat competition that accompanied men's programs. The cautious women were labeled "old school," and their voices were drowned out by the equal rights advocates. In 1972, Congress passed the education amendments to the Civil Rights Act, and this included Title IX, which forbade sex discrimination in schools receiving federal funds. As a result of Title IX as well as the fitness movement of the eighties, more women and girls play sports, including highly competitive sports, than ever before.

What has this meant for women? They are getting pleasure out of sheer physical competence. They are taking physical risks, and having fun in the process. Women athletes now have female stars to model themselves after, and those stars are gaining more fame and fortune than would have been thought possible twenty years ago. Sports participation has given millions of women new self-confidence and has taken them to where they never were before—onto what used to be male turf.

In high school, 1.84 million girls play interscholastic sports, up from 294,000 in 1971.[1] Of college athletes, 34 percent are female. Women made up 36 percent of the 1988 U.S. Olympic teams. ESPN, the cable sports network, covers women as a matter of course, and *USA Today,* in a marked improvement over most daily papers, devotes between 15 and 20 percent of its sports pages to women. Although women still don't have their share (50+ percent) of scholarships, financial rewards, or media coverage, the gains are great.

Yet every gain includes a loss. As women's sports have become more popular and lucrative, men have claimed leadership positions. In 1982, the National Collegiate Athletic Association (NCAA) began offering televised women's championships, leading to the demise of the Association for Intercollegiate Athletics for Women (AIAW), the body of female teachers, coaches, administrators, and students that since 1971 had made decisions about women's college sports. The NCAA, which now governs both men's and women's sports, is predominantly male. More than half of all women's college teams are now coached by men.[2]

The executive director of the Women's Tennis Association is a man, as are the heads of the Ladies Professional Golf Association and the Ladies Pro Bowlers' Tour. The United States Olympic Committee has 105 members on its executive board: 91 are men. Of the 38 national governing bodies of sport (such as the U.S. Figure Skating Association), 34 have male presidents.[3] Male corporate representatives dispense endorsements. Information about women athletes is filtered through male writers, photographers, broadcasters, and publishers: approximately 9,650 of the nation's 10,000 print and broadcast sports journalists are men.[4] Now women play in the "men's" gym, under male rules, male officiating, male coaching, and, too often, male harassment.

By contrast, male athletes play in a homogeneous environment. Coed sports are changing this somewhat, but because few women coach or officiate men's games (fewer than 1 percent of men's college teams are coached by women)[5]; because women are almost never the agents, scouts, or broadcasters of men's sports; and because men still exclude women from many sporting fields and functions (such as golf courses and football banquets), men play games that are defined by other men.

The act of sport remains a human act, unrelated to gender. There is nothing male about throwing a ball or practicing lay-ups. There are long moments when women athletes do not feel the presence of men. Entire games are played, entire races run in which women never see or think of men. As Temple University professor Carole Oglesby has noted, sport requires traditionally feminine characteristics—intuition, grace, flexibility, finesse, dependence, passivity, trust, beauty, receptivity—as much as power and strength.[6]

But even the best women seem to have doubts about whether they belong. Sprinter Florence Griffith Joyner once said of her technique, "I run more like a guy than a girl."[7] As in, "I don't throw like a girl"? Just how does a woman run? To paraphrase Sojourner Truth, Ain't she a woman?

Between 1974 and 1978, I played varsity basketball at Stanford. Those years bridged the transition from female-controlled to male-controlled women's sports. For the first two years, we played in the "women's" (read: old, tiny) gym. We wore plain red shorts and white blouses; over those we tied "pinnies," a word only women seem to know. My teammates and I spent our spare time in the athletic department, begging the male athletic director to enforce Title IX. In my junior year, we finally received uniforms, a more experienced coach, and playing time in the men's gym. In 1978, my senior year, Stanford offered its first women's basketball scholarship. In 1990, Stanford won its first national championship.

It was during the late seventies—the beginning of the more public, more privileged years—that I started to observe the influx of male coaches and began to feel intensified pressure to conform to male standards of beauty, male notions of "feminine" behavior, and the male-originated "no pain, no gain" value system. Reporters started asking if I had any men in my life, and, if so, how they felt about my playing basketball. I saw coaches, male and female, scream at players until the players were in tears. During one game, much to my horror, a woman on another team punched me.

I developed cartilage problems (chondromalacia) in my knees, but since I was setting school records and receiving awards, it did not occur to me to stop playing. The trainer taped both knees and I kept shooting hoops until years later I realized that, like untold numbers of football players, I had done irreparable damage to my body. Don Sabo, a leading sports sociologist from D'Youville College in Buffalo, New York, says I "got caught up in the body-effacing, rather than body-embracing, practices and rationales that typify masculinist sport."

I played professional basketball for a year in Europe after college, then returned to the United States and played in the misguided and short-lived Women's Pro Basketball League (WBL). The owner of the California Dreams sent us to John Robert Powers' Charm School. The New Orleans Pride hired a cosmetician to apply makeup to "the girls" before each home game. The league owner was a man; all the head coaches were men.

After bilateral knee surgery, I retreated to cycling, golf, swimming, and rowing. But even at the recreational level, I sometimes see men brutalize each other in the name of victory, and I see intimidated women unsure of their own power. As a writer, I've been disturbed to hear advertisers and editors express discomfort with female strength (bodybuilders, power lifters, rugby players), preferring to portray traditional feminine beauty instead.

So I wondered: Just how are women faring in this integrated sports arena? Now that women have increased opportunities to play *with* men, are they playing *like* men? How is women's sporting ethic evolving? Were women better off in the all-female domain?

To answer my questions, I interviewed ordinary runners, riders, rowers. I also talked with champions: Olympic heptathlete Jackie Joyner-Kersee, race car driver Lyn St. James, bodybuilder Carla Dunlap, Ironman triathlete Paula Newby-Fraser, dogsled racer Susan Butcher. I chose athletes who seemed to represent some of the dilemmas and challenges American women face today. We had long conversations; we also pumped iron and pedaled bikes together. And I spoke with coaches, sports psychologists and sociologists, athletic directors, and professors.

I found that women's responses to the male-dominated sports system are as diverse and complex as their responses to the male-dominated social, political, and economic system. Some are confused about sport; some have been abused by sport. Some use male achievement to inspire and teach them; others insist on an all-female sports environment, even when this means that a team will go without a coach rather than turn to a man for guidance. Aware of their tentative status in the men's gym, some try to play by the men's rules, including destructive competitiveness and tyrannical coaching styles. Others implement a deliberately gentle sports system.

What makes women interesting to talk with is that they've analyzed themselves and their participation. Most men seem to be able to play sports without thinking, without becoming introspective or political or sociological about it. Most women can't. Even now, when they are being offered some of the perks of the male system, women retain an outsider's perspective and an outsider's tendency to evaluate, judge, and devise alternatives.

As I listened to women athletes, through the diversity I began to hear a chorus singing the same song. Dismayed by the "winning is the only thing" ethic that presides over what Don Sabo calls "manstream" sport, many women are once again questioning the dualism and danger inherent in the male model. They're not just greedily gobbling up their thin slice of the sports pie. The old-school voices are resurfacing.

"Must we play as the men play?" they ask. "Should we celebrate women boxers? Should we take drugs? Must college athletes suffer so many injuries? What are we doing to ourselves in the name of winning? Are sports still fun?"

. . .

A new model of sport is emerging. I use the term "partnership model"[8] to emphasize that teammates, coaches, and even opposing players view each other as comrades rather than enemies. Players with disparate ability levels are respected as peers rather than ranked in a hierarchy, and athletes care for each other and their own bodies. "To compete" is understood from its Latin source, *competere:* "to seek together."

Contrast this to what I call the military model, characterized by obsessive ranking of teams and individuals according to playing statistics or earnings; authoritarian, derisive relationships between coaches and players; antagonism between opponents; and the inevitable question, "Who won?"[9] The language of the military model says it all: A quarterback's arm is his weapon. Opponents are to be feared and destroyed. Teams battle for honors. Even bowling can be a war. "Why does bowling satisfy?" wrote Art Plotnik in the *New York Times.* "Think of it. Ten bouncing, noisy maple pins tauntingly lined up at attention. Hit us! Hurt us! A shiny 16-pound cannonball all yours to fire at the enemy . . ."[10]

The partnership model is a compassionate, egalitarian approach to sport in which athletes are motivated by love of themselves, of sports, and of each other. Power is understood not as power-over (power as dominance) but as power-to (power as competence).[11] Like early physical educators, partnership athletes maintain that sport should be inclusive; in balance with other aspects of life; cooperative and social in spirit; and safe. Many agree with their foremothers that women's sports should be coached, officiated, and administered by women.[12]

But this view is not anti-competition. In fact, some of the most competitive athletes demonstrate elements of the partnership model.

Chris Evert and Martina Navratilova established a fourteen-year friendship/rivalry that came to symbolize a female bonding that seemed shocking to reporters but familiar to women.

Jackie Joyner-Kersee says, "I don't have to be enemies with someone to be competitors with them."

Kirsten Hanssen, after winning a speedskating, snowshoeing, and cross-country skiing event called the Mountain Man Winter Triathlon, was asked about the last stretch of the race, where she finally passed the woman who had been leading. "It was probably really tough on her," Hanssen said. "I tried to be real nice." The reporter smiled in disbelief. "No, I'm serious," she said. "Because she had led for so much of the race, and all of a sudden there I was. I felt like she deserved some encouragement."[13]

Not all women are such good sports. But for the women I talked with, sports tend to be more about affiliation and cooperation—the joy of playing together—than about one-upmanship. Even at the Olympic and professional levels, where fame and fortune beckon from beyond the finish line, women seem to be finding ways to develop friendly rivalries. They are bringing their sensitivity and intelligence into athletic arenas. What is emerging is a new relationship of athlete to athlete, athlete to coach, athlete to self.

Also emerging is a new relationship of woman to man. When a man sees a strong woman drive a golf ball, it changes the way he thinks about golf, and about women. He tells his wife, daughters, and male friends. He reevaluates his own skill. His expectations of women begin to change.

This book is about how female athletes are making out—both how victorious they are and how happy they are—now that they've left the women's gym and entered the public domain.[14] It's about how women, like all assimilated peoples, are gaining access to some of the privileges of the dominant culture while struggling to retain their unique heritage and values. It's about Olympians, professionals, and everyday cyclists and swimmers who are redefining athlete, and reinventing sport.

Alone at First

It was exciting, of course, but it was also lonely. It was hard, being with all those men.
        —ANN BANCROFT, on returning
        from Will Steger's 1986
        expedition to the North Pole

*F*OR every man with a baseball story—a memory of a moment at the plate or in the field—there is a woman with a couldn't-play-baseball story.

Billie Jean King's story began in the early fifties, when she was eight or nine and her father took her to see a professional baseball game. "Right away, I loved it," she writes in *Billie Jean*, "but it was unfair of me to love it, I understood soon enough, because there was no place for an American girl to go in the national pastime."[1] Tennis was her second, substitute love.

Diane Sweeney, a twenty-nine-year-old physician from Washington, D.C., says she's still sad about not having been allowed to play baseball. "My dad said, 'We'll find you a softball team,'" she remembers. "But I was a pitcher. I didn't want to pitch underhand."

My own story dates to 1962, when I was six, my brother, eight. Before that, we'd spent every free hour on the make-shift baseball diamond behind an abandoned church. Suddenly a chasm called Little League yawned open between us. Pete got the uniform, the cap, the stretchy stirrup socks, the cleats, the soft leather glove, the catcher's face mask, and the chest protector, while I was relegated to the unrewarding role of spectator. I watched as our entire neighborhood league— Tommy Mitchell, the two Daves, Lefty Wright, the four Bidwell boys, and Pete—hustled onto a field from which I was barred.

Pete became enthusiastic about things that held no meaning for me: baseball cards (he still has 2,800, including seven Roger Marises and four Mickey Mantles); the batting averages of the Philadelphia Phillies. He grabbed the *Philadelphia Inquirer* every morning and pored over box scores. He idolized men with odd, little-boy names—Cookie Rojas, Johnny Callison, Whitey Ford, Willie Mays—and within our Philadelphia suburb he became a bit of a hero himself.

Thanks to a twelve-year-old named Maria Pepe and her supportive family, Congress in 1973 rewrote Little League's federal charter, so today a few young women have their own fond and frightful memories of game-saving runs and missed pop flies. Sometimes, when one of these pioneers has a winning personality or has encountered forward-thinking boys or men, she will recount stories of friendship, respect, and the community feeling that can develop on a team, a bonding based not on gender but on spirit, on passion for the game. Human bonding.

But often, because girls in Little League still generally play on otherwise all-boy teams, because most junior high and high school programs are closed to girls, and because baseball remains in the minds of many Americans an inappropriate activity for girls, these young athletes tell stories about rude questions, demoralizing coaches, jeering teammates, loneliness, and lawsuits.

Entry into previously all-male sports clubs might be easier for girls if they joined in groups, or even duos. As it happens, girls tend to shove their way onto baseball diamonds (and football fields, ice hockey rinks, wrestling mats) one by one, and as the lone girls they are anomalies, subject to scrutiny and often, abuse.

Julie Croteau, the first woman to play college baseball, started her career on a Little League team in 1976, when she was six years old.[2] Half of her teammates were girls. By the time she turned fourteen, she was the only girl in the neighborhood still jamming her first into a glove, but she was accepted by the boys on her team. The first time she hit a home run, even the other team cheered.

On a late spring afternoon in Washington, D.C., Julie, eighteen, is the one cheering. "Hey, big Charley Bolen," she calls to her teammate, "piece of cake." Julie sits on a bench in the dugout, which is not dug out but at ground level, protected from foul balls by a chain-link fence. She and her St. Mary's College teammates have driven two hours from southern Maryland to the grass-scented campus of Gallaudet College, the liberal arts school for the hearing-impaired. Charley, the St. Mary's pitcher, is at bat.

"Piece of cake," Julie says again. Then, to her teammates, "Come on, guys. We have to want this."

Julie is frustrated with these guys. They haven't won any games, for one thing, and the season is half over. They don't seem to mind. They don't seem to want to win badly enough. As a first-year student, Julie is hesitant to step into a leadership role, but she eggs them on anyway.

"That's what the bat's for, to hit the ball," one man chimes in, joining his hands in a single clap.

"Way to look it over, Charley B."

Julie is shorter than most of her teammates, about five-foot-seven. Her ponytail protrudes so perfectly from the hole in the back of her blue baseball cap that it gives the impression caps were designed to accommodate ponytails. Bolen and the other men have holes in their caps, too, but without ponytails their caps seem, by contrast, empty.

13

Beginning to shiver in the cool air, Julie rubs her hands together furiously. A black-and-white-haired woman calls from the bleachers, "Julie, why don't you put your jacket on?"

Julie swivels on the bench and frowns, but there is no anger in her eyes. Two teammates glance at her sympathetically. "Mom," says Julie, making the word into its own sentence, its own command.

"Sorry," Nancy Croteau says quickly, laughing at herself.

St. Mary's takes the field for the first time. The first Gallaudet player trickles the ball down the left sideline. The third baseman nabs it and whips it over to Julie, at first base, but the throw is a little wild. This is college ball but NCAA Division III, so this guy is no Brooks Robinson. Julie has to stretch, leaving her toe on the base and reaching her gloved right hand toward the outfield in a lunge that would please Mary Lou Retton. A moment before the base runner arrives, the ball lands in Julie's glove with a satisfying *whock*. Batter up.

To her teammates, Julie is simply a baseball player. These men had a girl or two on their Little League teams; they had a girl or two on their soccer teams; they have mothers or big sisters who shoot hoops or run marathons. Legally, Julie's participation is a big deal; historically, it's a big deal; personally, it isn't. Julie is just an eighteen-year-old lefty with a good arm.

So the players say things to Julie like, "Whad ya think of the pitcher's curve ball?" and Julie, well acquainted with the nuances of baseball lingo, belches. The players, pointing to her thigh, say, "Hey Julie, ya ripped your pants," and Julie, accustomed to her status as the team's lone female, jokes, "Yeah, next time up I'm going to show the pitcher some skin and distract him."

When another player approaches the seated crew, stands in front of them, and taps a baseball deliberately against his crotch, Julie, like the rest of her teammates, ignores him. They look elsewhere, bored or too mature to acknowledge such antics. The knocking of ball on cup reverberates, filling the air with a hollow, echoing sound—surely not what he intended.

Despite her unique status, Julie does not feel alone or lonely. She knows and understands boys better, she figures, than do girls who simply date them. "Every spring I played with sixteen boys," she points out. "I've made so many friends. They're not hesitant to say things in front of me that they normally wouldn't say in front of a girl."

"After the first few practices, you forgot she was a girl," says Charley Bolen.[3] She has lost her status as "other."

The hearing officer who in 1973 ruled that Little League must be sexually integrated stated: "The sooner little boys begin to realize that little girls are equal and that there will be many opportunities for a boy to be bested by a girl, the closer they will be to better mental health."[4]

But for the girls who teach the boys these lessons, the road can be rough. Julie credits her parents for helping her survive when the pressure was worst for her, in high school. They also supported her and her interest in baseball when she was little, the way many parents support their sons.

In fact, Ray Croteau had wanted sons but got daughters instead, so he made do, tossing balls at baby Julie until she learned to catch them. Her cousin John Croteau lived next door in rural Manassas, Virginia, and was also supportive. "They did what any boys would do—played ball all day," reports Nancy. "He'd throw it as hard as he could to hit her in the face, and she'd catch it."

Her first year at Osbourn Park High School, Julie didn't make the baseball team; she was short, about five feet, and she wasn't good enough. But by trying out she served notice. The junior varsity coach tried to steer her toward softball. She wasn't interested in softball. "It's not my sport," she says.

She tried out again her sophomore year and again the coach talked softball. He had already discussed it with the softball coach, he told her; there was a uniform waiting. But

Julie had grown a few inches, had continued to develop her skills through Little League, had become a good player—not "good, for a girl," just good. She made the team.

It was a terrible year, though. The coach brought in an outfielder to play Julie's position; then, when that boy was suspended, he brought in someone else. He wouldn't call ahead to tell other teams to open a girls' locker room, so Julie would have to track down a janitor and change in a bathroom.

In her junior year, the varsity coach said that because so many players had returned, juniors would play junior varsity. There was a new JV coach that year, and he liked Julie. She was better than most of the other JV players now and began leading warm-ups. The coach assured her she'd make the team, even suggested that she might be captain. Then he cut her. "I know the varsity coach got to him," says Julie.

For the only time in her career, she thought of quitting. "I thought, Maybe I'm taking this too far. Softball even entered my mind—once. But I'm too stubborn, I guess. And I love baseball too much to quit."

She tried out for her high school team once more, as a senior. This time she was sure she wouldn't be cut. Clearly, she was better than most of the guys on the varsity squad. The coach cut her. That's when her parents sued the school's principal and coach for $100,000.

The judge—who interrupted the proceedings to tell his own baseball story—ruled against the Croteaus, saying that Julie had received a fair tryout and that the decision was unrelated to gender. Nancy says "there are many ways to win" and cites the good publicity that may pave the way for other girls in the future.

Other girls such as her daughter Nicole, a twelve-year-old who runs track and plays basketball and baseball. If Nicole is excluded from middle school baseball, as the Croteaus fear, Ray and Nancy, who are both lawyers, may find themselves in court again. "People think lawyers are eager to sue. We're not," says Ray. "It's just as expensive and time-consuming and draining for us as for anyone else. But we will exhaust all possible remedies, up to and including going to court or filing a class action suit. Nicky is a superb athlete. There's no reason she shouldn't play baseball."

Baseball is the national religion, some have said, but that's not true—it's *men's* religion. During baseball season, radio and television reporters (and even airplane pilots) recite game scores, statistics fill the newspapers, and baseball-capped boys seem as common as mailboxes. Even the government gets involved. Distressed by stalled labor negotiations in March 1990, the ninety-eight-percent-male United States Senate passed a nonbinding resolution calling for prompt settlement of the baseball strike and resumption of spring training. ("We're wasting everyone's time and we just look like fools," protested Senator Warren Rudman, a New Hampshire Republican.)[5]

Men worship a male deity who ordains male players, managers, umpires, grass cutters, ticket takers, team owners, stadium builders. They do not want to worship Julie Croteau or her little sister, Nicole.

It's not just baseball. Men protect what they perceive to be the male turf of racetracks, basketball courts, football fields, and even billiard tables with a vengeance.

What's it like for other female pioneers? Billie Jo Mann, fourteen, wrestled with the boy's team at McKinley Junior High School in Kenosha, Wisconsin. The school administration resisted—until her lawyer threatened to sue—but her teammates were supportive. They even signed a petition to convince the school to let her play.[6]

Eleven-year-old Sara Naison-Phillips played basketball in an otherwise all-boys' league for three years before anyone complained. Then other teams in the Brooklyn Catholic Youth Organization league began to grumble that Sara, one of the best players, might get hurt. One team refused to play a game unless Sara sat out. Her teammates came to Sara's defense, refusing to play without her. "If she wasn't so good, they wouldn't care," said eleven-year-old team co-captain John Lucadamo. Eventually the two teams, including Sara, played the game.[7]

For most girls and women, pioneering is a rough road. Nancy Winnard, one of the first girls to play Little League, was kicked out of a game in Detroit in 1975 for not wearing the requisite protective cup on her groin.[8]

Beth Balsley, a New Jersey girl who gained national attention in 1986 when a judge ruled that she had a right to play on her high school football team, was repeatedly harassed by her teammates. One day after practice they ganged up on her, tackled her, and threw football equipment at her. "Why do you want to play football?" reporters asked her. "You're not even very good." She wasn't very good, apparently, but the school had a no-cut policy. Until Beth tried out, they had been committed to "participation for all." Does someone have to be good to enjoy a sport? She liked colliding with people, Beth once explained.[9]

Shauna Winemiller, the first female high school ice hockey player in Illinois, reported that the boys on other teams "know I'm a girl and tend to hit me harder. They've been giving me cheap shots left and right."[10]

Lakeal Ellis, a football player at Theodore Roosevelt High School in Washington, D.C., once said of her teammates, "They didn't take me seriously. They'd hit me harder, for no reason. The quarterback wouldn't throw me the ball. Boys would make goo-goo eyes and throw kisses just to be funny."[11]

Tamara Dakis wrestled during her junior year at Meade High School in Severn, Maryland, but didn't go out for the team again as a senior. "The team was cruel, and it never got better," she said. "The last match I went to, even on the bus home, they were still mean."[12]

When money is involved, male resistance escalates. Female jockeys have been boycotted by male jockeys, have been forced to go to court before being granted licenses, and have had their homes stoned.[13]

Jean Balukas, who has been the best female billiards player

in the world since 1972, when she was thirteen, has played in men's tournaments (where there is more money) since 1987. Her attempted entries, eventually successful, were originally met with men's threats to play in women's tournaments. As if to reaffirm its stance, the Professional Billiards Association recently changed its name to the Men's Professional Billiards Association.[14]

For Julie Croteau, the struggle to be "just a baseball player" continues. When she first tried out for the St. Mary's team, she was warned by her new teammates, most of whom were supportive, to stay away from one player who, she was told, "hates you."

She tries not to take seriously other players' comments. At the Gallaudet game, where the opposing team was deaf, she joked, "I'm smiling at them and they're probably saying 'you bitch' in sign language."

Accustomed to cameras that film her games, she feels proud that crews now come to watch her play rather than to see *if* she can play. She is used to reporters, having fielded questions from, she estimates, about a hundred so far.

The three stupidest questions, she figures, are: (1) Where do you change? ("I think it's rather apparent I don't change with the men"); (2) Why don't you play softball? ("If I had a nickel for everyone who asked me to play softball, I'd be a rich bitch right now"); and (3) Do you date? ("I feel like saying, 'Do you?' ").

To those who emphasize her pioneering role in baseball, she says coolly, "If I'm the first, it's not because I'm the best. It's a mixture of circumstances and stubbornness. At first it felt silly that all these people were coming out to cover the story. I'm a freshman. I like to think of myself as a very good ball player, but I'm not an exceptional athlete. I'm just trying to do what millions of people are trying to do.

"But then I sat down and thought about what I was doing. If it weren't for the women who fought to play Little League, I wouldn't have been able to play Little League. If someone had done this last year, maybe I wouldn't have been cut from my baseball team as a senior. It's all building. By me fighting in the court and coming to play here, maybe I've made it easier for someone else."

Part of blazing a trail for others involves absorbing some media abuse that, presumably, will not continue once "female baseball player" is not an oxymoron. When Julie was honored as Sportsperson of the Week on NBC's *Today,* cohost Bryant Gumbel said of Julie's entry into college baseball, "Is nothing sacred?"

While appearing on the morning television program *Live: Regis & Kathie Lee* ("She's Number One with the Guys Now" was the title of the segment), Julie was given a glove and asked to play pepper, a fielding drill. ("What was I supposed to do, refuse?" she says, laughing at the thought: "No, I don't feel like it.") Cohost Regis Philbin stood five or six feet away, then "nailed the ball right back at me," Julie remembers. "The first one he hit out of my reach. Another one he hit in the air; it hit the top of my glove. I caught the rest of them, but the whole thing was ridiculous. It felt like a freak show."

When asked to fly to Los Angeles for *The Pat Sajak Show,* Julie opted to stay in Maryland and study algebra instead.

The insults and barriers have made Julie stronger, more articulate, more politically astute. Her scars have formed a thick skin that comes in handy. But she is rare not because she loves baseball—grown women would not still mourn their exclusion if this game were not appealing—but because of that thick skin. Like black baseball player Jackie Robinson, who also sometimes played first base, Julie is not necessarily the best player in her excluded class; rather, she is the most persistent, determined, durable.

Pioneers by definition have no role models. Julie does not identify with the men who play her sport professionally, and cannot name the starting nine of any pro team. She did not realize that her number (3) was Babe Ruth's. She knows about the All-American Girls Pro Baseball League, which flourished from 1943 to 1954, but she doesn't envy their segregated status; she sees no reason not to play with men.

Some of Julie's strongest support comes from male teammates. She describes Jeff Austin, a St. Mary's pitcher, as her best friend. In her senior year of high school, when she was suing the school and the coach was claiming she wasn't good enough to make the team, several of her teammates—including longtime friends—sided with the coach. That "hurt a lot," she admits. But a few supported her publicly. "They essentially gave up their baseball careers to back me. They came out on my side in the trial, knowing there was no way they'd play next year, which would essentially cut them off in college."

Little League is still overwhelmingly male. In fact, Little League channels girls away from baseball through its 270,000-member softball league, created specifically for girls in 1974, the season after Little League was forced to desegregate. The organization does not keep statistics on how many of its 2.5 million baseball players are female. "We get rosters, but it's too hard to tell the Pats and Lees," says executive director Creighton Hale, who refuses to estimate. He does admit, however, "We don't see too many girls on the baseball side."

Julie has been accepted on the St. Mary's baseball team because she "fits into the male system," as Coach Hal Willard puts it. Julie "talks the game, knows the game real well; she's not just along for the ride." Willard coached the St. Mary's women's basketball team in the early eighties, and he was "a little leery" that Julie would be like those women—not "intense as far as wanting to win."

Fortunately, she has "a good attitude." She is neither brash nor flirtatious. She says with some embarrassment that she has met at least one girl who played baseball just to find a date, and she is determined to give no one that impression about herself. Her persona has taken years to develop; Julie's mother reports that when she was younger she swaggered on the field, then tried to revert to a daintier method of locomotion elsewhere. Now she has developed a walk and a personal style that seem a careful compromise: not too boy-like, but not too girl-like either. She could be criticized either way.

Julie is a good player, and that helps. She bats two for eight in the doubleheader with Gallaudet and is errorless halfway through the season. Coach Willard ranks her among his top ten players in terms of skill and knowledge of the game. Although she is not a big hitter, she rarely strikes out. She claims to be stronger than at least two men on her team, and Willard concurs. Some of the coaches who had discouraged Julie from applying to their schools have now told Willard that she would have made their squads.

Still, like most Division III players, Julie is not pro material. "It's not because I'm a woman, it's because I don't have the strength," she explains carefully, adding that when a woman finally does play pro, she'll be her biggest fan. Instead, Julie has her sights set on becoming a civil rights attorney. "It's the only thing I've really cared about—people getting a fair shot. I want to change the world."

She'd like to help her sister, for instance. "After me being able to play NCAA baseball, my sister can't try out, as a twelve-year-old, for her middle school. I think that is ridiculous," Julie says. "It makes me angry. A twelve-year-old is going to have to fight that. It's hard. That was a hard experience for me. It's not something a lot of teenagers want to take on.

"As long as the high schools and middle schools cut girls off, they're going to keep them out of college [sports]. Hopefully, more will get through now. But if girls are allowed to play in fifty percent of America's schools, that's still only fifty percent. And guys will be able to play in a hundred, and there will be better guy athletes."

Fifty percent is a long way off. In the 1988–1989 season, 902 girls played high school baseball in the United States, compared to 412,825 boys. Still, things are changing: just one year earlier, only 372 girls played.[15]

Julie is still too young to help her sister directly, but Ray Croteau is chipping away at the "baseball is for boys" myth. He is "semi-retired" at age fifty and spends most afternoons practicing baseball or basketball skills with Nicole and her friends. Ray, who with Nancy was a Berkeley activist in the sixties, has become further radicalized by his older daughter's passion and pain. "You sit at games with other fathers," he says, "and you feel funny, because they're talking about their sons' going on to play in high school or college, and some have hopes that they'll play pro. They don't feel your daughter is in direct competition with their son, because even though she may be better than him now, he has maleness in his favor."

To make sure Nicole becomes an indispensable player, Ray is teaching her to pitch.

In a recent interview, Little League executive director Creighton Hale couldn't place the name Julie Croteau. While women's groups such as the Virginia chapter of the National Organization for Women have honored Julie, Little League—which could claim her as an example of the success of an integrated League—has ignored her. Hale minimizes the meaning of her accomplishment for other young women. "It's the exceptional girl who will be able to play college ball," he says.

Julie's coach shares the "exceptional girl" view. "I don't want to call her not the normal girl," Willard begins carefully, "but normally females, once they reach teenagehood, choose between being an athlete and some traditionally female activities. Baseball has traditionally not been one of those."

Julie's teammates also accept Julie as the exceptional girl, the honorary boy, the tomboy: some version of a boy who won't flinch at their dirty jokes. A girl you forget is a girl.

Her presence and the presence of girls on baseball diamonds throughout the country have not yet become part of America's collective consciousness because the pros are still exclusively men. But many women I've talked with know of this "female Jackie Robinson" and have been inspired by her story. At the Gallaudet game, at least half of the fifty or sixty spectators are women, and they cheer for Julie. At eighteen, she has become what she never had—a role model, even for much older women. Moreover, she has become a hero, the kind only athletes can be.

In the last inning of the first game, Julie hits a single to center field, beginning a streak that brings the score from 6–0 to 6–6. St. Mary's loses that game on a two-run homer in the bottom of the inning, but by the time Julie comes to bat again in the second game, the fans are filled with anticipation.

"Hit a home run!" yells one gray-haired woman enthusiastically. Nancy Croteau laughs a little—after that first home run when she was fourteen, Julie hasn't hit any more. Nevertheless, Julie swings hard and connects. The ball travels directly up, then back, over the backstop, toward the street. The woman—who no doubt hasn't a couldn't-play-baseball story of her own to tell—leaps up from the bleachers and runs down the short slope behind the field. Uncontested, she retrieves the ball before it comes to rest and triumphantly raises it overhead in an inadvertent imitation of the Statute of Liberty. "Julie hit this! This is Julie Croteau's ball!" she shouts. "This is the highlight of my life!"

Her voice resounds across the field. The Gallaudet pitcher, unable to hear, winds up for his second pitch. Julie Croteau, accustomed to blocking out heckling from the stands, does not react either. Crouching, she waggles her bat.

Staggered Starts

When I first started running I was so embarrassed I'd walk when cars passed me. I'd pretend I was looking at the flowers.
—JOAN BENOIT SAMUELSON[1]

*B*LOND, green-eyed, and almost fifty, Kitty Porterfield is wearing a boat on her head. It is a long, narrow shell, unbelievably long and so narrow that if you were looking from above—from atop the boathouse, for instance—you'd see Kitty's two elbows poking out from under the shell's shiny black belly, her bent arms forming little triangles with the sides of the boat, at the same angle as the riggers.

Kitty maneuvers her craft carefully down the ramp that leads from boathouse to dock. A team of eight young men marches uphill, their heads hidden under their even longer boat, so they resemble something from a camp skit, a poor imitation of a centipede. Kitty, the director of a scholarship program in the Alexandria, Virginia, public schools, smiles at them as they pass.

At the very edge of the dock, the clean water of the Occoquan Reservoir nipping her toes, Kitty removes her heavy hat, lowers it to her waist, stretches it out over the water, and lets it rest. It floats. She inserts one long oar and then the other into oarlocks the shape of cupped hands. Storklike, she perches on one leg in the middle of the shell, lowers herself slowly onto the tortilla-size sliding seat, laces her feet into nailed-down sneakers, sighs. She is on the water. She is ready to begin.

Kitty Porterfield's only early memory of athletic competition is a three-legged race. But in her early forties, as the mother of three teenagers, all rowers, she had an idea that transformed her life. She had spent innumerable afternoons standing on riverbanks, watching her children's regattas. She had endured endless evenings listening to their complaints about sore backs and blisters. She had carpooled, raised money, baked brownies, organized events. She served as president of the Alexandria Crew Boosters (ACB), an organization for parents of rowers, for two years and sat on its board of directors for nine. Finally, when she was forty-four and her youngest child, Michael, was a senior in high school, she told the ACB board, "I've stood on the shore far too long. It's time to put down the gavel and get into the boat."

For Kitty Porterfield and the millions of women who have joined what is condescendingly referred to as the "fitness craze," sports are new. Boat-carrying, boat-rowing, balancing on one foot, all of it is new. Because they did not grow up with sports and are only later, as adults, learning what their bodies can accomplish, these women do not think of themselves as athletes. ("Maybe 'athlete' is a male word," suggests Kitty, who now rows at least three times a week and competes in races.) These women did not grow up playing catch with their fathers and cousins, do not have drawers stuffed with T-shirts or mantels topped with trophies. They work out at lunchtime or after the kids' bedtime or on weekends, before cleaning the house. The terms "interval training" and "lactic acid" mean nothing to them.

Competition is a foreign concept. Winning has sometimes been forbidden. "In school it was always, 'Do well, but don't do better than him,'" Kitty recalls. "It was terrific to be number two. I learned that lesson really well. I could have graduated magna cum laude [from Radcliffe], but I didn't do it."

Now a masters-division competitor in both single and double sculls, Kitty says, "At the start of a race, there's a lot of terror about doing badly. At the same time, the thought of winning is very scary. I have great trouble visualizing winning a race. That's a hell of a way to go into a competition."

Midway through her first race, the Head of the Potomac, Kitty "caught a crab"—dipped one oar too low—and her boat capsized. Treading water and catching her breath, she heard some fishermen on shore laughing. Angry, she hoisted herself into the tipsy boat—no easy feat—and finished the race in a respectable time for a novice.

Kitty's second daughter, Deborah, a medical student at the University of California, San Francisco, witnessed Kitty's second competition, the Head of the Charles, a tortuous three-mile regatta in Boston. Then a college rower waiting for her own race to begin, Deborah watched Kitty from the Radcliffe boathouse with a group of friends. "She'd rowed only that summer and that fall," Deborah recalls. "It was quite an adventure for her. She was not very fast. She was way off course. It was a little embarrassing. But my friends thought it was great because no one else had a mother rowing in the Head of the Charles. So at the same time that it was amusing that she was far behind and way off course, it was fine. My mother has always been very supportive and pretty visible, so a lot of my friends know her. We had a big cheering squad, laughing and cheering."

Kitty says, "I have never been so frightened in my life as when I went through the chute at the start. I was terrified. Here I was, in my second athletic competition in my whole life. I had no idea what to expect. I had no reservoir of what it feels like to be in a competition—to know that it does end and that you are alive when it's over, those basic things that as you compete a lot you begin to take for granted.

"Coming down the course, there are all these people who

are yelling and encouraging you. After you come under the first bridge, the banks are lined with people. You are surrounded by this incredible amount of sound. It's like walking into a football stadium for a Super Bowl game. It's most extraordinary. No matter how far behind you are, it's a wonderful experience."

Women make up the majority of new participants in several sports, including weight training, running, cycling, and basketball. More women than men now swim regularly.[2] It's poignant, this mass movement of women toward the water, the aerobics studios, the playing fields. They have not sweated from exhaustion since giving birth, yet here they are, more women than ever, becoming athletes—even if they cannot relate to the world. Women are physically educating themselves, and it's an exhilarating, challenging process, as momentous and natural as children's learning to walk.

Many are tentative, and with good reason: they are reentry students, middle-aged beginners finding their way in a world that has changed considerably since they were young. They associate sports with embarrassing gym suits, mandatory showers that ruined hairdos, too many laps around a hot track. They feel uncoordinated, and often are.

As with proficiency in language, what San Francisco State University physical education professor Roberta Bennett calls "movement literacy" takes time to develop, ideally a lifetime.[3] Despite the fitness boom of the eighties, women remain to a large degree physically uneducated, even retarded. Their competence has been slowed, delayed; their physical proficiency has been hindered.

How many women athletes started playing sports after childhood? Most. In 1970, fewer than 300,000 girls participated in interscholastic high school athletics, compared with 3.6 million boys.[4] Some teenage girls played sports through swim clubs, Girl Scouts, or other groups, but the total number of participants was small. Women who attended high school in the early seventies or before are likely to be either late-blooming athletes or not athletic at all.

Unlike the teachers and fellow students she remembers from Radcliffe physical education classes, Kitty Porterfield's current teachers and teammates are usually men. Ninety-five of the 110 members of the Occoquan Boat Club are men. Her doubles partner is a thirty-eight-year-old former high school rower, John Meehan.

Kitty's husband, Jovan, enjoys what the husband of triathlete Joanne Ernst has called "aerobic spectating." Jovan has become the family photographer, compiling a vast collection of family rowing photos that are displayed in the Porterfields' Alexandria home.

Kitty learned to row at the prestigious Craftsbury Sculling Camp in Vermont. All but one of her coaches were men. When she needs coaching these days, Kitty calls on her son, twenty-two and a member of the U.S. rowing team. She and Michael are planning to buy a double; Michael and Deborah will use it to compete in masters races when they reach their late twenties. Sports have become a family affair, beyond the old father-son model.

Even Kitty's mother, a former field hockey and tennis player who gave up sports to bring up her family, has recently become a rower. At seventy-two, Kay Burnett purchased a Concept II rowing machine and made plans to attend Craftsbury.

Karen, Kitty's older daughter, lost interest in rowing after one year of college competition, but now, at twenty-six, she takes lessons in weight training from her mother. And the sport of rowing continues to bond Deborah, Michael, and Kitty. They're always talking crew. "Before, I had no experience with athletics, so I had no idea of the stresses they were under," says Kitty.

But while fathers, sons, and male friends often assist or participate in sports with women, men and women are not yet athletic peers. This is partly because of strength or size differences but largely because men have had a head start. Kitty Porterfield missed out on decades of practice. So too did the majority of American women now discovering the joys of athleticism.

Kitty grew up "not connected to" her body, not knowing what she could accomplish and not knowing that movement, even momentarily painful movement, could yield pleasure. "As a kid I avoided pain," she says. "Fifteen or twenty years ago, I was in terrible shape because I avoided hurting. I was more protected than pushed, for all the right reasons, but I missed being encouraged to know that you can do a lot more than you think you can do. Now I'm involved in an exploration of how much I can push myself. I make my body feel bad and nothing happens. In fact, there are extraordinary benefits. I've gotten stronger. I'm learning that I don't have to be afraid, that my body doesn't break, or if it does, it mends. That's a nice thing to know about yourself. There are a lot of women who don't know that."

Nor do many women know how to execute some basic sports skills. Kitty admits she still can't throw a ball. "Not only is there a typical style of throwing like a girl, but there is a more or less typical style of running like a girl, climbing like a girl, swinging like a girl, hitting like a girl," writes Miami University philosophy professor Iris Marion Young. "The whole body is not put into fluid and directed motion. . . . The woman's motion tends not to reach, extend, lean, stretch, and follow through in the direction of her intention."[5]

Women are timid, Young points out, fearing injury,[6] fearing they might appear awkward, and at the same time not wishing to look too strong. Studies have shown that both women and girls consistently underestimate their abilities. "We decide beforehand," Young says, "that the task is beyond us, and thus give it less than our full effort. At such a half-hearted level, of course, we cannot perform the tasks, [we] become frustrated and fulfill our own prophecy."[7]

Young wrote those words in 1980. I'd like to believe that women are more competent now; surely they are. But the flashiness of Florence Griffith Joyner, the power of Steffi Graf, and the fluidity of female joggers and aerobicists tend to obscure the fact that women as a group still lack fundamental movement skills.

Can your women friends—even the ones who lift weights—throw a ball? Is your street filled with girls on bicycles, girls on skateboards, girls building tree forts? In my neighborhood, it's the boys who do wheelies off sidewalks, the boys who convene for football games in the middle of the street. Boys take up space, developing their bodies. Where are the girls? Inside playing with their Flo-Jo dolls?

Thirteen fundamental motor skills have been identified by physiologists. They include walking, running, leaping, hopping, jumping, skipping, galloping, sliding, throwing, catching, striking, kicking, and bouncing. They are cumulative: once you learn to slide and to run, you can learn to ski. And they translate from one sport to another: the motion for a baseball throw is similar to the motion for a volleyball spike, a tennis serve, and a badminton clear.[8]

The *principles* of movement also translate from one sport to another. Once you learn that a ball rebounds off a surface at the same angle at which it hits the surface, you can, intuitively or consciously, apply that knowledge to basketball, billiards, and even the choice of clubs in golf. This is the sort of thing most women don't know, because they haven't experienced it. They don't know about transferring weight in the direction of a throw in order to generate power, or about putting the opposite foot forward before throwing or rolling a ball. They don't know the language—or even the alphabet—of sports.[9]

To make matters worse, women are often given misinformation. "Speed determines distance and force," says sports physiologist Linda Bunker, who also teaches golf. "But one of the pieces of advice I hear continually given to women is, 'Don't worry about swinging the club too fast. Just swing it nice and easy.' The faster you can swing the club and still control it, the farther the ball will go. Yet we continue to reinforce for women and girls the qualities of movement that are slow."[10]

Physical retardation is caused not by abnormalities in the chromosomes but by abnormalities in the socialization process. Female babies are overprotected, understimulated. Parents teach boys to throw and catch at a very young age; girls often don't have their first experience throwing and catching balls until a grammar school kickball game. In an emotional presentation at a Women's Sports Foundation banquet in 1988, actor Gregory Hines confessed that when his daughter reached age four he realized if she had been a boy, the two of them already would have been playing ball. His daughter had missed two years of physical training. So he started taking her out to play catch.

Boys are allowed to run, and to explore the space around them. Girls are restrained by clothing ("Don't let your panties show") and attitudes. Watch in public places: boys race all over the place; girls sit quietly next to their parents. It's not that boys have more energy. They're given the permission to express it differently.

Women still buckle flimsy, slippery-soled shoes on their daughters' feet—and their own. The comparison to traditional Chinese foot-binding seems extreme until one considers how critical shoes are to agility, balance, and one's sense of being safe, grounded, spontaneous, and competent. Women who have been stuck in a snowstorm or who have suddenly had to run after a child while wearing heels, women who have nursed corns, bunions, blisters, and calluses know what I mean. Many women now wear practical shoes during the commute to and from the office. This is progress. But many professional women still spend eight hours a day in shoes that are as restrictive to natural movement—including running from danger—as were corsets.

Any clothing that inhibits spontaneity inhibits athleticism. How often do women show up at a barbecue in a dress, then regret not being able to join in the volleyball game?

At the root of women's physical illiteracy is the deep-seated belief that girls and boys are different sorts of people and therefore should be treated differently. From these gender-associated expectations flow institutionalized norms that stunt girls' development. A ten-year-old girl can earn the President's Physical Fitness Award patch, for example, by completing such tasks as forty sit-ups, three pull-ups, and a mile run in 9 minutes, 19 seconds. A ten-year-old boy won't earn his patch until he does forty-five sit-ups, six pull-ups, and a mile run in 7 minutes, 57 seconds.

Discrimination against boys? Hardly. Lower expectations lead to inferior performance and, perhaps most damaging, to a belief on the part of both girls and boys that boys are naturally superior athletes.

Muscles—a symbol of strength—have been deemed inappropriate for women. How paralyzing this has been, and continues to be, despite the recent muscle mania. Health-club instructors of both genders still assume women fear big muscles, and prescribe exercises accordingly. During one of my brief forays into weightlifting, a fitness instructor said to me, "Don't worry, if you do just one set of ten, you won't bulk up." Had I asked him how not to bulk up? Had I told him I was repulsed by my own potential muscle mass? No. He had assumed all of that, on the basis of gender alone.

Nancy Croteau, inspired by the accomplishments of her daughter, Julie, recently began competing in masters swimming meets. One day as we watched Julie play baseball, she told me she planned to enter the 50- and 100-meter butterfly in a meet the following day.

"I hope you enjoy swimming alone," I said.

"What do you mean?" she asked.

"Most women in their forties don't do butterfly," I explained. "As kids, they were herded away from the event, told that it would make them develop broad, unsightly shoulders. Now, most can't swim fifty yards of it because they haven't developed the strength it takes." She later reported that she'd won both events—unopposed.

. . .

In a Women's Sports Foundation (WSF) survey of 1,682 athletic women, 45 percent of the respondents mentioned "lack of involvement and training as children" as a barrier to increased participation by women in sports and fitness.[11] In another WSF survey, almost 50 percent of nonathletic girls reported that they "don't want to play sports because they lack the necessary skills."[12]

Yet tragically, many women and girls seem to believe their physical retardation is genetic, gender-based, or mysterious. "I'm just not coordinated," women have told me more times than I can count. "I'm a klutz. I was never good at those boy things."

"You can't play because you're a girl" is how exclusion has been justified. Of course, the problem isn't *being a girl;* it's that organizers of sports teams have forbidden and often still forbid girls and women to play. But children, who tend to be literal, often believe: "I can't be athletic because I'm a girl."

When these women begin to develop skills, they bring to sports an unnamed, largely unacknowledged athletic grief, like that of miscarriage, a mourning for something that never had a chance to develop its potential. It's a difficult, nebulous grief I hear about often, sometimes in a quiet, sad voice, sometimes with anger or envy. "I loved sports," these women tell me, "but there weren't any teams for me to play on. For girls, it was cheerleading or nothing."

Kitty Porterfield still mourns. Her son was recently asked to row in a high school alumni race, and Kitty realized with sadness that she'll never row in such a race; she has no athletic past.

In 1977, the Women's Studies Department at San Francisco State University offered a class called "Physical Education Without Fear." The women learned skills such as throwing, catching, running, and moving among and in relation to other people. "Their early responses exhibited fear and confusion—the results of learned, taught helplessness," write

Roberta Bennett and her colleagues. "They were afraid of getting hurt, of being bumped or bumping someone else, afraid of large, fast movements, afraid of themselves. They would duck away from objects, take forty or fifty strides to cover a space that should take twenty strides to cover, become . . . frozen when encountering barriers. When asked to move sidewards, or backwards, or to be upside down, the women experienced extreme disorientation."[13]

I see these women everywhere. They have no idea of their own body's capabilities, or even its orientation in space. But I see the other women too, women with newly muscular backs, proud posture, springy steps. Even my own sister, the self-defined klutz in our family, has suddenly become an athlete, inspired by some offhand praise my mother offered recently, when they were swimming together. "You have a nice stroke," my mother told Carol casually.

"I do?" said Carol. "No one has ever told me that before." She swam a few extra laps. Then she joined a health club. Next thing I knew my "unathletic" sister, a thirty-eight-year-old trial lawyer and the mother of four young children, was running laps around a track—one the first day, four the second—and hanging out in a gym, shooting baskets. "I was always good at shooting baskets," she says. "I just wasn't good at running back and forth, so I never made the teams."

Some excellent women runners were late bloomers. Sherri Hall, thirty-eight, is a student athlete on the Southern California College women's track and cross-country teams. She didn't start running until age thirty-one. Priscilla Welch of England placed sixth at the first women's Olympic marathon in 1984, with a time of 2:28:54, just four minutes behind winner Joan Benoit. Welch, forty-five, didn't start running until she was thirty-four. She has also won the New York City Marathon and placed second in the London Marathon, breaking the women's masters world record with a time of 2:26:51. Forty-eight-year-old Joan Ullyot, author of *Women's Running* and *Running Free,* has run more than seventy marathons and been the overall winner in "about ten" of them, she says. She began running at age thirty to lose weight; with a best time of 2:47, she holds the national masters record for women aged forty-five to forty-nine.

Eighty-five percent of the 22.2 million participants in aerobic dance are women, and women make up the majority of stationary cyclists and treadmill runners.[14] Even though many of these women are motivated by fear of flab, it's likely that they will, along the way, develop self-confidence and physical pride.

Women are studying the basics of motor learning, acquiring the kinds of skills and confidence little boys acquire in their backyards. "I feel more in charge of myself," said one woman after the "Physical Education Without Fear" class. "Why didn't anyone bother to teach me these things before?" Said another: "I have a whole new sense of who I am as a woman and as a person, and I'm angry that I was not allowed to understand myself this way before."[15]

Too ashamed of their lack of coordination to risk the taunts, stares, and humiliation of ineptitude in public—too afraid of how their bodies will appear to others—untold numbers of women remain physically incompetent. Ironically, poor body image keeps women from participating in the activities that could enhance their body image.

But even this is changing. Kitty Porterfield finds it refreshing that rowing is an unpretentious sport, where athletes are more likely to wear old gray sweats than Lycra tights. "I grew up in an era of sleeping on curlers so you could look nice the next morning," she remembers. "At the boathouse that's not what one is prized for, and that's a nice feeling. Appearance is not an issue."

Kitty has developed a new appreciation for callused hands, and for bulk. "I was this height [five-seven] when I was in seventh grade," she recalls. "It wasn't good for a girl to be big. If she was big and bright, that did not make her enormously popular." She felt pressured to diet, to view her body "only as something to make smaller, something to minimize." Nowadays, she says, "to be around my daughter and her friends—women rowers who are wonderfully big—I love it."

Painful though it can be, there are advantages to starting late in life and to being, as a class of people, denied privileges. Women don't take participation for granted. They revel in their newfound opportunities with a passion and intensity more often seen in the young.

Kitty Porterfield gets a kick out of "buying dog food and tossing the forty-pound bag in the back of the car myself." Three years ago, she says, she would not have been able to do that. And she's passionate about rivers, shorebirds, and purple sunsets.

"I love the water," says Kitty. "It's incredibly beautiful. And rowing is a lot cheaper than therapy. You feel better when you get out. Your life is more orderly. Or it hasn't changed at all, but it seems it has. Rowing recreates the soul."

Unlike her male teammates at the Occoquan Boat Club, many of whom rowed in college or high school, Kitty has the pleasure of developing rather than deteriorating with age. Each year she gets faster. Although she doesn't keep track of her victories, when pressed she'll add up four third-place finishes and two firsts. The firsts were in the 1986 and 1990 Mid-Atlantic Erg Sprints, a silly but somehow serious annual rowing-machine contest in which competitors row for what's called 2,500 meters while in actuality never leaving the gym. Finally she's winning. Not just second or third place, but first.

"I've learned a lot about competition that I never learned as a kid," Kitty says. "Sitting at the starting line, waiting for the gun to go off, you feel naked and alone. I'd never risked that way before. And you see all sides of competition—the politics, how some of it has nothing to do with athletic skill."

Along the way, she keeps learning about teamwork. "They're always saying that boys learn teamwork that helps them in business, and there's a lot of truth in that," she remarks. "My lessons from rowing are standing me in enormous good stead."

Having discovered sport's sweet offerings, late bloomers make a commitment, sometimes for the first time, to themselves. "I had nothing in my background to prepare me for this—spending hours and hours by myself," says Kitty. "I'm having to build up inner resources. I'm having to learn discipline."

Kitty is also making a commitment to other women rowers, lobbying for more coaches, better boats, and broader opportunities. It's women, she says, with whom she feels the most affinity. She names Carlie Geer and Holly Metcalf, former national team rowers, as two of her role models. "With the exception of Michael, who remains my main coach," Kitty says, "all of my courage and inspiration comes from my associations with women."

Kitty is "giving back to her sport"—many athletes use the phrase, a trite term for something that actually is not a bad idea. In 1990, she was elected vice-president for women on the board of directors of the United States Rowing Association.

To be an outspoken, politically active athlete, a woman must stand her ground with men. Kitty says she developed this skill earlier in her life, when she was involved in the women's ordination movement in the Episcopal Church. "I was one of very few women among very powerful men in combustible situations," she recalls. "I learned to handle myself."

So she knows how to respond when, on the dock of the Occoquan Boat Club, a man asks whose boat she's rowing. "Mine, of course." And she knows how to respond when, in a club meeting, the male membership refuses to acknowledge women's needs for, among other things, coaching. "You rowed in college," she'll remind them. "Women didn't have that opportunity."

Kitty has acquired the patience she needs to deal with the

obstinate men, the ones who, as she gently phrases it, "couldn't care less if women row." She learned how to gain their respect, and "how much of that respect I need and how much I can do without."

For the past two years, Kitty has served on an otherwise all-male committee that organizes a youth regatta. She recently attended her first meeting—before that, the men in the group "forgot" to notify her of the meeting times. Some of the "old boys" got rather tipsy during lunch, before the business of the day began. When someone made a motion, Kitty seconded it. She wasn't prepared for what happened next. She recalls, "One old man, well in his cups, leaned over to me and whispered, 'Oh, dearie, I don't think you can vote.'"

Twenty years ago, Kitty says, she would not have had the courage to contradict him. Ten years ago, she "would have been so angry that there would have been a terrible scene." Now, she found it hilarious. Smiling, she told him, "Oh, I think I can."

The last time I saw Kitty, she and her partner, John Meehan, were rowing in the Head of the Potomac, a three-mile race that twists past Georgetown in Washington, D.C. Kitty "stroked" the boat, sitting in the stern and setting the pace for the approximately twenty-minute race. John sat in the bow, where it was his job to crane his neck around periodically and keep them on course. ("I don't like taking responsibility for not crashing into things," says Kitty.)

They began at Fletcher's Cove, wove through several sets of buoys and around some rock outcroppings. They didn't talk much, just rowed, stroke after stroke after stroke, listening to the now familiar sounds of long oars dipping and gripping the water, then, during the recovery part of the stroke, dripping droplets back onto the river. The exertion required to yank a boat through the water, fast, precludes chitchat. ("Part of the trick is learning how hard you can pull and manage to get to the end and not fall apart completely," Kitty said later, laughing.) Occasionally John called—"Turn coming" or "Ease off on starboard." When the wake of a passing powerboat threatened to flip them, he said "Shit."

If only Deborah could have seen her mother this time. Kitty and John were steady, strong, swift, and for the most part right on course.

Because the starting times had been staggered, each boat leaving twenty seconds after the previous one, Kitty and John couldn't tell for sure how they were faring compared with other mixed double teams. They just rowed, past the Potomac Boat Club, where fans waved enthusiastically, and past Thompson's Boat House, where Jovan Porterfield had meant to take photos; he went to the grocery store at the wrong time, however, and when he returned they'd already rowed past. Finally, Kitty and John muscled the boat across the finish line. Both of them collapsed, panting dramatically the way rowers always do at the end of a race.

Then they rowed unceremoniously upstream to the boathouse, stepped carefully out of their double shell, and smiled at each other. It was the first time they'd been face to face in a long while. They hoisted the boat over their heads and strapped it onto their club's trailer. Then Kitty, John, and Jovan sat on the back of John's pickup truck, dangling their feet, downing apple juice, and munching on peanut butter and banana sandwiches. Other rowers stopped by to chat. The results were not yet posted, but Kitty wasn't terribly curious.

"At the starting line, I looked around and it dawned on me that I was ten or fifteen years older than everyone else," she recalls. "They also had more experience. So it didn't make sense for me to say, 'We should win this race.' I just hoped it would be the best race we ever had together, and it was. Luckily, we still have more races coming up."

Kitty is still a beginner. She can't throw a ball, but she can heft a thirty-pound boat overhead and toss a massive bag of dog food into the trunk of her car. She can row now, with precision and power, and she's in good company. Most of the male members of her club respect her because she competes, she says; she ignores the rest. Her daughters cheer for her, her son coaches her, and her husband dangles his feet next to hers, holding her callused hand.

When she finished the last sip of apple juice, Kitty crunched the empty paper cup in her fist. Then the proud athlete hopped off the back of the pickup and, exhausted and happy, went grocery shopping.

I Never Thought
A Woman Could Go
This Fast

It's so acceptably easy for a woman not to strive too hard,
not to be too adventure-crazed, not to take too many risks
. . . not to live in a state of rampant amazement each day
because she can't get over the shock of living—being here
at all, in the midst of lichens and aromatic grasses and
octopi and golden-shouldered parakeets. It isn't seemly for
a woman to have that much zest.

—DIANE ACKERMAN[1]

*O*N October 22, 1988, Paula Newby-Fraser, a twenty-six-
year-old white woman from Zimbabwe, ran from the shores
of Hawaii's Kona Coast into the Pacific Ocean and promptly
became anonymous—a red-capped sardine flailing her well-
muscled arms and legs partly for locomotion, partly for self-
defense. When she emerged, dripping, almost an hour later,
most of the other 1,274 swimmers were still thrashing
through the waves.

Paula ran to the transition station to find her bike. She had
just completed the first third of the Ironman, the grueling
race that began as a beer-inspired bet in 1978 and gave birth

to the word "triathlon." Fifteen men had entered that first swim/bike/run competition. By 1988, a decade later, the Bud Light Ironman Triathlon World Championship had ballooned into a televised event offering $150,000 in prize money to the top fifteen male and ten female finishers in an international field of 1,275, including 240 women.

Paula Newby-Fraser had won this competition before, in 1986. As happens in road races, female and male Ironmen begin at the same time and cover the same distance, in this case a 2.4-mile ocean swim, a 112-mile bike ride through hilly lava fields, and finally a marathon—a 26.2-mile run, walk, or stumble, depending on one's condition. The best men finish first; to say Paula has won is to say she has won the *women's division.*

Were the Ironman a truly integrated race, with women and men judged on the same standards, as is the case in horse racing, equestrian events, car racing, and the Alaskan Iditarod dogsled race, for example, female contestants never would have been declared winners. The best woman had, until 1988, always finished more than an hour behind the best man. In 1987, the female winner placed twenty-sixth overall. Which is why Paula Newby-Fraser's eleventh-place-overall finish in 1988 shocked the triathlon community—and Paula herself—and upset long-established notions of what women can do.

During the bike ride Paula gained momentum, pedaling past each of the four women who had outswum her, including Erin Baker, the record holder from New Zealand. Paula didn't know how fast she was going. She had a watch on, but she didn't look at it because she didn't want to feel hurried. "I felt happy enough that if I blew up at the Ironman, that was too bad," she said. "I had a very relaxed mental attitude."

Paula relaxed through the marathon as well. The run has an out-and-back route, and as she approached the turnaround point, she saw her boyfriend, Paul Huddle, running at a slower pace. She had never passed him in a race before, and had never dreamed that she would. "It's terrible," she says, "but I didn't want to pass him. When I saw him, I'm going, 'No, that's not him.' When I got closer, I'm going, "Oh my God, it's him.' "

Paul Huddle, twenty-six, is a six-foot-two, 175-pound professional triathlete. He finished fifteenth in the 1987 Ironman. Paul and Paula live together in San Diego (she retains Zimbabwean citizenship) but rarely train together, partly because he's stronger than she is ("He could beat me in any sprint") and partly because, as with many couples, it makes the relationship easier when they don't share a workplace as well as a home.

Paula passed him without so much as a nod. "I didn't know what to say," she explains in a still strong accent. "I want Paul to excel in his chosen sport as much as I want to do well. I didn't realize at the time that he was doing well." She was thinking: If I'm passing him, he must be having a terrible day.

He was having a fine day. He eventually finished fifteenth among the men again—sixteenth overall, because of Paula's eleventh-place finish. "Good job, keep it going, you look really strong," he called as Paula, eight inches shorter and sixty pounds lighter, sped past.

Chris Hinshaw, a friend of Paul's, was near them at the time. "Let's go with her," he suggested to Paul.

"*You* go with her," Paul said, gasping. He explains: "She was moving twenty seconds a mile faster than us at the time. I would have exploded if I tried to go with her. At that point in the race, you just want to finish. But a lot of guys were in shock."

Some teased Paul: "She's in front of you, she's beating you."

"Shut up, she's beating you too," came his reply.

Paula crossed the finish line with enough energy left over for a triumphant raised-arms salute; she had sliced more than a half-hour—34 minutes, 24 seconds—off the women's record. She finished a mere 12 seconds after the tenth-place man and just 30 minutes, 1 second after the male winner, Scott Molina. Her time of 9:01:01 would have been fast enough to beat all of the men in any of the Ironman triathlons before 1984.

"I never thought a woman could go this fast," she said.

Now, from the men's times in the previous four years, she knew that a *person* could go that fast. She knew that, in a sport merely ten years old, improvement is inevitable. Nevertheless, she had developed in her mind a limit not on human performance but on female performance. She had thought that on a particularly good day she might finish in 9:25 or 9:30. Erin Baker had recently predicted that she, Erin, could eventually finish in 9:15, and Paula had thought Erin grandiose.

In a way, Paula was right to be shocked. Everyone was shocked. The consensus is that men are better athletes than women, period. Those who gaze into the crystal ball of sports consistently make predictions about how good men will get and how good women will get, and the women's times are slower than the men's. Like others, Paula had decided that relative to men women would always be slow. She had believed the myth of female inferiority.

Tennis, golf, basketball, volleyball: it's easy to rattle off names of sports in which the best men outdo the best women. Men fare even better in sports from which women have been and to a large degree still are barred: football, ice hockey, wrestling, baseball. It's impossible to find sports in which *all* men are better than *all* women, but it's true that many male athletes are better than many female athletes, and that the overall world records in most sports belong to men.

Men often act as if women athletes were inferior, racing to cover women's positions in coed softball or volleyball games, offering unsolicited advice on golf courses, tennis courts, anywhere sports are played. Although many women bristle at these intrusions, others collude in the belief that men know more about sports and are more capable. Sometimes the very design of a playing field reinforces this idea. "As soon as I step up to the red tee, there is an expectation that I will underperform a male player," says Cathryn Thorup, a novice golfer and the director of studies and programs at San Diego's Center for U.S.–Mexican Studies. "That assumption of inferiority is reinforced on every hole."

That assumption starts in childhood. Temple University professor Carole Oglesby asked two groups of children to imagine a bicycle race between a boy and girl of the same age. Both kids have new bikes and similar skills, she told them. Who would win? In the younger group, five-year-olds, the kids were evenly divided as to who would win. In the older group, aged nine to eleven, the majority of both girls and boys predicted that the boy would win. Despite the success of women's professional tennis and golf, despite the visibility of women in the Olympics, despite the integration of Little League, preteen children seem to believe that somehow, even with equal equipment and equal skills, boys emerge as better athletes than girls.

I posed the question to my nine-year-old neighbor, Lora Cary, forgetting to mention the "equal equipment" clause. The boy would win, she said decisively. Why? "Because boys get better bikes," she asserted. "My brother's bike has eighteen speeds, and girls his age [thirteen] usually only have five."

In fact, given equal equipment, training, and encouragement, the average young girl would probably be physically superior to the average young boy, since girls tend to mature faster than boys. But like many myths, that of female physical inferiority becomes true the more people act as if it were true. "'You can't do that, you're not that strong, you just can't'— that's what you're told," says bowling Hall of Famer Betty Morris. "If you hear that enough, you can't. That's one of the things that's keeping [men and women] apart. A lot of the ladies feel, deep down inside, Well, I can't. Because they've been conditioned for so long to think that."[2]

When I talked with Paula Newby-Fraser in June 1989, she had just returned from winning the World Triathlon Championship in Nice (yes, the sport of triathlon has two world championships, and no, it doesn't make sense). "The respect women get there is horrible," she reported. "You get up on-stage, and everybody [says], 'Oh, look at these attractive young women, isn't it nice they have this hobby.' When the top men get up, there's a complete standing ovation." Paula won $11,000 for her efforts; the winning man took home $12,000 plus a jeep. She has threatened to boycott the event in the future.

To sort out natural differences from environmentally created ones, physiologists speak of sex-linked characteristics, carried on the Y chromosomes, and gender-associated characteristics, carried on through the culture. Height, weight, and strength are sex-linked, physiologists have decided. The average man is naturally taller, heavier, and stronger than the average woman. Yet there is considerable overlap: many women are taller, heavier, and stronger than many men.

Differences also exist in average cardiorespiratory capability, percentage of body fat, and thermoregulation. In other words, the average man has a bigger heart and lungs, he is leaner, and he sweats more.

Exactly how much these differences—or others, such as shoulder breadth—matter, and in which sports, remains unclear. Men have an advantage in endurance events, some argue, because they have more efficient lungs and less fat to carry around. Women have an advantage in endurance sports, others argue, because they can cash in on that store of fat, they are better able to withstand heat, and they have less total weight to carry around.

Comparing women with men is an imprecise science partly because researchers have usually compared trained men with untrained women. More recent studies have found that the male strength advantage shrinks when trained women are studied alongside trained men. But even if researchers measure the strength or speed of the best women athletes, they can never track down a woman who was reared in an environment where at least half of the most highly paid and highly visible athletes were female; where parents, friends, coaches, and teachers all rewarded and developed her talents; and where she was inspired by and chosen from among millions of other girls similarly developing athletic skills.

Male athletic superiority seems so obvious not only because men have been given lifelong physical training and indoctrination that they are the stronger sex, but because two of the most visible, most revered sports (in the United States, at least)—football and basketball—capitalize on men's natural assets. If one were to design sports specifically to favor men's strengths, football and basketball would be ideal.

In other sports, however, such as distance swimming, riflery, and horse racing, men's physiques do not make them the best all-around athletes. Height can be helpful (basketball, volleyball), but it can also be a drawback (gymnastics, horse racing). As steroid use is proving, testosterone boosts strength and bulk, but bulk in itself is useful only in certain sports and can be disadvantageous in others. Strength is important but overrated as the decisive factor in most sports. In ice hockey, for example, skillful stickwork is more important than sheer strength, and short people with a low center of gravity have an edge.

It's not clear what women's sex-linked advantages are. Body fat seems helpful for cold-water swimming and it may be for other endurance events, but some marathon swimmers and most runners are lean. Flexibility is helpful, but if men spent as much time stretching muscles as contracting them, they might be as flexible as women.

Women's relatively lower center of gravity could be an advantage in most land sports, including golf, tennis, and baseball. Squash pro Karen Kelso says that being short helps her win games against men. "In most sports, it pays to bend your knees," she explains. "Small people can bend easier, with less low-back pain. Muscularity helps, but there's more to sport than muscles. If a man is stronger, I don't try to outmuscle him. If he slams it, I lob it back. If he slams it again, I lob it back again."

In equestrian events, it is often said that women have a better relationship with the horses. Women are more sensitive, or the horses respect women more; they feel safer in women's hands. People have explained the success of Susan Butcher, four-time winner of the Iditarod Trail Sled Dog Race, by saying she has a maternal way with the dogs. Susan laughs that off. "It was funny—when I was coming in second, it was always: 'Susan's never going to win, because she babies her dogs too much.' Now that I'm winning, it's: 'Well, Susan wins because she takes better care of her dogs.' "

"What women lack in brute strength, they make up for in toughness," contends endurance athlete Julie Ridge. Women are tougher, she and others have postulated, because they were built to endure childbirth—"the most painful thing a human being has to go through." A higher pain tolerance leads to a more gutsy performance, she says.

Pain tolerance is difficult to measure. Even if what Ridge says is true, it's not necessarily an advantage. Successful athletes have to learn not only to tolerate some pain but to respect it, and to rest. Victories are not, despite popular conceptions, achieved by ignoring pain. Especially not second and third victories.

We do know that physical characteristics, to whatever degree they may be sexlinked, tell only part of the story. Does the tallest, strongest, bulkiest man always win? No. Case in point: Michael Chang, five-eight and 135 pounds, won the 1989 French Open in men's tennis, defeating larger, heavier opponents. Persistence, courage, desire, patience, humility, intelligence, and self-confidence—none of which is sexlinked—play a huge role in athletic accomplishments, as do technique and skill.

Comparisons between women and men must be tempered further by the fact that the women athletes who rise to the top are the cream of a very small crop. Women's participation has increased dramatically in the past two decades, but of the 5.26 million kids playing interscholastic high school sports in the

United States, only 1.84 million are girls. Only about one-third of college athletes are female.

Few if any women are good enough to play pro baseball, but it's not because they're all shorter or weaker. Lisa Rubarth, a six-foot-one, 185-pound first basewoman for the UCLA team that won the 1978 women's college world series, says she "definitely" could have played pro baseball had she been raised on Little League, high school, and college baseball. "Lots of the best women softball players could," she says.

Really? Lots of them? Although not known for their speed or endurance, baseball players do tend to be rather large and strong. Could women really keep up?

Back in 1931, a woman named Virne "Jackie" Mitchell, in an exhibition baseball game between the Chatanooga Lookouts and the New York Yankees, struck out both Babe Ruth and Lou Gehrig.[3] More recently, in 1981, softball pitcher Kathy Arendsen of the Stratford, Connecticut, Hi-Ho Brakettes struck out Reggie Jackson three times in three meetings.

But Donna de Varona, chair and founding member of the Women's Sports Foundation, cautions that in the process of comparing women's and men's achievements, we must be careful not to let women's traditional arenas of success become devalued. "In some ways, the question of whether men and women can compete equally is a trap," she says. "While it's exciting to watch women match men's feats of speed and strength, the comparison implies that those events that women have traditionally excelled in—like the barrel race [a rodeo event] or figure skating—are somehow not as important. While challenging the boys, we must not forget that there is genuine athleticism in grace and beauty."[4]

Helen Lenskyj, in *Out of Bounds*, counters that women's involvement in sports that they are "naturally" good at—"individual, aesthetically pleasing activities that show their beauty and grace to good effect while making relatively small demands on strength and endurance"—has "a deceptive aura of common sense and naturalness. They reinforce 'what is' in terms of relations between the sexes: females are the smaller, slower, weaker sex, needing the protection of the bigger, stronger, faster men. The alternative strategy, encouraging participation in the areas in which each sex is weaker, with the goal of equalizing performance and promoting full human potential, provides a tantalizing glimpse of 'what might be.' "[5]

Many companies that sponsor athletic events seem to be more interested in tantalizing glimpses of female flesh. When women started entering triathlons in the late seventies, they changed from one outfit to another at the transition stations, or they wore the skintight "trisuits," reminiscent of men's turn-of-the-century bathing suits. Next they wore one-piece swimsuits. Now, to appease and appeal to sponsors, they wear as little as possible. "Obviously there's the fashion side of what you race in as far as marketing goes," says Paula Newby-Fraser, now a businesswoman who rakes in more than $100,-000 a year in prize money, and at least another $100,000 in product endorsements.

But she has her limits. She says that Murphy Reinschreiber, her agent/manager, "is trying very hard to let [Aerodynamics, her clothing sponsor] know I'm no, as he puts it, 'piece of meat.' When you go there, they do a real job on your hair, your makeup. I just went for a photo shoot the other week, and the marketing woman is going, 'I don't like your hair. Why was it cut like this?' I'm like, 'It wasn't cut for this photo shoot, it's cut so I can tie it up for training.' If I was a model, then they could pick on the way my hair looks."

More dangerous than trying to please sponsors is trying to compete with other female triathletes in an unofficial beauty contest. They compliment each other for losing weight, Paula says, thus reinforcing the notion: The skinnier the better. Paula says she's catching this weight obsession like an infectious disease.

When she entered her first Ironman, in 1985, she carried 123 pounds on her five-foot, six-inch frame and felt fit. In

1986, at 120 pounds, she won. In 1987, she had shrunk to "about 110 or 111." She remembers, "My logical brain told me, 'You have to have reserves.' I knew I should put on about five pounds the week before, and I never did. I suffered cramps, something I've never had. Everybody tells me I looked emaciated before that race." She finished a disappointing third.

Now, at 115 pounds, she says her body image is "pretty bad." She doesn't like her legs or buttocks. "I always feel like, 'Gosh, I'm not thin enough.' I always go, 'Do I look fat?' Paul has heard it more times than I care to remember. He gives up. He says, 'You're really thin.' What can he do? I always ask. I realize it's a little bit destructive."

For noncompetitive women, weight obsession can be psychologically devastating and, in the cases of anorexia and bulimia, even fatal. Athletes share those risks; they also risk undermining their achievements.

"Do you ever eat less than you need for training?" I ask Paula.

"Sometimes, but I realize what I'm doing," she replies. "I try not to get into it. I've seen girls out there who are getting too thin. They're not eating enough, and they're getting sick and weak."

Male logic and lore create more problems. When she began entering triathlons in 1985, Paula was shocked that the sport was still so male-dominated. "All the literature was by men," she says. "The mileages, the distances we were socialized into thinking we needed to do, were oriented toward the top men in the sport." The name of the Ironman competition remains unchanged, although women have participated since the second year, 1979.

Paula has established her own training regimen and is considered unusual because she trains so little. Before the 1985 race, she had never ridden a bike 100 miles. As a teen, she had been an Olympic-level swimmer, but she didn't accept college scholarships because her coach had overtrained her, she says, and she'd grown to hate the water. Now Paula averages a mere 10,000 meters' swimming, 250 miles' bike riding, and 55 miles' running per week—which, believe it or not, is a cake-walk by modern triathlon standards. Paula says these distances are appropriate for women—and perhaps also for men.

Another factor that limits women's performance in a way men don't experience is what sports physiologist Linda Bunker calls the "ceiling effect" of boyfriends and fathers. When a father, for instance, says, "Have fun bowling, but don't beat him," the girl, wanting to please both her father and her boyfriend, often balks.

The example sounds dated, but women still choose to assuage male egos, to the detriment of their own success. "I was always taught never to beat the boys," says swimmer Nancy Hogshead, winner of one silver and three gold medals at the 1984 Olympics.

Sometimes, at the professional level, instead of women's slowing down, men drop out, withdrawing from both the race and the romance. During the 1988 Ironman, Paula watched Erin Baker's former fiancé, John Hughes, quit when Erin passed him. "As soon as Erin caught him, he hopped on the nearest motor scooter" and rode to the finish, reports Paula. "He was still in the top twenty—having a perfectly good day. He was not prepared to stay in the race with her in front of him."

Later, Hughes, a New Zealander like Erin, said to Paul Huddle, "Mate, how did you do it?"

"Do what?" asked Paul.

"How did you stay in the race after [Paula] passed you? When I heard Erin was coming up, I just dropped."

"I was having a great race," explained Paul. "I was still in the money. I could have dropped out, but what's the point?"

(In 1989, a woman dropped out of the triathlon, also for romantic reasons, but different ones. Julie Moss, who made Ironman a household word by crawling across the finish line in 1982, dropped out in 1989 because she got news that her fiancé, Mark Allen, was winning and she wanted to cheer him on. Julie had been in seventh place among the women. She had been swimming, cycling, and running for about eight hours, and she was two hours from finishing. But she hitched a ride in a television truck and rode the rest of the race in front of Mark, encouraging him onward.)

Despite discrimination and despite female collusion in the myth of male superiority, women are gaining on men. What were once huge gaps between male and female performance are no longer. It's as if Woman and Man are running a race; he has a head start, but over the years her speed increases and his stays relatively constant. To look at a chart marking the decrease in men's and women's world-record times in many sports is to see one fairly flat line tilting gradually downhill and another plummeting as dramatically as a ski slope.

Women and men already compete equally in several arenas, among them equestrian events, archery, auto racing, and horse racing. In riflery, the only coed sport at the NCAA Division I level, women won three of the four individual crowns at the 1989 and 1990 national championships. In artistic sports such as skating and gymnastics, some would argue that women's performances outwow those of their male counterparts.

The best female bowlers are, according to them, as good as the best men. Some male bowlers dispute this, claiming that scores from different tournaments with different lane conditions cannot be compared, but at the 1988 Gold Rush Mixed Doubles Shootout in Las Vegas, women's and men's averages were virtually identical.

Runners are catching up. Women have finished first overall in several marathons, 50- and 100-mile runs, and twenty-four-hour runs. In September 1989, Californian Ann Trason became the first woman to win an open national championship, the Sri Chinmoy TAC/USA 24-Hour Race, with a national record-setting distance of 143 miles. The second-place finisher, Scott DeMaree of Colorado, ran four fewer miles. The fourth-place finisher was also female. Kathy Switzer, the woman who sexually integrated the Boston Marathon in 1967 by entering the race under the name K. Switzer, contends that after about sixty miles, women are faster than men. "The marathon is too short," she says.[6]

Even sprinters are not that far behind. In 1988, Florence Griffith Joyner's 100-meter world record of 10.64 was just .72 of a second slower than Carl Lewis's record.

Janet Evans's 1988 world records in the 800- and 1500-meter freestyle would have been world records for men in 1972. In other words, she is slower than today's male swimmers, but she is not slower than yesterday's. Her record for the 400-meter freestyle beats Mark Spitz's 1968 world record by more than two seconds. Back in 1968 and 1972, women did not share men's access to early sports training, including college scholarships. They had not been taught to believe in their own sports potential. The number of female competitors was much smaller than the number of males. Is it possible that, all those things being equal, Janet could have beaten Mark Spitz?

Who knows what might have happened in the 1988 Olympics if Evans, a triple gold-medal winner, had been permitted to swim her best event, the 1500-meter freestyle. "She would have beat everyone by twenty-five seconds," says her coach, Bud McAllister.[7] But it was not an Olympic event for women—only for men.

In the long distances, women are the better swimmers. Californian Penny Dean has held the English Channel record of 7 hours, 40 minutes since 1978, when she was just thirteen. In the 28.5-mile swim around Manhattan, Shelley Taylor-Smith won three years in a row, from 1987 through 1989.

Another Californian, Lynne Cox, thirty-two, holds the overall records for swimming the Bering Strait and the Strait of Magellan. She is the only person to have swum across southern Siberia's Lake Baikal and around the Cape of Good Hope.

In endurance cycling, the top women are closing in on the men. In the 1989 Race Across America, Susan Notorangelo, the first female finisher, placed seventh overall with a time of 9 days, 9 hours, 9 minutes—which would have been an overall first-place time as recently as 1987.

In the triathlon, it is likely that Newby-Fraser or another woman will soon catch the top ten men, thus mixing the races, so to speak. Just a month before Newby-Fraser's victory, Erin Baker finished eleventh overall in the Nice Triathlon, just *one minute* slower than the 1987 men's winner. "The implications of both of these outstanding performances are fascinating, if not frightening, for many men," wrote C. J. Olivares, Jr., the editor of *Triathlete* magazine. "Will race directors finally distribute prize money equally among men and women? Will women be allowed to collect prize money for both women's and men's places if there is an overlap? Is there the possibility that men and women will someday compete against each other in a new open division?"[8]

In other words, might we eventually give up the notion that men are naturally, biologically better athletes? I raised the question with women friends while working on this book. "You're not going to see women playing professional football, are you?" one said.

Even women have come to think of football as the most important sport. Note how often both women and men intone "Men are stronger" as a justification for female exclusion from sport, whereas "Women are shorter and lighter" has never been used to keep men from becoming jockeys. (Nor has the fact that Hispanic men tend to be relatively short kept Hispanics from pro baseball.)

Maybe, because of testosterone-based strength differentials, the best women and the best men will never compete equally in football, basketball, weightlifting, power lifting, or other sports—volleyball, tennis, rowing, wrestling—that depend on strength or what physiologists call the ability to generate power. Maybe women will compete equally only in equestrian events, swimming, diving, running, cycling, triathlon, skiing, softball, baseball, golf, gymnastics, riflery, archery, horse racing, table tennis, skating, windsurfing, field hockey, curling, fencing, bowling, and billiards.

Ideally, sports would be organized not according to gender but according to height, weight, or skill level. Eliminating the gender category would go a long way toward offering women a fair shot at sports, and offering men the myriad lessons of integration.

Children's soccer leagues, organized only by age, and coed softball leagues, organized only by ability, have set two precedents for non-gender-related sports opportunities. Recreational tennis leagues, swim clubs, and high schools are not far behind: they divide people first by gender, but then according to skill, with A and B, or varsity and junior varsity teams. Wrestling teams classify boys (and an occasional girl) by weight; basketball leagues sometimes offer a men's "under six-foot-two" division.

What if women had no cultural disadvantages? What if as children they had access to sports opportunities that specifically encouraged girls and included many visible, respected, well-paid women athletes? If women were never segregated from boys, never called tomboys, never dressed in restrictive clothing, never admonished to "act like young ladies," and were taught sports skills—what then?

We can only imagine. Julie Ridge, herself the world record holder of a swim in which she circled Manhattan five times in five days, predicts that even with the smaller pool of competitors and the numerous cultural disadvantages, a woman will win the Ironman by the year 2000. "I'd say sooner, but I don't want to be wrong," she adds.

We need a new paradigm, a framework for comprehending competition that includes women and men as peers. "I never thought a woman could go this fast" won't do. "I want Paul to excel in his chosen sport as much as I want to do well" sounds more like it. Paula doesn't need to drop out of the race to stand by her man, and Paul doesn't have to shrivel in shame when Paula sprints past him. They can support each other just as triathlon twins Patricia and Sylviane Puntous do, accepting the fact that, come time to cross the finish line, one will inevitably finish before the other. They can use each other's accomplishments as inspiration.

Paula experienced her own paradigm shift after the 1988 race and began comparing herself to the best people, instead of just the best women. It makes her angry now when she can't beat Paul in a 10K running race.

Paul says, "Paula, I've been running for ten years. You've been running for four. Think how fast you'll go in ten years' time."

We Are the Best

Alaska: Where men are men and women win the Iditarod.

—Popular T-shirt slogan
in Alaska

*T*O play with men is one thing. To defeat men is something else entirely.

Susan Butcher has defeated boys since she was a little girl growing up in Cambridge, Massachusetts. Canoeing, sailing, running, mountain climbing: she was always the best. Not the best in the women's division, the best of all.

Eventually she made defeating men a career, although she doesn't think of it that way. Because of her love of dogs, snow, cold, wilderness, competition, and adventure, she became an Alaskan dogsled racer, competing each year since 1978 in the Iditarod Trail Sled Dog Race, a grueling eleven- or twelve-day, 1,049-mile trek from Anchorage to Nome along an old route of the Alaskan gold rush.[1] For three years in a row, from 1986 to 1988, and again in 1990, Butcher won the race. She didn't win the women's division—there isn't such a thing—she won the race.

It's nothing personal, this beating-men thing. Susan doesn't see it as anything with deep psychological significance. She doesn't trace her competitiveness to her father, who, before divorcing her mother, taught Susan and her sister to sail and ski. She doesn't say, as many women do, that her father wanted a boy. Analysis and introspection are distasteful to her. That's one thing she likes about living in the Alaskan bush: people are too busy working to spend time sitting around thinking about things.

"I'm lucky to have grown up feeling there were no restrictions on me because I was a woman," Susan says. Does it have any particular relevance to her, then, that for five years she has dominated a sport that includes men as well as women? "Oh, it has tons of relevance. It's more of a challenge. I enjoy it. From the time I was a little tiny girl, I was the first girl to do this or the first girl to do that. At coed camps I would better all the boys."

What's so great about beating boys?

"I don't know," she says. "I was just trying to beat everybody, I guess. And that included the men."

This is how men get to feel—a few men, for a few moments, and all men, vicariously: the best. Not the best of one gender, but the best of all.

At this moment in history, the sports in which the best women are most likely to equal or exceed the best men are those that require flexibility or endurance or those in which horses, dogs, cars, go-carts, guns, or other machines or animals are involved. Susan Butcher came to this realization in her late teens, and it was upsetting. The boys she had been beating in every conceivable endeavor miraculously grew taller than she did and amassed muscles that dwarfed hers. If you want to be the best person, adolescence can be a drag. "Sure, I could still beat a lot of them in arm wrestling and things like that, but in all-out speed, I couldn't," she remembers. "Endurance I've always had, so in mountain climbing I could still be one of the very best people. I didn't pick it for that reason, but I was lucky to end up with a sport [dogsled racing] where I'm able to compete on an equal level."

Some women take particular delight in winning on this

equal level. Tennis sensation Jennifer Capriati says, "When I whip the boys, any boy, that makes me feel so proud. I hear them saying things like, 'Man, ain't no female going to beat me.' When I hear that, I really get psyched. . . . I make them respect me."[2]

Michelle Granger, one of the best softball pitchers in the country, says, "I pitch against the guys once in a while. They say, 'Oh, we can hit her [pitches].' They've never seen me pitch, or they don't really know how a softball pitcher pitches. Then it's a lot of fun. You go out and throw a couple of pitches and strike them out."[3]

Says baseball player Julie Croteau: "I used to have a friend on a team when I was thirteen. He was a big boy, six-two, and outplaying him was fun. There's something about beating somebody you're not supposed to beat that makes it twice as nice."

Newspaper editors see it as a big story when women beat men, even in obscure sports. Who besides Alaskans (who are nuts about dogsled racing) had heard of the Iditarod until Libby Riddles won in 1985? A nice twist: an activity being taken seriously because women are good at it.

Perhaps it's the "we are the best" feeling that appeals to the voting members of the Women's Sports Foundation. In 1987 and 1988, the Foundation chose Susan Butcher as Professional Sportswoman of the Year over richer, more visible nominees such as Steffi Graf and Pat Bradley—chose, in other words, Alaskan dogsled racing over international tennis and golf. It wasn't the sport that mattered, but the gender of the competition.

The "we are the best" feeling may also explain why Billie Jean King is better known for beating Bobby Riggs than for her twenty Wimbledon titles, and why race-car driver Lyn St. James is inordinately popular with women's business and professional organizations, whose members ask her: How do you do it? How do you beat the boys at their own games? Should we?

What does it mean to women, men, and society in general

when women are the best of all? What sort of winners are women? Gracious and ladylike? Toughened by the climb to the top? Or boastful and vengeful, so subsumed by the male sports systems that they defend and uphold the military model?

Do female winners identify with the men who preceded them? Or with the women who follow them?

Female athletic superiority seems a new phenomenon, but it is not. Over the years, female champions have beaten men in international rifle-shooting events, national bobsled championships, ultradistance running races, and other contests. Female marathon swimmers, billiards players, bowlers, equestrians, horse racers, and auto racers have won major coed events. At the recreational level, women and men compete daily, and women often win. Yet because men still dominate in virtually every aspect of society, female victories take on mythic proportions.

Greek mythology is full of women athletes and warriors, from the hunter Artemis to swimming naiads.[4] But it is the Greek myth of Atalanta that seems most to pervade modern-day thinking about women who supersede men.

Atalanta was a woman who didn't confine herself to the "women's division." Her father, disappointed that she was not born male, left his baby on a mountain to die. Hunters adopted her, a bear nursed her, and Atalanta became a courageous hunter, admired for her athletic feats, which included defending herself against centaurs and defeating the male hero Peleus in a wrestling match.[5]

Then her father reentered the picture. Maybe she had turned out to be "enough of a boy" for him. In any case, he suggested she get married and settle down.

Forget it, she said.

Eventually they compromised. She would marry any man who could beat her in a footrace; losing challengers would be killed.

(It was a new game plan, but one that caught on. Later, the

goddess Thetis made a similar offer, and Peleus—using techniques learned from Atalanta, perhaps—defeated Thetis in a wrestling match and won the right to marry her. Their son, Achilles, was also athletic but had some heel problems.[6])

Anyway, Atalanta outran the first several challengers, and they were put to death. Then a young man named Hippomenes stepped forward. He matched her stride for stride for the first half of the race but was unable to pull ahead. He grabbed three golden apples—given to him by Aphrodite—and rolled them across Atalanta's path. She stooped to pick them up, and lost a few steps and eventually the race.

For men, the lesson seems to be that one must be both swift *and* clever to keep up with women. But for women, the lesson is that no matter how talented and independent you are, men will think of ways to defeat you or "win you over." Some will even die trying.

As in the story of Atalanta, marriage remains inseparable from women's athletic accomplishments. Unmarried, boyfriendless athletes are subject to unending "Is she or isn't she?" scrutiny. Susan Butcher says reporters once asked her dog handler, a woman, "Do you live with Susan? In that small cabin? Well, where do you sleep?"

"She had her own bed, but what business is that of theirs?" adds Susan with characteristic forthrightness. "There were those who labeled me gay for years. I was labeled everything you can think of. What bothered me was not that I was labeled, but that I was asked at all. They weren't asking any of the single male mushers what their sexual life was, but they were constantly asking me."

Now that Susan is married, the questions focus on children. "People are waiting to see: Will Susan have a child?" she says. "I hope to have children. But maybe I can't bear them. And if I can't bear them I'm not going to feel like less of a woman."

Susan's courtship with David Monson, a lawyer turned musher, began, as Atalanta and her spouse's did, during a race. Susan and David got acquainted in a ditch they had both fallen into during the 1981 Iditarod. David told the story to

The Boston Globe Magazine this way: "Susan had already fallen in the brush, and Emmit Peters fell in after me. So we had forty-five dogs in there, one irate woman, and a musher who didn't know beans from catsup. That was me. When we finally got out, she told me, 'You've got to rest your dogs.' I said, 'Gee, sure. OK,' and that was the last time I saw her in the race."[7]

Never having beaten her in the Iditarod, David now enters shorter races, such as the Yukon Quest. That's fine with Susan. She brags about his victories. They share dog care and housework.

Yet the myth marches on. In a 1989 *Sports Illustrated* story about Julie Krone, one of the most successful jockeys, male or female, Gary Smith wrote, "And now that she wasn't a *female* jockey anymore [meaning not overtly discriminated against as such], she could be a female [meaning traditionally feminine]. She could wear dresses and talk now and then about retiring in ten years, having a baby or maybe adopting one, settling down on a farm in Colorado."[8]

The notion of a career-ending marriage comes up with virtually all successful women athletes, even those who don't compete directly with men. A *Sports Illustrated* cover at the time of Chris Evert's retirement in 1989 quoted her as saying, "I'm going to be a full-time wife."[9] As if marriage were an occupation.

Triathlete Paula Newby-Fraser says she's often asked when she and Paul Huddle will get married and when she will retire to have babies. "I don't plan on getting married and I don't plan on having children," she answers brusquely.

Even teenagers are not spared. After winning three gold medals at the 1988 Olympics, sixteen-year-old Janet Evans answered more questions about her boyfriend than about swimming.

Billie Jean King catapulted women's sports into the limelight not by playing against women but by defeating a man. In 1973, when she beat Bobby Riggs, she was married. She was also having an affair with a woman, but that did not become public information until years later. Nor was it widely known that she had had an abortion two years before, primarily because her marriage was on such shaky ground. With Larry King at her side, she seemed the good wife, an outspoken feminist who challenged the blatant sexism personified by Riggs but who did not openly challenge the deep-seated belief that women who outperform men should at least have the decency to temper that strength by allowing themselves to be "won over" by a husband.

Riggs, a former pro, was fifty-five when he played King. Her victory (6–4, 6–3, 6–3) was a triumph of youth over age, but it was certainly not covered that way.

There's nothing wrong with friendly competition. At road races and triathlons worldwide, men are spurred on by the women in their midst. During San Francisco's annual Bay-to-Breakers road race, costumed teams of men called "centipedes" try to beat Joan Benoit Samuelson to the finish line. Women and men are naturally curious about how they compare with each other, now that large numbers of women have entered the race. It seems all in fun.

But calling competitions battles of the sexes unnecessarily severs the population along gender lines. A horse race featuring a black jockey and a white jockey and billed as a "battle of the colors" would be unthinkable. A "battle of the sexes" between Julie Krone and all-time leader Bill Shoemaker drew no protests. (Krone won.) To pit women against men in such a way can only polarize and antagonize.

To cast athletic competition as intergender war is also to misinterpret women's participation. Increased strength may help women defend themselves against physical attacks, but most women don't understand or talk about their athletic victories in terms of domination, defeat, or control. They play for love or money, for fun or fat reduction, and test themselves against men primarily because they're there, like mountains.

If women are thrilled by victory, it's because men provide

a challenge or because there's joy in demonstrating to dubious men that women are competent. But it's not a battle, and the goal is not so much to defeat men as to elevate women.

I talked with cyclist Elaine Mariolle, winner of the 1986 Race Across America, hours before the conclusion of the 1990 Iditarod. Susan Butcher was in the lead, and Elaine was rooting for her. "I love that race. The dogs are the athletes. The power and strength differentials are taken out of it, and it comes down to management skills, and how you can get along with other creatures," Elaine said. But she was concerned about the standard being set. "When women get in a position where we have to be better than men in order to be taken seriously, it's the same old story. We shouldn't have to be better than them to be seen as equals."

Susan Butcher has come to New York City to attend the 1988 Women's Sports Foundation's annual banquet, where she will again receive the Professional Sportswoman of the Year Award. Already, she misses Alaska—the snow, the vast sky. She and David live in a log cabin, heat with wood, and haul water from a stream. They fish from that stream, and from the Yukon River; they hunt moose. "We call it Eureka," she says of their home, which is 50 miles from the nearest supermarket and 25 miles from the nearest phone. Fairbanks, the nearest city, is 140 miles to the southeast. When David moved in with Susan a few years ago, he brought a generator; he enjoys such modern conveniences as the radio. Susan would rather listen to the familiar, happy panting of her 150 Alaskan huskies, each tied to its own little doghouse, just outside their owner's cabin.

Susan says of the dogs: "My dogs are both my pets and my coworkers. In addition, I've raised them all, so they're my family. And they're my livelihood and my teammates. This trust is strong between us. They know that I depend on them and they depend on me. The relationship is amazingly close."

Lyn St. James, also in New York for this banquet, is somehow more traditional, although driving race cars is hardly a conservative occupation. Now forty-two, she spends most weekends strapped into her Ford, zooming along closed-course roadways, traveling at about 200 miles per hour for up to two hours at a time.

Like Susan, Lyn St. James is used to winning. She's the only woman to have won a race in the International Motor Sports Association Camel GTO Series, and she's won five of those. She has set twenty-one national and international speed records, five of them "best woman" records, the other sixteen "best of all." She has driven 232 miles per hour. She has crashed, "I don't know how many times," she says. ESPN is fond of replaying one particularly horrific crash from 1986.

"I didn't choose racing because men and women competed together and I wanted to beat men," she says adamantly. "I loved cars, loved driving, and loved driving fast."

It was her mother, a cabbie, who taught her to drive ("My father didn't know a front end from a rear end"), her mother who served as chaperone when Lyn and a bunch of boys from high school first went to an Indianapolis 500, which Lyn calls "the most incredible experience I'd ever had." Women weren't permitted in the pit area, but Lyn attended a drivers' meeting that was open to the public. There she saw A. J. Foyt and Mario Andretti. "I never in a million years thought I'd be doing what they did," she recalls. "There wasn't any point of reference for me. I was a girl."

Lyn won her first drag race at age seventeen. Women were expected to race in the Powder Puff division in those days, but Lyn refused. "All the guys laughed at that," she remembers. "It was a mockery. So my goal was to win overall, and not just be the best woman."

Lyn wants to beat the people who count, the contenders who are taken seriously: the men.

Karen Kelso wants to beat the people who get paid. Squash is such a piddly sport in this country that pro tournaments are hard to come by, and even fewer are the ones that offer prize money to women. In five years of professional squash, the most Kelso, twenty-seven, has earned for winning a tournament is $1,450. (Male tournament winners generally earn between $3,000 and $6,000.) Lately, when a tournament offers prize money to the men but not the women, Kelso will enter the men's division. She hasn't won any men's pro tournaments yet, but she has won several early rounds and can beat many of the top men in her home city, Denver. "I like to beat men. It's really fun. I can't imagine anything nicer than beating a man," Karen says, then adds without a smile, "I'd like to be the best male player in Denver." Currently, she's the second best female player in the country, unranked among the men.

At five-three and 115 pounds, Karen Kelso could pass for a gymnast. She gets a kick out of surprising people—at least the handful of people who attend professional squash tournaments. Her male opponents are sometimes a foot taller and a hundred pounds heavier. "They're strikingly more athletic-looking," she says. Because most people define "athletic-looking" in terms of men's bodies, what she says rings true: the men are large, wheras Karen is small. To see a small person, especially a small female person, outplay a large man does have shock value. The men, in particular, are shocked.

In one tournament in the fall of 1989, Kelso competed aqainst a six-foot, four-inch Australian man. The match looked strange, the man large and lumbering, little Karen buzzing around him like a pesky fly. He won the first two games in a best-of-five set, then made the mistake of relaxing. She won the next two games, asking for an umpire midway through to settle disputes about calls. The Australian was nearly frantic by the fifth game, banging his long racket into the wall, smashing the ball viciously. Kelso won the match.

"Men can always resort to pride in being male—that they shouldn't lose to a woman," Karen commented afterward. "Like this guy today—he thought he was going to win the match, so he started getting all nice to me. Then I think it occurred to him in the fifth game that he was going to lose, and he went wild."

. . .

Male dogsled racers have had more time than squash players to get used to coed competition. Women have been racing in the Iditarod since 1974, its second year, and from one to ten women enter each year in an average field of fifty-three racers. Susan Butcher was the first woman to place in the top twenty, the first woman to place in the top ten, the first woman to place in the top five, and the first woman to finish second. Libby Riddles was the first woman to win; that was 1985, the year a marauding moose attacked Susan's team, killing two of her dogs and injuring several others. So by 1986, when Susan began her unprecedented (by women or men) three-year winning streak, the men in the race had heard plenty of times about this "first woman" to do this and that.

"Tell me how men have responded to you," I say to Susan. "You must have stories."

"I'm leery of telling them," she answers. "There are some wonderful men who love the fact that I'm doing what I'm doing and that I'm a woman. Then there are the even better ones who don't even notice that I'm a woman. They are very respectful of my ability as a dog musher.

"Then there's the norm. Because the media has put so much attention on the fact that I'm a woman, men resent that. They get pretty sick of 'Are you guys ever going to win this race again?' But also, there's a jovial sort of, 'Oh, we can't let Susan win again, we've got to get it back.' "

There is a lot of ground to cover here, there are a lot of men in her life. She pauses, as if coming to a brief rest stop at the end of a snowfield. Then she takes off again. "In the beginning there did seem to be a we-and-you situation where I was the only woman running in the top pack. There seemed to be such a buddy system among them, and I was not included. Now that I'm winning, there are some who are very seriously against me, more so than if I were a male champion. I pay little attention to it."

This "pay them no mind" strategy is a deliberate, practiced

one. "When I ran into blockades, I didn't look at them," she says of her ascendancy to top dogsled racer. "I just went right through them. I was unaware that I was fighting a fight. When I would talk to some of my feminist friends and say, 'I've had it, I'm so sick and tired of it. Why is this happening?' they would say, 'Susan, a woman has never done what you're doing. You're hitting every wall.' There were so many men down on me, working against me in groups—yes, I felt it and knew it, but I didn't want to look at it. I'm not one to sit there and go, 'Boo-hoo, why are people doing this to me?' or ask for help from fellow women or the law or whatever.'

"We don't need to be condemning men, we don't need to ask men to move over. We're just there. We just have to do it now. I'm tired of the 'pity me, I've been oppressed' thing. I am not a pitiful person. I don't want [men] to move over and let me win the Iditarod. I want to win it on my own, fair and square. The fact that they sometimes team up against me makes it that much more of a challenge and gives what I do that much more credibility."

The people who team up against Lyn St. James are also men. But they're not other drivers; the drivers, Lyn says, have gotten used to her, although female stock-car racers are still rare. It's her teammates—crew members who can change a flat in the time it takes other people to strap on a seat belt—who can give her trouble. Lyn got along with them better in the days when she hired her own crew, but since 1983 she has represented Ford, which hires both her and the crew. She likens it to being a pro quarterback: "The quarterback doesn't hire the front line."

Crew–driver relationships are delicate and, it seems to Lyn, a bit mysterious. Racing is a team sport, and although drivers, like quarterbacks, get most of the credit, the post-race victory circle provides a place for crew members to join their driver and take a bow. In 1985, after one of Lyn's first major victories, none of her crew walked into the victory circle with her. "It really bothered me, and it really hurt me," says Lyn. "I never asked why. I feel that we communicate more by our actions than our words. I chose to plod forward. But after a number of years go by, you start to think. I bet there was some uncomfortableness that maybe they didn't even understand themselves. A lot of these things are deep-seated or part of society's conditioning that we don't even always understand as individuals."

Another lonely experience, also in 1985, same crew. She crashed early in a practice session. "Driver error," she admits. "I went out too soon." The crew refused to speak to her. "I've had people avoid me, but I've never had that reaction," she says. "It's like you live together, around each other ten hours a day, in a very small, confined area, the paddock. Like family almost. To go from being part of that to being totally ostracized—I almost quit racing that weekend."

She made it through the weekend. Her crew fixed the car. She's still racing, still with the same crew, and she says they're starting to believe in her, slowly realizing that her wins are not flukes. The drivers, meanwhile, have reaffirmed their support by making her the first female member of the Road Racing Drivers Club, which has an invitation-only membership.

Token women sometimes adopt the values and behaviors of the group to which they have been admitted. Karen Kelso tries to intimidate other squash players by whatever means necessary, whether that's by calling for an umpire or acting aloof. "I'd like to get big muscles and look scary," she says.

Even the language Karen uses to refer to herself reflects an assimilation into the male sports domain. "I'm just a little guy," she once told a man who was shoving her on the court. "I'd like to be the best male player in Denver." It's not that she wants to be male, but she is so identified with men that she emulates some military-model values, such as intimidation, even referring to herself as male with no sense of irony. "On the court, it's a battle," she says. "I'm very competitive, so it's for blood."

Yet even Karen retains some partnership ethic. "I like to be friends afterward," she says, and for inspiration she looks to women, naming Martina Navratilova and Billie Jean King as her heroes.

Neither St. James nor Butcher would call herself a man or a guy; neither deliberately intimidates. Men are their peers but women are their allies, and competitions are not battles. Rick Swenson, supposedly Susan's archrival, served as a "bridesmaid" at her wedding.

Susan would claim the word "person" before "woman," and "musher" before either of those, but her allegiance is with women; she is woman-identified. "Women can do anything they want to," she tells me. She does not feel exceptional.

"Alone?" I ask.

"Sure. You can do it alone," she answers. "But you're doing it with the support of women. All the Eskimo and Indian women in the villages I go through, all it takes from them is a smile, and you know they're behind you."

"Has sports participation changed women?"

"I'm not sure women have changed," Susan says thoughtfully. "I think the attention to them has changed. The way we live, with a pioneer lifestyle, the women work as hard or harder than the men. A lot of women [have] very traditional roles, being the cook, the housewife, the mother, raiser of children, but they're also in the bush, hauling water, doing all those things too. Sure, the man is out working hard during the day, but a lot of times he'll come home and be done for the day while the woman still has many more hours of chores to do. There's no doubt in my mind how strong women are."

Lyn St. James, having rejected the Powder Puff league for herself, now supports all-women's races (no longer called Powder Puff) because they encourage women to pursue racing. "But then if women are motivated, they need to go to the next step," she says. "There's nothing wrong with being the best woman, but if you're going to test yourself, you have to take risks."

Lyn also runs her own school, the Lyn St. James For Women Only Driving School of Atlanta. "I struggled with that for a while," she admits. "I talked to other driving schools, and they said that of twelve students, they'd have one or two women. The women were intimidated. They had to take some grief, and some ribbing. They also didn't seem to catch on as fast, maybe because they were afraid to ask questions, though by the end of the course they were often better students."

Lyn gives talks to dozens of women's business groups every year. What the women in these groups want to know is not whether women *can* beat men but whether they *should*. Whether it's proper. They ask Lyn, "What if a client invites me to play tennis? Should I beat him? How about the boss at the company picnic?"

Lyn tells them that competitiveness is an asset, and that both women and men in positions of power often appreciate that drive, whether the challenger is male or female. "As with other assets, it may not earn you friends," she cautions. "But that's different from trying to get ahead."

It disturbs Lyn to see women holding themselves back. "Women fought so hard to be considered players. But we still have to learn to win. And we have to learn that you don't win all the time."

But so what if women win? Who cares?

Even when sports are organized by criteria other than gender, and even when individual female victors are oblivious to the social implications of their success, it means a lot to society that some modern-day Atalantas defeat men, particularly in arenas that have been defined as male. Such victories lay bare the "only men are good enough" myth. They toss the myth of male supremacy overboard, at least symbolically. Male reaction is one indication of the power of female victory: when a man finally won the Iditarod in 1989, after four years of female victors, *Sports Illustrated* ran a feature story entitled "Man's Best Friends." When Joe Runyan crossed the finish line first, men reportedly wept with glee, presumably because he was male.[10] (Butcher, whose dogs had contracted an intestinal disease during the race, finished second.)

Because Susan Butcher has become the best in the world at a sport no one heard of until women started winning, women get to say, "We are the best." ("She won!" cyclist Elaine Mari-olle excitedly told my answering machine when she heard that Susan had won the 1990 race, breaking her own record in a time of 11 days, 1 hour, 53 minutes. "I feel so wonder-ful!") No matter that still no one outside Alaska knows mush about dogsled racing. No matter that Bobby Riggs was fifty-five. We won. We are the best. Or at least, we are the best too.

Women and girls need heroes, as Merrily Dean Baker, assis-tant executive director of the NCAA, often says: female heroes. It's not so much that they need heroes who defeat men, but they need heroes who are successful in the larger world, in the public domain; women who climb mountains and drive fast cars and win notoriety and have adventures not in the Powder Puff league, but real adventures, where the adventurers are not defined by femaleness. *I'm lucky to have grown up feeling there were no restrictions on me because I was a woman.*

Women need Chris Evert, who showed them that they could play sports and simultaneously play the feminine role, but they also need Susan Butcher, who refuses to play any role. Just as her skin tone and height are no big deal to her, not character-defining qualities, so it is with her femaleness. She happens to be a woman, happens to have brown hair. Now, where's the dogsled?

I tell my little neighbor, Lora Cary, about Susan Butcher's victories. The next day I'm spreading gravel in my driveway, assisted by Lora and the boy next door, Jaimie Graham. "Lora, you can't push the wheelbarrow, you're not strong enough," Jaimie tells Lora. Jaimie is a year older than Lora, and bigger. The son of a feminist, Jaimie may be referring to

Lora's relative size and youth, not her gender. He knows that women are not weak.

No matter. Lora, an inveterate soccer player, has already heard "You can't because you're a girl" so many times that she hears it even when that's not what's being said. "Girls are just as good as boys, Jaimie," she tells him. "Some are better. Like Susan Butcher."

Lora needs Susan Butcher as I needed Babe Didrikson Zaharias, the only female athlete I knew about as a child. As role models go, Susan is even better than Babe: she's not just good, for a girl—she's good, period. She's the best of all. Therefore, Lora has a right to hold the wheelbarrow. It's a giant leap from Alaska to a Virginia driveway but a small step in the mind of a nine-year-old girl.

At the awards banquet, Susan's hair is woven into a tight French braid; makeup traces the bold features of her face. She wears a long paisley peasant dress, not inappropriate but humble, the simplest of the many, sometimes extravagant outfits women have worn to this formal affair. Lyn St. James and jockey Julie Krone are here; Martina Navratilova; marathon swimmer Diana Nyad; 1956 Olympic figure skater Tenley Albright. Here, too, are Mary Lou Retton, Florence Griffith Joyner, Wendy Lian Williams, Phoebe Mills, and Connie Paraskevan Young, all Olympians. During an opening "Grand March of Athletes" that is disturbingly reminiscent of beauty pageants, these champions walk, balancing tentatively or expertly on heels, from the wings to center stage, smile, receive grand applause, then stroll toward the crowd. As they make their way down the few steps from the stage, they are taken by the arm and "helped" downstairs by waiting male athletes such as Olympian Al Joyner.

When Susan walks that path in reverse, from banquet table to stage, to accept her award, the crowd applauds as enthusiastically as they did for Amateur Athlete of the Year Jackie Joyner-Kersee moments earlier. Susan says she's honored to be in the room, among her heroes. She dedicates the award to her ninety-nine-year-old grandmother, Gretchen Butcher, and tells the story of a recent visit they had in Massachusetts. Susan took her grandmother out to dinner one night, and afterward they discovered it was raining. Susan instructed her grandmother to wait while Susan ran to get the car. Misunderstanding, Gretchen Butcher chased Susan down the street and through a parking lot until Susan, hearing footsteps, turned around and saw her. "She was keeping up too," Susan says.

The audience laughs. "So I'd like to thank my grandmother, and all the women in this room," she concludes simply.

Mythology aside, Susan Butcher isn't really racing against men. She's racing with men.

There's no doubt in my mind how strong women are.

And she's racing for women.

Different Strokes

We have no reason to sacrifice well-being, harmony, sharing, cooperation and pleasure to symbolic superiority. The
very notion of superiority of one kind over another will
have to disappear, although differences among kind will
remain.

—MARILYN FRENCH[1]

*S*USAN BUTCHER feels lucky to have found a sport
where she can compete on an equal basis with men. Most
women are not so lucky. Even though women's performances
are improving faster than men's; even though, in some sports,
women and men compete on a par; and even though a particular woman may beat a particular man at any sport if she
happens to be more skilled, the majority of women in coed
situations find themselves less skilled than their male partners or opponents.

So then what happens? Are women defensive or embarrassed? Are male partners helpful or condescending? Are
women influential in determining the ethical standards of the
game, or do they play by male-established mores? How do
coed sports work for women who are not lucky enough to
compete on an equal basis?

Coed sports date to at least 2200 B.C., when pairs of young
people—one female, one male—would leap over bulls to the
delight of assembled crowds in ancient Crete. Frescoes from

77

that pre-patriarchal era[2] depict gymnasts who "evidently executed as great a variety of somersaulting leaps as a modern athlete on the vaulting horse."[3] Unlike bullfighting, bull-leaping was not a battle, and neither athletes nor bulls risked death. The bulls may even have been chosen for their docility, or trained. Since bulls were a potent religious symbol for the Cretans, this cooperative venture among woman, man, and animal had religious as well as entertainment value.

In modern times, the sports American men worship are the all-male ones. Because men control decisions about which sports are broadcast on television and which are reported in the newspapers, male spectator sports reign.

But beyond the range of television cameras, coed sports are quietly thriving. Coed softball and volleyball leagues abound. Women and men skate, ski, swim, bowl, golf, run, and play racket sports together daily.

In some sports, players construct special rules that attempt to compensate for gender differences (and preclude male domination) by mandating, for example, that a woman bats every other time or that women play key infield positions. Some leagues stipulate that each team must have an equal number of women and men or a minimum number of women.

Golf and bowling have handicapping systems that allow two players of disparate skill to compete together. Golf also offers what used to be called "ladies' tees," now sometimes known as forward or red tees, which give the user what amounts to a head start. These systems enable novice or unskilled women—or seniors, juniors, beginners, or otherwise less proficient players—to compete on a more equal footing with proficient men or women.

In pairs figure skating and roller skating, duos perform routines that require intimacy, synchronization, and at the highest levels, immense athleticism. But skating, like classical dancing, usually reinforces and recapitulates traditional, oppositional gender roles.

The most popular, most enduring form of female-male athletic cooperation is one in which there are no designated gender roles and, usually, no special rules or handicaps. In the mixed-doubles partnerships of squash, racquetball, and tennis, how each couple divides responsibilities, makes decisions, and communicates is entirely up to the individuals.

In tennis, women tend to be the weaker players. Mixed-doubles games can be frustrating for all parties. Yet men and women, particularly couples, enjoy playing tennis together—or the idea of playing tennis together—so mixed doubles is a mainstay of recreational tennis.

Sydney Jacobs has no trouble admitting that her tennis skills are inferior to her husband's. She uses a wheelchair; he does not. In their version of mixed doubles, the rules have been altered slightly to accommodate her disability. Her physical limitations are more obvious and more extreme than those of most women. But the problems she, her husband, and their peers confront are similar to those faced by women who, although they are not in wheelchairs, are nevertheless, as disabled activists might say, differently abled.

Sydney Jacobs and Mark Otto met in a tree-identification class at the National Arboretum in Washington, D.C. Sydney, the director of the Watkins Nature Center in suburban Maryland, made some witty remarks the first night that piqued Mark's interst. She sat toward the back of the class, and Mark didn't notice, at first, that she was in a wheelchair. He impressed her too: he wore a T-shirt, and Birkenstocks, and a beard. "He didn't seem like your usual Washington jerk," she recalls, laughing.

They began dating, paddling sea kayaks and wandering through forests, searching for rare birds. She decided he was her "favorite person to bird with."

He thought, Here's somebody who'd be nice to know for the rest of my life.

They dated for a year, lived together for a year, and were married. While they were dating, Mark, a former competitive swimmer and water polo player, wrenched his knee in a volleyball match and tore a ligament. Sydney, accustomed to devising creative ways to stay athletic despite disability, loaned him an old wheelchair, and the two of them began playing wheelchair tennis. When his knee healed months later, "he didn't want to stand up anymore," teases Sydney. "I had to say, 'Get out of that chair!' "

He walked around to her side of the net, they discovered a tennis subculture of wheelchair/able-bodied pairs to play with, and their mixed-doubles partnership was born.

Sydney, also a former competitive swimmer and skier, severed her spinal cord in a climbing accident seventeen years ago, when she was twenty. Although she identifies with disabled people and lobbies for rights for the disabled, particularly athletes, Sydney does not feel disabled. "If someone says to me, 'You're disabled and I'm not,' I say, 'Maybe you ought to think about that some more.' We all have limitations." She misses hiking with her dad, a family tradition; she misses running; when swimming, she misses flip turns. But the things she thought she'd miss, she doesn't. "I thought I would die because I couldn't ski, but I realized I'd skied for a reason—it was a kick to do it—and from an emotional need. It was just a matter of finding another sport."

Within months of leaving the rehabilitation hospital she was setting national disabled swimming records. She competed in international meets, including the Paralympics, the Pan Am World Championships, and the Stoke-Mandeville Games, from 1975 through 1980. She tried a disabled version of skiing called sit-skiing but it didn't hold her interest. She learned to scuba dive ("My mother thought I was crazy") but had ear problems. She played around with inner-tube water polo. She fell in love with kayaking ("On the water you're pretty much equal with everyone else") and came to enjoy tennis because it "takes a certain kind of maturity. It's not a brute-force kind of thing."

Currently, tennis is her favorite sport. "I'm obsessed with it," she admits. Mark, who would have preferred to spend more time in the kayaks, has gamely joined Sydney on the courts. Sometimes they play singles, Mark hitting with his right hand—he is left-handed—to make the matches more even. Sometimes he serves as ball boy for Sydney and her opponent at wheelchair tournaments, which tend to lack such amenities as ball kids and umpires. Most often he is Sydney's partner in the unique form of mixed doubles called one-up/one-down.

In one-up/one-down, one partner must be in a wheelchair, the other able-bodied. Otherwise, the rules are the same as for any mixed-doubles match, except that there is a handicapping system, a way of making the game more fun and more fair: wheelchair players can let the ball bounce twice before hitting it (as is the case in all wheelchair tennis). One-up/one-down exhibitions have been played at regular tennis tournaments nationwide, but the Washington, D.C., area is the first to organize leagues and tournaments.

The regular, non-wheelchair mixed-doubles format has been popular, even at the professional level, since the early 1900s, but has never received much attention. The first major mixed-doubles tournament was not held until January 1974, a few months after Billie Jean King whipped Bobby Riggs. While many people—women in particular—remember the exact spot on which they were leaping up and down as King defeated Riggs, who remembers that first mixed-doubles tournament? Billie Jean won that one too, with a man named Owen Davidson. Are Americans so invested in the concept that women and men are intrinsically antagonistic—or necessarily seductive—that we overlook examples of successful, egalitarian, nonsexual cooperation?

Tennis magazines run articles about how to hone a mixed-doubles partnership, but they focus on technique, such as when to lob. They ignore the larger implications of competition between women and men. As far as I know, the interpersonal dynamic of mixed doubles has not been studied by any sports scholars.

When not ignored, mixed doubles is maligned. Like the

game of bridge, it is reputed to destroy courtships and ruin marriages. But does it? Could it be that by playing together in close proximity, women and men learn how to—or could learn how to—mitigate differences in temperament, goals, or skill levels? Mixed doubles offers men the chance to depend on women's physical strength, concentration, and intelligence, and challenges women to believe in themselves enough both to play on a par with men and to ask for help. It requires a working partnership, a female-male bonding that is sweaty without being sexy, cooperative without being coital. Mixed doubles asks the question: Can women and men get along?

Twelve teams and a few dozen fans converge at the Severn Valley Racket Club near Annapolis, Maryland, one July Saturday in 1989 for the biggest one-up/one-down tournament of the season. The club's small parking lot is filled with players excitedly unzipping racket covers, unfolding wheelchairs, and stretching.

Mark Otto, slightly built, blond, and still bearded, straps on a giant blue "Joe Namath" brace that he needs to stabilize his knee. Sydney Jacobs, trailed by a long brown ponytail, rolls onto one of the three indoor courts in a sleeveless T-shirt that highlights her rounded biceps, the product of a lifetime of stroking, pulling, lifting, and more recently, pushing and hitting. With a wide Velcroed binder, she wraps herself into her custom-made lightweight quick-pivoting chair. She didn't like wearing the binder until she noticed that her idol, Donna Miller, one of the best wheelchair players in the region, wears one. Besides, she needs it: once, reaching for a ball, she fell out of her chair and sprained her ankle.

She reaches for plenty of balls in the first match, doubling over in the chair, extending her arm, groaning. "It's got to be frustrating," says a spectator, shaking his head as a ball whizzes by, just past Syndey's outstretched racket.

It's not, she says. She hated tennis before, when she had to run around. "Now I roll after the ball," she says, smiling, "and it's not so bad."

Still, Sydney and Mark get "knocked off the court," as Sydney puts it, in the first match. The second match, in a consolation round, is more their speed. On the other side of the net are two friends, Beth Ziebarth and Mark Ziebarth, Beth's brother-in-law.

Mark likes to tease Beth that she met her hsuband at a college fraternity party where she got so drunk she fell out of her wheelchair. She denies it—"That was a different party"— but there are many wheelchair stories and jokes in these circles. Watching the matches, I overhear tales about a man who smuggled dope in a wheelchair, a man whose toe was crushed when run over by a wheelchair basketball player, and a man who plays wheelchair golf, whacking the ball from his perch on the passenger side of a cart.

One-up/one-down, like regular mixed doubles, takes a while to get used to. Newly disabled players must learn the intricacies of chair control. Arm burns are common, since in the heat of the game players will brake their chairs using forearm pressure rather than a hand. The "up" partners must learn to trust the "down" players to get to the ball, and they must learn just how fast chairs can roll. There are times when, because of the two-bounce rule, the wheelchair player can reach a ball that the able-bodied player cannot.

Since Sydney and Mark are new to the game, their racket skills are not as impressive as, say, the precise, hard-hitting style of Brenda Gilmore, who was instrumental in organizing one-up/one-down tournaments in the area and first invited Sydney to play. What is impressive about Sydney and Mark is their communication. "Switch!" Sydney will call. "Oh, good idea!" Mark will respond.

Mark looks less comfortable on a tennis court than he must be in a swimming pool. He has not yet mastered the low, bent-kneed stance that behooves able-bodied land athletes; so although he is diligent and not unathletic, compared with

Sydney zipping around in her fancy four-wheeled low-rider, his movements take on a hippity-hoppity look. Sydney says she enjoys playing with Mark because, "We laugh a lot. Sometimes I can't hit the ball, I'm laughing so much, watching him bound around the court."

Today they are somewhat more serious. They win the first set. They lead in the second set until the "up" player across the net shifts into frantic overdrive, poaching here, lunging there, dashing in front of Beth and leaving her forlorn in a far corner. She could have spent the set filing her fingernails and she would not have been missed. They tie at 4–4, but Sydney and Mark win the next two games.

I ask Sydney and Mark what they thought of Mark Ziebarth's constant poaching.

"They gave us a bunch of points by doing that," says Sydney. "It's not a very smart strategy."

Poaching is a time-honored tactic, however, and one with which able-bodied female players are achingly familiar. Pauline Betz Addie, 1946 Wimbledon champion and now a teaching pro at Cabin John Indoor Tennis Courts in Bethesda, Maryland, played mixed doubles in pro tournaments in the thirties and forties with such luminaries as Pancho Segura and Bobby Riggs. Segura "wasn't very macho," Addie reports, but "Bobby's philosophy was to place the woman in the alley and say, 'Don't hit anything that isn't going to hit you.' " ("Yes, Bobby," she'd respond, then ignore him.) Now in their seventies, Addie and Riggs are still friends, and she chides him every chance she gets. "He denies it now. He says, 'I couldn't have said that.' "

Addie no longer competes, but she plays for fun, either singles or women's doubles. Why not mixed doubles? "Oh, occasionally I do, but I prefer the camaraderie among women," she says simply. I ask her if mixed-doubles partnerships appear to be more egalitarian these days. "It depends on who's better. The men playing with Martina, they let her hit her share, that's a cinch."

· · ·

There was a time when mixed-doubles ethics, at the recreational level at least, called for gentler hitting to the women and balanced hitting to both opponents. Tennis began as a sport of the upper classes; what could be more uncouth than for a gentleman to blast a tennis ball down the throat of a lady? Chris Shelton, a former pro tennis player and now a professor of exercise and sport studies at Smith College, thinks men's attitudes changed as women got stronger. "Now men figure anything goes," she says.

Even many recreational players have adopted the motto of former tennis star Bill Tilden, who advised, "Hit at the girl whenever possible."[4] If "the girl" is weaker, and one's goal is to win, this strategy contains a certain logic. But it makes for a ridiculously lopsided game in which the women hit the ball almost exclusively to each other, trying desperately to keep it away from the men, who crouch, waiting, their rackets drawn like revolvers.

Coach Larry Strickland says that because women playing mixed doubles tend to have more balls hit to them, "it's usually the woman who wins the match and the man who loses the match. The women are the ones who are going to be dominating most of the play. They have to be very steady. They have to set up and make the winning shots, whereas the male players—unless they poach all the time—are not going to see the ball as often." The teams that win, he adds, are those in which the female partner is the better of the two.

In fact, when any two doubles partners, regardless of gender, have disparate skill levels, the game will be fun only if the opposing team does *not* hit consistently to the weaker player. If the weaker player feels attacked and his or her partner feels bored and ignored, neither will go home happy, win or lose.

With all these difficulties, why bother struggling through coed sports? Do women who play with and against men benefit from male status, facilities, and expertise? Or should women retain a separate women's world, one that protects a different sports ethic and gives women more opportunities for relative excellence? Historically, these questions have been raised in terms of coed, interracial, and disabled/able-bodied education. Is separate but equal ever equal?

Most often, integration (or what African-Americans frequently call desegregation) has been chosen as the only equitable route. But some African-Americans are reconsidering this stance, noting that blacks often fare better academically in all-black colleges.

In wheelchair sports, consensus has not been reached. As a swimmer at the Paralympics in Holland, Sydney felt "like a real Olympian." So too do the handful of wheelchair track athletes who now compete in the "real Olympics," no doubt. But if integration becomes the goal, how many of the 4,000 people who competed in the 1988 Paralympics will be invited to the Olympics—a festival already bursting at the seams from its unwieldy size? Would integration yield fewer opportunities?

Nor has the coed sports issue been resolved. Sports sociologist Don Sabo asks: "[Will] cross-sex sports humanize male participants or . . . dehumanize female participants? Will cross-sex athletic socialization curb men's use of cheapshots and controlled violence or make women more violence-prone?"[5]

Clearly, coed sports have psychological benefits. When lunging for a soccer ball one cannot be overly concerned with whether or not one's hair is in place. Working together, individuals can't help but develop mutual respect. Coed team sports incidentally but inexorably break down stereotypes about who women and men are.

"Extensive research shows that if you want to create intolerance and prejudice, if you want to maintain stereotypical attitudes between two groups—in this case, blacks and whites—the best thing you can do is to pit all blacks against all whites," says Sabo. "If you want to break down intolerance, the ideal social psychological conditions for that are such that you mix teams, blacks and whites on one team, blacks and whites on the other. This facilitates cooperation across races, within teams."

Sabo adds that the "myth of the coed catastrophe"—that coed sports will break up marriages or lead to wild, wanton sex—is contradictory and irrational. "The patriarchy will always manufacture arguments against changing patterns of female-male relationships. It doesn't matter if the arguments are grotesquely inconsistent. They still exert ideological influence."

In fact, coed sports seem to have numerous benefits for women. A 1985 Women's Sports Foundation survey of athletic women found that women who as children had played with boys had a more positive body image as adolescents than women who had played only with girls.[6] (Heptathlete Jackie Joyner-Kersee grew up rough-and-tumbling with brother Al Joyner. Asked how she feels about her body, she answers, "I love myself." Her body is not an object to be liked or disliked; it's who she is.) The WSF study also found that women who are most athletic as adults tend to have played mostly with boys or in mixed groups rather than just with girls.

Theoretically, men who play mixed doubles come to respect women athletes who they hadn't realized were as talented or tough as they are. Theoretically, women athletes gain confidence, recognizing just how talented and tough they are. Ideally, women and men together define the unwritten rules, the spirit of play. In the one-up/one-down version, disabled players get to enjoy "regular" tennis with able-bodied friends, and spectators come to respect wheelchair athletes' skills.

Theoretically, coed sports "can be very instructive for men," says Don Sabo. A man may learn, for instance, to "allow himself to cooperate rather than compete, to feel vulnerable rather than powerful. Those are all dimensions of the human experience and sport."

Most of the women—78 percent—in the WSF survey agreed that "women can teach men about humane competition."[7] But it doesn't necessarily happen that way.

In mixed doubles, many women seem intimidated by male partners and opponents, and are eager to please and afraid to rock the boat. One woman told me that it makes her angry when the man on the other side of the net hits the ball directly at her, hard. "I know he's trying to intimidate me, and it works," she said. Could she talk with him, I ask, and tell him how she feels? Could she ask him not to do that? Could she initiate a discussion in which all four players talk about their goals and expectations for the game? "No," she said. "I feel like it's a man's game. I'm a newcomer."

While men *could* benefit from women's ways of playing, and while women believe that can happen, men more often set the tone of a match. As long as women feel like outsiders, believing that sports somehow belong to men, they are unable to influence the direction of sport. They adapt themselves to meet men's standards and practices instead of contributing their own values and ethics to the game.

Integration rarely arrives without conflict and compromise. Wheelchair athletes, like able-bodied women athletes, often have to insist that their partners stop dominating the court and let them play. Able-bodied athletes have to unlearn biases about what "disabled" means.

Women and men may express anger differently; they may have different styles of communication. Women may tiptoe around what they perceive to be fragile male pride. Men may be what former pro golfer Betty Hicks has called "compulsive instructors."[8]

Lifelong habits can be hard to break; I know a sixty-two-year-old executive who defers to her male tennis partner on the court, even though she is a self-described "raving feminist."

Another friend, also in her sixties, agrees: "I've never had a partner who was worse than me," she says, "but if I did, I'd look down my nose at him. If I were better than him, I wouldn't respect him."

Young women and men, raised in an era of feminism, may be less likely to struggle with sex-role restrictions. Spouses or lovers may enjoy the thrill of a unique rapport born of team-work.

Yet intimacy is often difficult, and because in sports the body as well as the mind is fully engaged, deep-seated beliefs, insecurities, and frustrations are bound to emerge. In other words, a mixed-doubles pair is subject to the same challenges as any female-male pair. Since women and men are from birth channeled into different activities and expected to behave differently, all marriages are "mixed," all heterosexual couples confronted by cross-cultural challenges. Within the confines of a tennis court, questions of power, cooperation, control, envy, admiration, territoriality, subservience, parity, and forgiveness are crystallized. Mixed doubles becomes a prism through which the strengths and weaknesses of a relationship and the individuals involved become clear.

Even when men are neither patronizing nor brutal, women must wade through institutionalized sexism. As a black disabled female athlete, Brenda Gilmore calls herself "a minority within a minority within a minority"—but says the only kind of discrimination she has experienced as an athlete is based on gender. At wheelchair tennis tournaments, men's singles and doubles take precedence over women's, although quadriplegic athletes of both genders are relegated to the side courts.

Timidly trying to score in the men's game, women can lose in innumerable ways. When men hit more delicately to women, women may feel insulted. When men and women play on an equal basis, but with the military model, women can find themselves attacked by bullet balls on every play. Even when the rules are changed to compensate for unequal abilities, women can still lose. At the Severn Valley tournament, with only free rackets and egos on the line, some able-bodied men still fired balls consistently at the wheelchair players in what seemed a seriously misguided attempt to win at all costs.

University of Iowa sports sociologist Susan Birrell, an advocate of sex-segregated sports, believes coed sports inevitably shortchange women because of the "subtle losses of power the accommodated class suffers when integrated within a structure already defined and run by others." Birrell differentiates between imposed separatism, based on discrimination, and chosen separatism, based on choice. She believes that chosen separatism—in a women's sports league, for example—works only when the administrators are also female: "Only when the entire system is segregated do women have complete autonomy."[9]

Chosen separatism is fine when that is what women want, but if women experience "subtle losses of power" in integrated sports, the thing to do is to change the dynamic between women and men, not necessarily to separate. Single-sex sports, like single-sex schools, may be good for women's development, but only through integration will the relationship between the sexes improve.

Increasing numbers of women are choosing integration, but they seem ambivalent about it. In the Women's Sports Foundation survey, only 50 percent of the respondents reported a personal preference for playing with women, yet almost 70 percent said that sports should be segregated by gender.[10] This might be explained in part by another survey response: 58 percent reported that women are often forced to choose between being athletes and being feminine. The women themselves do not experience "role conflict"; 94 percent believe participation in sports does not "diminish a woman's femininity." But they feel pressured by others, and seem to conclude that women need the safety of single-sex sports.

In general, sports are most satisfying when played among people with similar skills. But often a woman doesn't happen to share her husband's or male friend's skill level. What then? Must she always find another partner?

It is possible to create rules to adjust for unmatched ability levels and still have a respectful, competitive coed game. Slight alterations—giving the other player a few points, say, or extra serves—can easily make a game more evenly matched, and therefore more fun.

Why doesn't this happen more often? Primate research offers an interesting perspective. Female squirrel monkeys wrestle with each other, usually while hanging from a perch; their games result in no clear winners or losers. Male squirrel monkeys play more aggressively: one partner often pins the other to the ground. But the males will occasionally reverse the roles, with the more dominant monkey allowing the other to "win."[11]

Maxeen Biben, an animal behaviorist with the National Institute of Child Health and Human Development, found that when young male squirrel monkeys are housed with females or older males, they no longer play as aggressively as they do with other young males. They adapt their playing style, either by often allowing the other monkey to win or by playing noncompetitively.[12]

So there is precedence among primates for both males and females to alter their style of play to suit the needs or desires of playmates. Females don't seem to mind a male monkey letting them win, and males do not insist that winning is the only thing. Rather, it seems, playing is the only thing.

Female human beings, of course, bring to their play a history of gender discrimination and infinitely more complex emotions. To accept a handicap can be demeaning to women eager to prove their physical prowess to men. I know several women golfers, even beginning golfers, who refuse to use the "ladies' tees," preferring the challenge of the "men's tees." Yet in a golf competition with a stronger, longer-hitting man, it would make sense to accept the few yards' advantage.

Maybe it is only women who know the joy of athletic excellence who don't feel, compared with men, disabled. They can accept that in some sports they're differently abled (less strong, less swift) in relation to some men because in many sporting arenas they feel competent. I suspect such women have less tolerance for poaching on the tennis court, for patronizing advice, or for someone's deliberately trying to hit them with a ball. Because of their athletic self-confidence—an uncommon female attribute—they expect playmates to treat each other as peers, regardless of different talents. Once respect is established, handicaps—whether for women, people in wheelchairs, children, old men, or others—become insignificant.

Women who have the most difficulty playing with men probably lack the self-confidence (and the experience) to define a game's rules and mores. Intimidated by male muscles and male displays of power, they feel unable to assert their authority.

Bob Schmonsees, a paraplegic from Potomac, Maryland, plays mixed doubles with his wife, Judy, in a regular tennis league. Their opponents give him two bounces and he rolls rather than sprints after the ball; otherwise, the game is played in the usual way.

Schmonsees, the world's third-ranking men's over-forty wheelchair player and a former president of the National Foundation of Wheelchair Tennis, says the tennis partnership is good for their marriage. "Anytime you share common values and common frustrations and common joys, the relationship builds. It's something you do together, and you get better communication. There are times when the competitive aspect gets in the way, but if you've got enough self-confidence you just manage that competitive drive."

Before the injury that paralyzed him six years ago, Schmonsees was a better tennis player than his wife. Now she surpasses him. "It's great now, because she can beat me," he says. "Before I got hurt, I got frustrated with her level of play. Now she's the one who has to carry all that frustration. She handles it a lot better than I did."

Like Bob Schmonsees, Sydney Jacobs and Mark Otto believe the mixed-doubles tennis matchup enhances their relationship. Sydney, the more knowledgeable, more consistent player, says, "If it's close, and he blows it, I might feel a little like, 'What'd you do that for?' Or if he double-faults, I'll go,

'Why can't you get it in?' But I don't say anything out loud. I don't scream at him on the court. We don't get to that point. At least not yet." She laughs. "We've only been married three months. Ask us again after we've been married three years."

She adds, "It really bothers me to see people actually fight on the court. If we ever got to that point, man—I hope we never do."

Their one tennis-related argument occurred when they were playing singles with each other. Mark won the first set 6–0, then began losing the second. "I thought he was giving me points, and that pissed me off," Sydney recalls. "I thought, He just blew me out in he first set. Is he trying to lose? But we talked about it, and he said he wasn't, and I trust him."

Although Sydney is not yet as successful in tennis as she was in swimming and skiing, she and Mark travel annually to California for the United States Open Wheelchair Tennis Championships and spend many weekends traveling to other wheelchair competitions. When she praises Mark for putting up with her tennis obsession, he demurs, citing Sydney's support of his interests.

If there is a secret to their success it seems to be friendship, humor, and a casual attitude about difference. "Being in a chair didn't seem like much of an issue with her, so it wasn't a big deal for me," he says when asked about her disability.

The same could be said of gender. Sydney is a person, and that she is a female person doesn't seem much of an issue to either one of them. Nor does his maleness seem to inform many of his decisions or activities. He usually cooks because he enjoys cooking, does the laundry because the machines are beyond her access. He is her favorite person to bird with; she is someone he'd like to know for the rest of his life. When they play tennis, he wears a knee brace and she straps herself into a sports chair. They are two people who happen to have female and male bodies. They hope to have a child, and they enjoy sex. Otherwise, the fact of their genders, like their physical limitations, seems incidental.

· · ·

Ironically, the Severn Valley Racket Club is not wheelchair-accessible. Dan Andrews, the twenty-five-year-old tournament organizer, who is paraplegic, planned to hold the tournament outdoors, but it drizzled off and on, so the disabled players had to somehow make their way down the eight stairs leading to the three indoor courts. To go to the restrooms or reenter the lobby, where a spread of food awaited players on a buffet table, they had to somehow make their way back up.

Most of the players asked two friends to carry them and their wheelchairs in one fell swoop. One man crawled down on his hands, shoving his legs in front of him. Another rode down the stairs in his chair.

Sydney and Mark have their own technique of stair-maneuvering. At the bottom of the stairs, Mark leans over and lifts her out of the chair and into his arms. He then walks up the stairs and, carefully, Sydney's feet first, crosses the threshold of the lobby. This lifting and carrying is a practiced, professional-looking ballet, as graceful, charming, and loving as the much-replayed twirling hug Al Joyner gave Florence Griffith Joyner when she set a world record in the 200-meter run in the 1988 Olympics.

To me, it comes as a shock. What? This athlete whom I just saw race to the net, smash an overhead volley, chase down a lob, and hit strong passing shots can't even walk up the stairs? Sydney confirms later that people frequently forget that she is disabled. She takes it as "the highest compliment," but it's weird, she says. "One time I was sitting on a couch with a group of friends, and we decided to go out, and they were all at the door before they remembered that I couldn't just hop up."

In the lobby, Sydney and Mark wait for me to arrive with the wheelchair. I am less experienced at such things, and the grace of the ballet is broken when I place the chair a little too far from them, and Mark plunks Sydney down on the edge of it. For a second she tips forward. "Whoa!" she says, laughing.

Sydney and Mark's third-round match is their closest competition. They know these opponents too: both played in their one-up/one-down league this summer. In this pair, it's the woman, Barbara Dunn, who is up, and the man, Kevin Whalen, who is down. Kevin Whalen is a "high-functioning" quadriplegic, meaning he has some paralysis in his hands. Like other "quads," he straps his racket to his hand with a special Velcro band. Kevin and Barbara represent an integration of races as well as physical abilities and genders; Kevin is white, Barbara black.

So this match, with one married couple and one pair of friends, is about as integrated as one tennis match can be. But after a while, the scene—unheard of on country club courts— just looks like a bunch of people playing tennis.

Sydney swings hard for a shot, misses entirely, and laughs, burying her face in the crook of her arm. Kevin hits a ball into the net on a crucial point and Sydney calls, "Thanks, Kevin."

"No problem, Sydney," he calls back.

Mark lobs a ball toward Kevin's chair; it bounces in front of him and drifts up, over his head; as he reaches for it in vain, Sydney groans with empathy. That's one thing wheelchair players can't do: jump.

Despite the misses, they play some good tennis. Kevin, even from his seated position, has a good serve. Sydney and Mark, warmed up from their previous two matches, move together well, covering for each other, talking to each other, making well-placed shots then pausing before the next serve to congratulate each other, once with a quick kiss. It's a rhythm Mark will later say is "almost like dancing. You start being able to see how the other person thinks."

Okay, so they're newlyweds. They're lighthearted, tree-loving, noncutthroat folks, not your usual Washington jerks. "I'm not sure we're a typical couple," Mark warned me when I first told them about this book.

"You're not," I responded. "But I'm not interested in typical."

I'm interested in women and men who find ways to play

together, to celebrate each other and sports in whatever ways make sense, given their abilities and interests. My question is not: Who's winning the war between the sexes? But: Who's creating peace between the sexes? And how? How can we enable each other to have fun, develop athletic skill, and enjoy each other's company? And as women strive to be all that they can be, can they accept that in some sports they are, compared with men, differently abled? Can men accept that too, without being condescending or antagonistic? Can a game based on mutual respect prevail?

Sports are, at the recreational level, games. Can we lighten up? We've got Susan Butcher and Lyn St. James and Julie Krone out there defeating men, proving how competent women are. We've got Paula Newby-Fraser chasing the men's records, narrowing the gender gap. Women who compete "just for fun" in numerous sports, including those that favor male physiques, could relax now, and stop trying to prove anything at all.

Men have to get past the glory of victory and learn how to play. They have to realize that tennis does not have to be a "brute-force kind of thing." Men *could* learn some things from women about humane competition.

Women, for their part, must get past believing that sports belong to men. They must stop trying to fit in. They have to find their sense of humor, to begin to tease men, to mirror back to them how ludicrous it is to smash a ball at your friend or steal balls from your partner. Women have to act not as if they own the court but as if they have a right to share it, and to help decide the terms of engagement.

I don't know why Sydney Jacobs seems to know these things better than most female mixed-doubles players I've met. It probably has little to do with wheelchairs. But I do think the rights movement for the differently abled sets a good example for women. Disabled athletes insist on participating, regardless of ability level. They invent rules to suit their needs. They acknowledge their limitations, and within those limitations work to become superb athletes.

You Can't Just Be Muscular

> The culture industry hasn't invented "beauty" in
> order to control how we look, but how we are, and
> that's the scary part. How we think. How we *be*.
> —SCOTT BRADFIELD[1]

NEVER in my life have I felt so like Olive Oyl. Bodybuilder Carla Dunlap and I are standing in front of a mirror,
and it looks like a fun-house distortion: Carla is scrunched
into a compact black pack of energy, like a size D battery; I
resemble a piece of pink saltwater taffy stretched from floor
to ceiling. We are discussing "abs." Carla lifts her T-shirt,
curls her shoulders forward, contracts her abdomen, and out
pop six dark moguls arranged in two precise rows. "The
trick," she says, "is to practice in the mirror, because sometimes you think you're flexing, and you're really not."

I lift my shirt, and before I can stop her, Carla pokes my
belly. I flex, believe me. Her finger hits a wall just beneath my
skin but round mounds are nowhere to be found. "You can
have low body fat and firm muscles but still not have definition," she offers generously.

I am humiliating myself in front of Carla Dunlap in order
to learn about muscles. Why do women want them, all of a

sudden, and why are they afraid of them? What do women's muscles have to do with male muscles, and male approval? How do women get these muscles? Carla should know: she has been a bodybuilder since the infancy of female body-building more than a decade ago, and has won every national and international competition at least once.

If Diamond Gym were a bar, it would be called a dive. Instead it is called hard-core, which is appropriate: it is a hard core of a gym, a bare-bones place furnished only with essential metal and decorated only with mirrors and photographs of bodybuilding champions. The floor is concrete, covered with plywood and topped with strips of black conveyor-belt mate-rial. Stale sweat mingles with Brut and other manly odors. Six ceiling fans energetically attempt to cool the ninety-degree New Jersey heat, and unidentifiable music competes with radio static for airwaves. Everywhere, huge caricatures of men straddle benches, grip bars that bend under the weight of flat steel doughnuts, and grunt.

A modest marquee by the entrance says: "Welcome back, Carla Dunlap, Ms. Olympia." Carla has come to Diamond Gym this summer to train for the Ms. Olympia contest, the most prestigious of all women's bodybuilding competitions, three months away. She won several years ago, in 1983, but in 1984 Cory Everson began what became a seven-year reign, and Carla wants her title back. A week ago Carla drove to Newark from Boston, where she was living with her boy-friend, Phil Kaan, a judo champion and son of Mayo Kaan, the original model for the Superman comic book character. Phil had wanted Carla to keep training in his gym, a million-dollar facility equipped with all the Nautilus machines, juice bars, and Jacuzzis a wealthy Bostonian could desire. "He likes to say, 'Ms. Olympia trains in my gym,'" explains Carla. "I'm a selling point there, a business asset."

But never having seen a female bodybuilder before, much less a Ms. Olympia, gym members were fond of whispering, "That's disgusting, she looks like a man."

"It's an uneasy truce," Carla continues, "but I think Phil realized he was a little off base. It's a nice gym, but if I had my druthers, I'd not be training there."

"I notice you had your druthers," I say.

Carla laughs. "I usually do."

Shirley Kemper, as much as Diamond Gym itself, lures Carla back to Newark this hot August. Shirley owns the gym with her husband, John, and she and Carla have been training partners for seven years. Shirley is what Carla isn't: shy, fidgety, blond, married. They complement each other perfectly. If there were a Best Posture Award, Shirley would win it. She also wins bodybuilding contests, most recently a mixed-pairs event with John, a former Mr. Universe. I have never seen muscles like hers up close. She looks like an anatomy textbook—here are the deltoids, here is the sternomastoid, here are the origin and insertion of the biceps. I stare, figuring that's what they're there for. "Nice arms," I say.

"Good," she answers with a quick grin.

Photographs of Carla hang on the walls beside those of Serge Nubret, Frank Zane, Lee Haney, and other Messrs. Universe past and present. Over the stationary bicycles, the most high-tech equipment in the gym, one photo shows Carla smiling at the furious pedalers, her near-naked muscles bold and brassy. Next to the pull-up bar, Carla strikes a "most muscular" pose on the cover of *Flex* magazine, and over the small countertop that serves as an office, a photo shows Carla draped pseudo-casually over a bench, elbows on the floor, chin in hands. This last one is cheesecake, but Carla's arms are stubbornly remarkable. The ins and outs from shoulders to elbows remind me of long, curvaceous balloons.

John and Shirley are enshrined here too, and I learn from a framed magazine article ("Mother and Daughter Muscle") that the Kempers have three daughters, all of whom lift weights. I see a ten-year-old over by the counter who must be one of them. Shirley peers out the front window of the gym and says, "Here comes Daddy."

A squat man, John Kemper is most notably wide. Each thigh is wider than an average person's waist; his chest is so massive that his arms, instead of hanging straight from his shoulders, detour outward. He turns sideways to fit through the door.

For the next two hours, John answers the phone and does odd jobs around the gym as Shirley and Carla lift weights. They draw dumbbells together and apart as if playing accordions; hold 200-pound bars and shrug. Few words are spoken. "We know each other so well, training together is like breathing," says Carla. Lovers usually can't pull it off. "Phil loves training with me, but if I start cursing or something in the heat of the workout, he gets insulted and that night he mopes. Then the next workout, I tiptoe, afraid something will happen."

Carla was a muscular baby, no doubt, with guts to match. She started developing that strength through swimming, claiming New Jersey state championships in the butterfly, the most difficult stroke and the one that other girls in the sixties avoided for fear of developing large, unsightly shoulders. She became known as "Muscle Lady," as in, "Make me a muscle, Muscle Lady!"

In high school, Carla tried out for the boys' swim team, and in the process outswam every boy. The coach challenged her, and she beat him too. Still, he wouldn't let her on the team— no locker room for her, a distraction for the boys, all the old excuses—so she did gymnastics instead. After a tumbling accident she discovered a lump in her breast, and at age fourteen had surgery to remove a benign tumor. When a second lump was discovered and removed, her mother, afraid the lumps were related to tumbling, encouraged Carla to quit.

"Why don't you stick with swimming?" Anna Dunlap would plead.

"Ma, there's no dance in swimming," Carla would answer.

While working at a summer camp, Carla met some synchronized swimmers who invited her to join them. Carla's body was so dense she had to work harder than the others to stay afloat, but at last she could simultaneously be dancing and swimming, powerful and graceful, controlled and creative. After college she moved to San Francisco and then San Antonio to train with the best coaches, and became one of the country's top synchronized swimmers.

Synchronized swimming, however, doesn't pay. Bodybuilding didn't pay either when Carla began competing, but the training is more concentrated, and you can do it on your own schedule, and in your own town, even Newark. When a friend named Steve Wennerstrom told her she could be a bodybuilder, Carla decided he was right.

She competed in her first contest, The Best of the World, without ever having lifted weights, and placed fifth. The year was 1979, before women's bodybuilding films, television contracts, and Madison Square Garden competitions; before steroids. Contestants tottered around onstage in heels and bikinis in an event barely distinguishable from a beauty pageant. Still, a fifth-place finish for someone who had developed muscles primarily through the much-maligned sport of synchronized swimming was impressive. Carla, then twenty-five, decided that with some training she could probably get pretty good.

She came here, to Diamond Gym. Already strong, Carla didn't start with any five-pound weights—she grabbed the thirty-pounders. The members of the gym, all of them male and most of them gargantuan, were astonished. They gave her their highest compliment. "You've got balls," they said.

In a way, they were right. She made two gutsy moves at that first contest that forever changed women's bodybuilding. First, she walked onstage and kicked off the obligatory high heels. No American competitor ever wore them again (the Europeans still do). Second, she struck poses, such as the front double biceps, that actually reveal muscle. Women have been flexing ever since.

. . .

Carla lies supine on a bench, hoisting a barbell off her chest. She and Shirley have added progressively more weight to each end of the bar, picking up twenty-five-pound rings and slipping them onto the steel pole as if hanging up clothes. The barbell weighs 135 pounds now, exactly the same as Carla.

"Come on, come on, c'mon c'mon c'mon," Shirley says. Carla's face withers into a contorted mass of wrinkles, her mouth puckers as if to kiss, and with a final "hwoooo" she locks her elbows and plunks the bar into its Y-shaped holders. Shirley immediately lowers it to Carla's chest again. Over and over, Carla pushes the bar up as if her life depended on it, as if she were pinned under a car. On the last lift, Shirley puts a few fingers on the bar, offering token help. When Carla stands, her chest seems broader and more "ripped," as they say in weight rooms, or "defined," or "cut up."

Carla and Shirley change places. They are methodical in their training, and focused; among bodybuilders, concentration is key. I try not to disturb them as I follow along, mimicking them with miniature weights like an overgrown child. I suspect they are laughing to themselves. Here I am, dangling from an overhead bar where each of them did forty pull-ups. They had slowly raised and lowered themselves as if assisted by an invisible hydraulic lift. Can I touch chin to bar even once? Strain, wiggle, kick: no. On to the next task. I pull a bar down behind my neck, then grip dumbbells and bend them up toward my nose. Where they have done three sets of twelve, I do one set of six.

Pitiful performance notwithstanding, I enjoy myself. I pumped iron in college, back in the mid-seventies when only a handful of varsity women athletes considered such a thing, and my body is starting to remember. In the mirror, I can see triceps peeking out from behind my arms. Bodysurfer Lauren Crux told me she lifts weights not for the look but for the feel, and I understand what she means now: a current pulsates like neon through my body. Wandering from one set of weights to the next, I start to walk the way I did when my name was announced before a basketball game, as if applause might break out at any moment.

But when I was playing basketball, weightlifting had a purpose. Sitting on a stool and struggling to pull a bar down overhead, I'd think about rebounding. The stronger I became, the more effective I could be on the court, and that kept me groaning through the final set. From time to time I still end up in weight rooms, more out of habit than desire, as if acting out an old hypnotic command. But I wake up on about day three when, strapped into some machine or another and straining to lift some damn weight, I ask myself, Why? Added strength might help me row or swim faster, but so what? Invariably I release the bar, listening to the satisfying smash of metal on metal, and hit the showers.

Above the music-static, Carla and I can hear that same thud-clang, thud-clang as exhausted lifters drop the weights. "At my boyfriend's gym, he'd kick you out if you did that," Carla offers on her way to the next weight machine. "Here, we don't have to worry about damaging a carpet." Carla helped John and Shirley relocate Diamond Gym to this presumably nicer address several years ago, and has stapled fresh conveyor belt onto the floor, rolled paint onto the walls, replaced ceiling panels, swept.

When the Kempers first bought this building, it was a beauty salon. In a way, it still is. Bodybuilding competitions are, after all, new-age beauty contests. But only the strong survive, and the attrition rate is high. How many times will a woman line up next to other women and have judges declare that she is *not* the fairest of them all? Carla meditates and practices yoga daily to keep things in perspective. "Nine out of ten bodybuilders take the judging personally. You have to take it for what it is—just people's opinions."

Opinions change. In the past decade, muscles have become fashionable for women, practically mandatory. Models have them now—at least a little grape-size bulge in the upper arm—and even some store mannequins have them. But when female bodybuilders carried muscle mania to its logical extreme, saying, "You want to see muscles? I'll show you muscles," the general public balked and bodybuilding judges had torrid debates about how much was too much. Carla was deemed, in the early years, "too muscular." Judges used the Miss America standard then, trying to choose someone to represent American womanhood. Thus tiny Lynn Conkwright, no more muscular than today's average aerobicist but decidedly cute, won the 1979 world bodybuilding championship, although several women outmuscled her. Even as recently as 1983, Australian power lifter Bev Francis sent judges into a tailspin at the Caesar's Cup competition, which was immortalized in the documentary film *Pumping Iron II*. Although Bev's massive physique made the other competitors look like prepubescent waifs, she placed eighth. Carla, more muscular than most but no match for Bev, won. Yet this is America, where bigger is better. By 1987, Bev Francis had won the world championship, and no one expects svelte hundred-pounders like Lynn Conkwright to reign again.

Bodybuilding is hard work; there's the lifting, and then there's the not eating (fatlessness is next to godliness), plus even black women have to get tan (television lights bring out yellow undertones), and you have to choose music and choreograph routines, and buy or make bikinis. The sport requires "good genetics," as the competitors phrase it—the sort of muscles that respond to training by trying to burst out of the skin. It requires discipline, of course, and the desire to do something you probably won't get paid for and probably will get ridiculed for. In addition, you have to be or be made beautiful, for the judges take into account "overall appearance" as well as muscularity and symmetry. To this end, one successful bodybuilder hired a plastic surgeon to chisel her nose into a daintier form.

Carla fulfills the beauty requirement, although she doesn't think so ("I look at pictures of myself and cringe"). Nor has she always understood the role of traditional beauty in women's contests. It was Christine Little (then Chris Reed),

Carla's on-the-road roommate, who showed Carla the fine points of the game, in the summer of 1981.

At the United States championship in Atlantic City that year, Carla placed second in the middleweight division. (Amateurs now have three weight classes—light, middle, and heavy; for years there were only two because organizers feared women would resent being called heavyweights.) Middleweight Deborah Diana looked visibly upset when she was named the winner. "Everyone knew Carla should have won," says Christine. "It was obvious."

Four days later, they flew to Las Vegas for the Ms. America contest, the national championship. "Carla and I were exact opposites," Christine, now a nurse, continues. "I was off-the-wall nervous—yakety-yak like Chatty Cathy—and she was all calm; she used to do yoga before going onstage. All the way to Las Vegas I'm telling myself, I've got to be honest with Carla. I don't know how to do it, but I've got to do it."

When they arrived at their hotel room, Christine blurted out, "Carla, you didn't lose that contest on your physique, you lost it on your appearance. You're wearing the wrong color suit for your skin tone, you don't wear any makeup, and you're pulling your hair back like a chambermaid."

Carla paused for only a moment. "Will you go out with me tomorrow and get makeup?" she asked.

"You bet," said Christine.

Christine loaned Carla an extra suit, a white one (Carla's had been purplish gray), they bought makeup, and Carla fluffed out her hair. Two days later, Carla won the Ms. America.

"I still don't wear makeup when I can get away with it," Carla says. "It's a pain in the neck." For today's workout Carla wears no makeup and her hair is pulled into a bun at the nape of her neck. Feminized only with three stone earrings, she manages to look glamorous anyway. "I found that in bodybuilding, because you were sending so many mixed signals, if [people] looked at you and did not see a face they immediately recognized as female, the next place they looked was at your chest, and if you didn't have recognizable breasts, then you had to in some way communicate your femininity."

How refreshing it would be to meet, perhaps in the year 2020 or so, a female bodybuilder who did not mention femininity. But today, that would be like meeting a swimmer who did not mention water. Sex-role confusion is the water modern-day bodybuilders swim in.

"That's the first time you've used the F word," I tell her.

She laughs. "Femininity is such an old issue. So old and so dead."

She's right about the old but not about the dead.

Since women first started pedaling bicycles a hundred years ago, defenders of our nation's morality have been worried that muscularity would lead to masculinity. To defuse negative reactions, women came up with what sociologist Jan Felshin terms the "female apologetic"—an emphasis on femininity despite the traditionally masculine behaviors involved in certain sports.[2] According to researcher Patricia Del Rey, women athletes who are in the least socially acceptable sports—basketball, football, ice hockey, softball—are the most apt to apologize for their participation through makeup, dress, mannerisms, and other affirmations of "feminine" traits.[3] Bodybuilders, particularly vulnerable to attack for defying feminine tradition, are thus especially likely to overcompensate. Virtually every magazine article and book about bodybuilding contains the apologetic. One article put it this way: "No, bodybuilding won't make you a female Conan the Barbarian—just shapelier, firmer, sexier!" This sexualization of sports is disturbing for many reasons, primarily because women use sports as a way to become appealing to men, rather than a way to discover their own power.

It's difficult to be a strong, assertive athlete and cling to traditional feminine roles, most of which contradict athleticism. Even world-champion bodybuilders seem to confuse female gender with the feminine sex role:[4]

"Why should muscles be considered masculine? I think of myself entirely as a woman" (Lisa Lyons).

"I'm very female-looking. I don't look extremely masculine, whatever masculine is" (Rachel McLish).

"My idea of the perfect female bodybuilder is [one with] a body that is muscularly as close to the male's as possible, but with the expression and the personality of a female coming out" (Bev Francis).

Gloria Steinem once said, "We are becoming the men we wanted to marry," but she was referring to our professions, our assertiveness, our abilities to, say, fix cars. Some of us now have the muscles of the men we wanted to marry, and that flies in the face of a primal human assumption that the two genders should, even when clothed, be immediately distinguishable. "You can't tell the women from the men!" older folks moaned when boys grew long hair in the sixties. Now the pitch is higher, the tone more desperate. "Why do female bodybuilders want to look like *men*?"

Women *are* trying to look like men, in a way; they want to develop big muscles and show them off and have people exclaim, "Gorgeous!" I think many women are fixated on muscles these days in part because men have them. Pectoral envy. Muscles can be fun and somewhat useful, but more important, they represent strength, privilege, and competence. Weightlifting eliminates flabby upper arms, baggy thighs, and other such embarrassments of womanhood.

Female bodybuilders don't look like men; it's just that people still aren't used to seeing muscles on women. (Male bodybuilders don't look like ordinary men either.) And though Carla could put Joe Average to shame, she could never compete against John Kemper. Mixed-pairs competitions, in which a man and a woman pose together, seem designed to demonstrate just how tiny women are, how minuscule their muscles.

Muscles are male. Everybody knows that. For women to do "male" jobs shakes the structure of the economy; for women to play "male" games upsets cultural norms. But for women to become very strong, stronger even than men?

"When people see that I look strong, they immediately say, 'Don't beat me up,'" says Carla, who has not, to date, beaten anyone up. But what if she did? What if battered women battered back? A world in which women were not physically intimidated by men would be a different world indeed.

Despite her muscularity and self-confidence, Carla is still female, and therefore vulnerable. "That's one thing I like about living in Boston," she says. "It's nice not to have to always look over your shoulder as you do in this area, or L.A., or Washington. Bostonians complain, but I say, 'Are you kidding?' Some people in Newark go out of their way to threaten you. It's so nice to sit in a park after dark and not worry about being mugged or accosted or even 'Hey, baby,' that sort of thing."

"Don't your muscles help?" I ask.

"I'm five-three," she reminds me. "If it's dark, or my clothes cover me . . ."

Indeed, she is barely taller standing than she is when seated, and with a sweatshirt on she could look, at first glance, merely stocky. "People are always amazed at how small I am," she tells me. "Bodybuilding is illusion."

It is ironic that female bodybuilders, while bending over backward to prove that they are not men, also ingest synthetic versions of testosterone. At least many of them do; Carla estimates that 80 percent of professional women bodybuilders do. In the womb, testosterone is the substance that is responsible for the development of either male or female sex organs. Without it, the baby will appear to be female; with it, the baby will appear to be male. When a transsexual wants to change from woman to man, testosterone in the form of anabolic steroids is the drug of choice.

Through a quirk in human metabolism, anabolic steroids enlarge men's muscles but shrink their testes; a male bodybuilder who takes steroids for years is likely to be infertile and impotent. In women, the effect is consistent: muscles grow, facial hair grows, genitals grow. And while steroids produce in men a mass that makes Mike Tyson look wimpy, women who use them do not become grotesque.

Which of the women are taking drugs? "It's a secret society," says Carla. "No one tells the truth." Officials perform drug tests at all major contests, but few offenders are caught. Many drugs cannot be tested for, and detection avoidance has become a science. Bodybuilders believe they can discern a steroid user because of a hard, leathery, thin-skinned look and unusually rapid development. "When you see a woman who's only been training for two years and she has ten years' worth of muscle," says Carla, "you assume it's not natural."

Carla, it seems, is clean. She has added mass slowly, her peers say she's clean, and besides, after her breast surgeries, she feared that any ingestion of hormones would greatly increase her chances of cancer. Carla is not categorically opposed to steroids. "If a woman wants to enhance her physique, I can understand it," she says. "She just has to watch it or she'll start to look—especially in the face—very hard." Carla seems to weigh the pros and cons of steroid use the way other people decide about vitamin supplements. On the one hand, steroids can make your face grow stubbly with beard, make your clitoris grow to the size of a small penis, damage your heart and liver, and give you kidney, bladder, or breast cancer. On the other hand, they can help you win contests.

The stakes are high. Compared to Martina Navratilova's $15 million career earnings, purses are a pittance, but Carla won more than $75,000 between 1982 and 1987 (more than any other competitor) and earns another $40,000 or so each year from exhibitions, camps, videos, newscasting, and other sports-related activities and appearances.

"One woman told me, 'I don't know why there's such a fuss about testing, I'm off drugs more than I'm on them,'" Carla reports.

Carla thought, You just blew it with me, kid. What's that make you, a careful abuser rather than just an abuser? She explains: "It's illegal. When athletes who have taken steroids compete against athletes who have not taken steroids, it's taking money from them. It's theft."

If women are tempted to take steroids, one can see why. Side effects notwithstanding, they work. Although bodybuilding probably has the highest percentage of steroid users, female runners, swimmers, and cyclists have also admitted to or tested positive for steroid use. Angel Myers qualified for the 1988 Olympics in five swimming events, then was disqualified from the team for a positive steroid test, though she denied taking the drugs. Cindy Olivarri, one of this nation's top cyclists, admits to having taken steroids for three years, until being booted from the 1984 Olympic team for a positive test. Angella Issajenko, a top Canadian sprinter and a 1988 Olympian, also admits to having taking steroids. No one estimates that as many women as men take steroids, but no one denies that steroid use is increasing among female athletes.

In bodybuilding, steroid use is not that different from breast reduction, breast enlargement, facelifts, hair removal, liposuction, starvation, and myriad other means by which women compete for love, money, fame. It has the additional onus of being against the rules, but hasn't beauty always involved an element of deceit? Isn't bodybuilding just an obsession with appearance, raised to the level of professional sports?

Says former bodybuilding champion Rachel McLish, who even at her peak looked downright scrawny compared to today's hulks, "It's a perversion of the female gender. It's sad for me to watch these women trying too hard to be sexy, posing with these gyrating movements, overdone fingernails, too much makeup, and silly bows in their hair. They're overcompensating for what they've done to their bodies."[5]

A few other black women are starting to join Carla in the gyms and on the stages, but in general, black women seem reluctant to jump on the muscular-beauty bandwagon. Carla has a theory about that. Having traditionally been seen as matriarchs, black women are beginning to enjoy media attention for their glamour, their sexiness, she says. The last thing they want to do is go "back" to emphasizing strength. White women, on the other hand, are trying to escape media objectification—and thus have been quick to embrace at least weightlifting, if not bodybuilding.

"Then why did you get involved so early?" I ask.

"I always run contrary to the current," says Carla.

Back in her synchro-swimming days, black runners and basketball players complained to Carla, "What are you doing paddling around with those white girls?" Now, as one of few black female professional bodybuilders, Carla is overlooked for endorsements and other opportunities because of her race. ("It's also because I don't go after things," she adds. "I can be very lazy.")

None of this seems to bother Carla. "My parents never made a big thing about color," she says. "It was, 'You're black, and that's your heritage, and that's fine. As far as your values go, you're a human being. Now treat people as people.'" So she was comfortable with the Jews in her Newark neighborhood, the rainbow of races in her high school and college, the whites in synchro swimming. "My parents never saw race or gender as a limitation," Carla says, and that explains a lot.

But because Carla is a woman, she cannot, except in the privacy of her own thoughts, be simply a bodybuilder. She will be a bodybuilder *but* she wears makeup, a bodybuilder *but* she likes to date men, a bodybuilder *but* she is not as strong as the men. A bodybuilder *but* she's a woman. Never simply a bodybuilder.

After the workout, Carla strides over to the counter that serves as the Diamond Gym office. She is wearing green tights that end just below the knee, and I watch her calves move up and down like pistons. Her chest-first gait is the bodybuilder's pose—what judge would vote for a slouch?—but it is also, I have noticed, simple athletic pride. I can almost see gold medals draped around her neck.

Carla begins thumbing through bodybuilding magazines.

Her name is in all of them, her picture in some; she has made a new video for female competitors, she will host a television pilot, and she is quoted on such sundry subjects as judging standards and amino acids.

A few women are working out, each with a man. "It's a regular Peyton Place around here," says Carla, amused. "Everybody knows everybody's business."

"Do they leave you alone, then, because they've heard you have a boyfriend?" I ask.

"Oh, no." She laughs. "They know me better than that." She does not elaborate. Instead she says, "Phil loves to train with me, but every once in a while he'll touch me a certain way—just my back or something, but in that certain way, between lovers—and I can't stand it. There's no place for that during training."

Several post-spinach Popeyes, all wearing ripped T-shirts that could have been pulled from the same ragbag, dismount their machines and lumber over, greeting Carla shyly, the way children would greet a grade-school teacher. They come in assorted colors and sizes—black, white, and brown; large, huge, and humongous.

Carla dances a little, a casual hum-de-dum dance she might do while housecleaning. It doesn't seem to be the music that moves her as much as the workout; her muscles are humming, and happy, and they dance.

So it is when Carla is onstage. Bodybuilding may or may not be a "real" sport—the debate continues among those who enjoy semantic aerobics—but it is without doubt an interesting spectacle. Male bodybuilders are fascinating the way Ripley's Believe It or Not Museum is fascinating, and many are advertisements for synthetic testosterone, testaments to the miraculous combination of drugs and weights. But while the men flex and bulge in a rote manner ("It's so boring," says Carla. "You want to gong and pull them off the stage"), the women incorporate the compulsory poses into routines as varied as gymnasts' floor exercises, and almost as compelling.

"People expect muscle to move poorly," says Carla. "But that's where women have added polish to the sport."

Carla is perhaps the best poser among the few dozen professional women bodybuilders. "Feline grace," some have said, but her passion and poise remind me of ballet dancer Gelsey Kirkland. "I like to make people feel," Carla says. "In other sports, you don't have to worry about how your body looks, as long as it functions. In bodybuilding, it's personality, projection of an essence, a joie de vivre. You can't just get up onstage and be muscular. Your body has to have a soul."

Observing this soul in motion, I am amazed to discover that Carla does not rehearse. Christine Little told me, "I'd practice my routine at least a half-hour a day for at least two weeks before each contest. And that was after spending two weeks or so choreographing it. I'd show up in Vegas or San Jose or wherever and say to Carla, 'Let's see your routine.' She'd say, 'Listen to these three tapes, and tell me which one you like.' Then she'd go out there and ad lib, and I'd be blown away."

"I never know how I'm going to feel when I hit the stage," explains Carla. "If I find music beforehand, I practice in my mind, seeing how the music might move me, but in order to preserve the raw feeling of feeding off the audience, I don't actually do it until I'm onstage."

Does anyone else wing it?

"No." She laughs. "It's not something everybody could do."

Neither is bodybuilding. It takes energy to develop and maintain muscle—women have to work harder at it than men, they say—and then what? All you have is muscle. An anaerobic activity, pumping iron doesn't even condition the heart or lungs. The perfect body is every woman's dream (feminism notwithstanding), but like all things material, its pleasures are superficial. "I see people all the time who are grasping for things outside themselves to make their lives meaningful," says Carla.

"Things like muscles?"

Carla nods, smiling. "Absolutely."

. . .

I spent a weekend with my sister recently, and she started talking about my thighs. "I still can't get over how different you look now from when you were playing basketball," she said.

"About twenty-five pounds thinner," I agreed. "I have cheekbones now."

"What I remember is your thighs, how huge and solid they were, how they bulged with every step."

She's right: my thighs were thick marble pillars, and I showed them off shamelessly, like trophies. "Here," I'd say to friends and near-strangers, grabbing a hand and placing it on my quadriceps, "feel this."

I loved those thighs, and the more time I spend with Carla, the more I am tempted to travel from gym to gym in search of them. But I'm closer to my sister now than I was ten years ago, and somehow I think it has something to do with my thighs. When I was busy being strong, and vain about that strength, I let people feel my thighs, but I'm not sure I let them know me. "You're softer now, more accessible, more human," one friend told me when I'd reduced my workout schedule from ten to three times a week and had shrunk to what for me is a more normal size. I miss my thighs but the friend was right. I insulated myself with muscles and athletic performances, remaining on display, an object for public viewing. No longer muscle-bound, I now feel free to be fallible, and to be—horror of horrors—ever so slightly flabby. That's not to say it's impossible to be Herculean and humble, enormous and intimate. It just hasn't been my experience.

I ask Carla if any of this makes sense to her. "Sure," she says. "I'm maybe too much of a loner. I don't form bonds."

Bodybuilding is about making oneself seem larger than life. It's about creating the illusion of perfection. Along the way one also builds protection, a suit of armor that shields whatever delicate organs may lie hidden beyond the massive chest, the padded back. An essential part of posing, Carla tells me as we look in the mirror, is learning how to disguise a weak hamstring, how to flex even during the "relaxed" pose, how to draw attention to one's strengths. Carla presents her body to the judges in such a way as to hide all flaws; that is her job. To reveal imperfection would be unprofessional.

So in the precarious balance between professional athlete and target of ridicule, in the no-woman's-land between beauty and beast, Carla is alone. She is friendly with other women on the tour, but they are, after all, her competition. She can have boyfriends, but she must instruct them not to flirt with her while she is working out. Lacking a coach or trainer, she depends on Shirley Kemper ("Some people change training partners like they change their underwear; I can't"), but she seems uncomfortable with this need. "I am a complete person," Carla tells me, and when she says it I hear the echo of other athletes in other places who have felt the need to tell me the same thing.

Even in the 1990s, to be female and athletic takes courage, including the courage to go it alone. No wonder Christine Little's favorite story is the one about helping Carla buy makeup. Carla finally had let someone in.

Carla finishes ninth in her last Ms. Olympia competition and retires soon afterward. I'm not sure she is the kind of complete person judges are looking for anymore. She can out-dance everyone, swimming across the stage as if still doing synchro, her femininity ("whatever that is") intact, but her body is shrinking, in comparison with reigning champion Cory Everson, former power lifter Bev Francis, and other relative newcomers to the sport. Carla has learned from meditation that "we're all the same under the skin," she tells me, which is an interesting insight—and a useful one—for someone with her physique.

Drugs played only a small part in Carla's decision to retire. "Women can still compete without steroids," she argues. "I was still placing in the top ten without them. It's just time to move on."

I have a feeling that Carla's transition to dancing or sportscasting or some new sport will be as smooth as her swimming stroke. Her muscles are defined but she is not defined by them, and that makes all the difference.

It is difficult but not impossible to pose while looking in one's rearview mirror and barreling down the New Jersey Turnpike, away from Diamond Gym. I really must start lifting, I find myself thinking as I twist the mirror and turn a shoulder so I can peek at my triceps. I take my foot off the accelerator and flex my leg. I should have shown Carla my right calf, I say to myself. It's my best muscle. Ah, well.

Running Scared

Carol hangs out with the boys at recess, and is often chased by two or three of them. They like to throw her into snowbanks and rub snow into her face, or, when snow is lacking, to tie her up with skipping ropes. When she runs away from them she flings her arms around a lot. She runs in a funny wiggling way, slow enough to be caught, and screams loudly when she is.

—MARGARET ATWOOD, *Cat's Eye*

WHAT happened to Andra Chamberlin and Barbara Logan is not what happens to most women runners. It's what they're afraid will happen.

Andra's nightmare began on a November morning in 1987, before the sun was up. A cardiologist's secretary, twenty-nine-year-old Andra was in training for her first marathon. She awoke at four-thirty and drove the half-hour from her country home to the nearest city, Midland, Texas, to run on a par course, a 1.5-mile loop. Often friends from Midland would join her for a prework run. That day her friends stayed in bed, but there were lights at the course, and houses nearby. Andra ran about two miles, warming up. The moon was full, outshining the lamps dotting the course. She felt relaxed and happy.

A man ran toward her.

"My first thought was, Here's another runner. My second

thought was, Gee, he's running awfully fast. By the time I realized he was coming right at me, he was an arm's length away. He body-slammed me into the ground."

He began choking her, both large hands on her throat. She struggled to free herself, then started to black out. "I thought, I can either fight him and he will kill me, or I can quit resisting and maybe stay alive. When I quit resisting, he quit choking me."

He led her to a dark area under a tree. She trembled, her stride so rickety the earth seemed unsteady beneath her step. In an instant she had been transformed from confident athlete to quivering victim. "Why are you shaking?" he asked. "Are you scared?"

"Yes, I'm scared, this has never happened to me before," she told him.

"You don't need to be scared, I'm not going to hurt you," he said.

"Then what are you going to do to me?"

He didn't answer.

She had worn two T-shirts that morning, planning to remove one when the sun rose—her favorite part of morning runs. Andra would sometimes run on country roads near her home, timing the runs so she'd reach the halfway point just as the sun was beaming its first thin spotlights over the edge of the earth. "It was God's way of saying, 'Look, Andra, this is just for you, because you had the discipline to get up,'" she says. "It was so beautiful and so peaceful. Then, later in the day, when things got so busy and I was feeling frazzled, I'd stop for a minute and remember what I saw that morning."

Her assailant lifted one of her shirts off partway, leaving it over her head as a blindfold. The other he pulled up around her shoulders. Her running shorts he tossed into some bushes. He raped her.

"Are you married?" he wanted to know afterward. "Do you have any children? Are you going to tell the police?" She answered him honestly: Yes to the marriage, no to the children, and of course she would tell the police.

Finally, he pulled one shirt down over her chest and patted her hip "like I was a dog or something," she says.

"You shouldn't be running out here alone," he told her.

"Don't worry, I don't plan on doing it again," she replied.

He instructed her to wait five minutes before getting up. How the heck am I supposed to know when five minutes is up? she remembers thinking; this is stupid. But she listened for his footsteps, then heard a car pull away. She sat up, dressed herself, gathered her keys and water bottle, and drove to the police station. She pushed open two sets of double doors and found herself facing two male officers behind a counter. "Can I help you, ma'am?" one asked kindly. Andra sobbed uncontrollably.

Police do not keep statistics on the incidence of rape and assault of women runners. One out of twelve women will be raped at least once after the age of twelve, according to the Department of Justice estimates,[1] but there are no separate statistics for runners.

Individual cases come to public attention. Kari Swenson, once the United States' best biathlete (cross-country skier and rifle shooter), was running near her home in the Big Sky region of Montana in the summer of 1984 when she was abducted by two men. They chained her to a tree overnight and, during an attempted rescue, shot her in the chest.

Henley Gibble, the first female president of the Road Runners Club of America (RRCA), was assaulted in 1981 while running on a bike trail in Alexandria, Virginia. The man exposed himself to her, then grabbed her. Sweaty, she was able to slip out of his grasp.

A gang of boys raped, and severely beat a Wall Street investment banker who was jogging in New York City's Central Park at about ten at night on April 19, 1989. The teenagers joked afterward that "it was fun" and called the rampage "wilding," thus introducing mainstream Americans to the euphemism. There was a great hue and cry from the press about race relations, since the woman was white, the boys black and brown. Television's talking heads debated whether perhaps it was more an issue of class than race, an attack of the have-nots on the haves. *Newsweek,* in its lead sentence of a full-page story, insinuated that the woman was partly at fault because she was "out jogging by herself, rather daringly for that late hour."[2] Writers Anna Quindlen, Letty Cottin Pogrebin, Ellen Goodman, and others pointed out that gang rape is not a new phenomenon, despite its new name, and that the central issue is gender, not race or class. Pogrebin wrote: "Escalating male aggression has become a form of terrorism in women's lives."[3]

Women runners keep track of these stories and the fate of victims, memorizing a female version of sports statistics that bears no resemblance to batting averages or winning streaks. Local statistics have particular import. "There have been notable cases where women have been abducted from bike trails," offers Jean Hacken, an Arlington, Virginia, runner who covers twenty to twenty-five miles per week. She remembers their names: "Judith DiMaria, a tennis instructor out in Vienna, was running on the [Washington and Old Dominion bike trail], and her body was found weeks later." Hacken remembers that four runners were raped in nearby Bethesda, Maryland. "Also, if you read the crime stats, there have been a fair number of exposures. Somebody's hitting the women with visual assaults."

A few women's running groups have compiled statistics as well. The North American Network of Women Runners surveyed women marathoners in the Avon International Marathon in Ottawa in 1981.[4] Of fifty-two respondents, 72 percent had experienced "annoying comments, heckling or harassment." Almost 60 percent had experienced "attempts by drivers to interfere with their running." More than 80 percent reported that concern for the possibility of rape or harassment influenced when, where, or how often they ran.

The Washington, D.C., RunHers surveyed its members in 1983, after three women were murdered in separate incidents while running or walking on bike trails in the city's Rock

Creek Park.⁵ Of the hundred women who completed surveys, 41 percent answered that they had been threatened by a man or men. Incidents included being followed by men on bikes, chased, grabbed, slapped, and pinched. Drivers of cars had thrown things at the women; men had exposed themselves. Seventy-eight percent of the incidents occurred in the daylight.

Twenty-eight percent of the women who were threatened reported that they avoided more serious harm by such tactics as outrunning men who were chasing them, running toward crowds, screaming until help came, and wrestling themselves free from the strangers' grasp. Because of the harassment, 76 percent changed their running habits by varying routes and times of runs, not running on isolated trails, being more alert, running in the street, staying away from doorways, running familiar routes only, or running with a partner. None stopped running.

Hacken, a contracting officer for the federal government, runs only on city streets; she avoids "the country trails, which would be more pleasant to run on, but which I deem less safe because there are far fewer people around." What is she afraid of? "Getting killed."

Murder and rape are the far end of a spectrum of abuse women runners become familiar with, if not accustomed to. When asked, "Have you ever been harassed?" Hacken responds, "No. Fortunately." Then she adds, "Nothing other than honking, leering, the usual 'Hey, baby, lookin' good,' that sort of stuff."

How would things be different if she had nothing to fear? "I would run with abandon," Hacken says. "Certainly with less fear. I'm very tight when I run. When somebody honks to get my attention, I tense inside. When I pass a solitary man or somebody who in my judgment doesn't seem safe, I look over my shoulder after I pass. Were I to feel perfectly safe, I wouldn't do that. I wouldn't avoid bushes. I have been known to cross the street to avoid somebody I think may be threatening. A car slows down, maybe they're just dropping somebody off, but I dodge that stuff. I fear being grabbed into a car. All those precautionary things I wouldn't do; therefore I'd be far more relaxed. Obviously, I wouldn't run on crowded Washington Boulevard, I'd run at Teddy Roosevelt Island, the woody areas, isolated areas, some of the bike trails. I'd also probably run at night.

"The other thing I might do is wear skimpier clothing," she continues. "They have new jog bras that you wear on the outside. It's neat because your stomach shows. It would be cooler, and I'd probably wear one if I weren't afraid."

It is a paradox, exclusively female: the stronger a runner gets, the more likely she will be to assert herself, venturing into a world where she will be rudely reminded of her fragility. Running, an activity that usually relaxes the mind and muscles, can make women tense and hypervigilant. Women runners develop a distinctive stride: run a few steps while looking over the left shoulder, run a few steps while looking over the right. Were it a comedy rather than a tragedy, it could be called the damsel dash.

Barbara Logan was just twenty-one in 1977, when she was attacked while running through the town of Williamsburg, Virginia. A senior at William and Mary College, she had grown up in the small, safe, and unusually athletic town of Blue Bell, Pennsylvania, where she had swum competitively in the summer and played field hockey, basketball, and lacrosse during the school year.[6] A short, stocky blond, Barbara—incongruously but inevitably nicknamed "Barbie"—was known for her easy laughter, aggressive hockey stick, masterly piano-playing, and intelligence. She was valedictorian of her graduating class in high school.

"Sports are the underlying theme of my life," Barbara says now. "My father used to take movies of us. He has one of me doing a sack race when I was about six. I look so determined. I was falling down, but I was happy."

Barbara was an intense athlete, with a stubborn game face that included a tongue curled over her upper lip. "I loved the physicalness of sports, the sheer playing of it," she recalls. "I liked competition because the vast majority of my teams have been winning teams. I always played attack, and when I got a goal, I felt like, 'Got you!' It's kind of a snotty feeling. But sports were something I was successful at. You hear horror stories about people who were picked last for teams—well, I was one of the first ones picked."

Her assault occurred on a rainy October Friday, the day she and her college field hockey team were planning to travel to Maryland for a tournament with several other schools. Barbara often supplemented her daily practices with a four-mile round-trip run between her apartment and the Williamsburg campus ("I wasn't speed, so I had to be endurance"). It was a busy street for a small town, lined with houses, shops, and hotels. On some days she'd be stopped several times by tourists needing directions, so she wasn't suspicious when a sedan rolled up beside her and the thin, nervous man inside asked how to get to the Williamsburg Pottery Factory. Barbara looked in the car.

"Get in," he said, pointing a gun at her.

Later, she thought of ways she might have acted differently. "I should have run, I should have just bolted, in a zigzag pattern, like they do in the movies. I wonder if he would have shot me. But at the time I didn't think of that. I was too scared."

She got in. The man sped out of town, driving so erratically Barbara feared she might die in a car accident. She tried to jump out when the car stopped at a light, but he had locked the doors from his side. When they reached a farm on the outskirts of town, he ordered her to strip and lie down in a cornfield. She had had some time to think by then. She had been memorizing his young face, had stared at his black pistol. He was dangerous, possibly on drugs. She took off her clothes.

Like many rapists, the man was impotent. After numerous failed attempts, he commanded her to lie facedown and shot her twice in the head. "I think he shot me because he was impotent," Barbara says. "Rape is a power crime and he didn't even have the power to do that. But he could eject a bullet. That's the only explanation I can make. I wasn't resisting. Why pick a random person to murder?"

The first bullet felt like "a grapefruit exploding." She didn't feel the second.

The man fled and it began to rain harder. Barbara remained unconscious. A farmer in his tractor came upon her and called an ambulance. On its way to the hospital, the ambulance skidded on the slippery pavement and crashed, and Barbara's gurney flipped. She heard a paramedic say, "I thought we'd lost her." But she knew she'd survive.

Andra Chamberlin's recovery has been primarily psychological. Four days after the rape, she forced herself to return to the par course, husband, Chuck, in tow. A month later, surrounded by her friends, she completed the marathon she had been training for ("I couldn't let him take the marathon away from me"). Then, her goal achieved, she stopped running, gained twenty pounds, and "felt terrible." Friends offered to run with her in the mornings, but she had enjoyed the solitude, and resented having to have company. "My attitude was bad," she says. "I thought, 'If I can't run by myself in the mornings, then I'm not going to run at all.'" Finally, a year after the assault, Andra began running again, always with friends.

For Barbara Logan, the recovery was also physical. She spent almost four months in a hospital. She was confined at first to a bed, then to a wheelchair. Her left side was paralyzed, but she was in such good shape that her right side was often able to compensate. She could sit up, for instance, using only the muscles in the right side of her abdomen.

The first time she went to physical therapy, the therapist said, "Wow, you must have had huge leg muscles." That made Barbara feel good. She had been proud of those muscles, and she worked hard to regain use of them, applying to her recovery the same athletic discipline that had compelled her to run that morning. "My physical therapist was just a year older than me," she remembers. "I'd ride a stationary bicycle and we'd kick a soccer ball around—it felt almost normal." She abandoned the wheelchair, then the cane, then the leg brace.

Still captain of her hockey team, Barbara traveled with her teammates to England, where they met Constance Applebee, who introduced field hockey in the United States. Soon afterward, Barbara testified in court. Her assailant was convicted and sentenced to prison.

Barbara graduated a year after her original class. Fourteen years later, her left hand and arm are minimally functional, so she cannot play the piano. She cannot see out of the left half of each eye, so she does not drive. Instead she walks the mile from her home in Peoria, Illinois, to the community college where she works as a guidance counselor.

She can run, but her left ankle is weak, and even when walking she limps, the way someone who had polio or a stroke does. She is more cautious now, never running at night. "I have enough trouble tripping over stuff in the light," she says without self-pity.

Daily, she swims. "I'm kind of neurotic about it," she says. "I have to swim every day. My doctor said, 'You're going to have to work harder than most people just to sustain some kind of grace.' " She competes in masters swim meets, specializing in endurance events. In the pool she does not limp, except with a one-armed butterfly.

Sometimes Andra Chamberlin wakes early and looks out her window at the West Texas countryside. She doesn't want to drive into town; she doesn't want to converse with friends. She wants to lace her sneakers and sprint toward the sunrise, feeling joyfully alone and free and blessed. "I think, Today I'm going to go out there and run," she says. "Then I think, Great, you're going to get to the end of the driveway and be scared to death. Then I think, This makes me so mad!"

Even walking to her car in the early-morning darkness is scary. "I feel my heart in my throat. I'm more cautious, which is good, but then there's the fear. It's not as crippling as it was before, but it's something I'm going to live with for the rest of my life."

Chuck, a supportive spouse but not a morning person, runs alone some evenings. "He doesn't have to worry about going with somebody or making arrangements; he can just go," says Andra. "I'm so envious of men."

Yet Andra says she hasn't been "consumed" by the anger, as have other women with whom she's talked. When told about Barbara's experience, Andra says, "I might have been quite a bit more angry had I been physically harmed. Strange as it may sound, I do feel lucky I was able to walk away from it."

For Barbara, the greatest loss is in her coordination. Because of her limited field of vision, she bumps into things and feels embarrassed; the new clumsiness clashes with the athletic self-image she grew up with. She also misses team sports. "It still bothers me that I can't be a good volleyball player or play on a recreational softball team or a coed soccer team or anything," she says. "Or even just Frisbee. Ray [Gozzi, her husband] and I throw the Frisbee around, but it would be neat to play Ultimate Frisbee. Or golf. I play, but I have to have someone spot the ball, and my arm hurts after a while." She stays as involved as she can: in addition to swimming and running, she announces college basketball games.

Like Andra, Barbara feels lucky: "He could have shot me in the back, which would have been tons worse." Like Andra, she struggles with fear: once when she was walking to work, a man shouted obscenities at her from his car, and she panicked.

Both women have channeled their anger into trying to make the world safer. Barbara became an advocate of strict handgun laws (her assailant had borrowed the gun from his girlfriend), and has given public talks, appeared on radio programs, and written a chapter for *Guns Don't Die, People Do.*[7] Her husband encouraged her to answer innocent questions about her disability honestly. "When I was working in high school, girls would ask me, and I didn't know what to say," Barbara recalls. "Ray said, 'You should tell them.' I started to look at it like, People can learn from this."

Andra became a volunteer at the Midland Rape Crisis Center. She learned self-defense and now helps teach classes. "It takes a lot of practice, and a lot of mental practice, because even in class, when you're faced with a man, it's scary." She practiced on her husband. "Poor Chuck got so tired of being thrown off the bed," she says, laughing. "But it works. Our oldest student was eighty, and she threw one of the instructors—I think he weighed about 230 pounds—into a wall and cracked the plasterboard." Now Andra feels confident that she could defend herself from rape or attack. But she still wouldn't run alone. "I just think it's a stupid thing for a woman to do."

"It's a very sad commentary that women who are doing something so harmless have to worry—and that men don't have to worry," says Road Runners Club of America president Henley Gibble. When she reported her attack to the police, they already had a composite drawing of the man from several previous reports. "The most infuriating thing was that this guy had been out there for four months, and the police hadn't warned anybody," says Gibble. "They hadn't put up fliers, hadn't called local running clubs." Henley became an activist, calling newspapers to get the word out.

Coincidentally, a year later the same man attacked a friend of Henley's, and the friend noted his license number and prosecuted him. He received six months' probation.

The RRCA has published a safety flier entitled "Women Running Smart," which lists fourteen basic tips, among them: don't wear headsets; ignore verbal harassment; carry identification; wear reflective material at night; carry a whistle or noisemaker. In January 1990, the RRCA sponsored the Women's Safety Summit, featuring police officers and FBI agents who spoke to women runners about protecting themselves. (The flier and a videotape of the summit are available from the RRCA.[8])

Less than two months after the investment banker was attacked in Central Park, the New York Road Runners Club created a safety patrol that now numbers more than three hundred trained volunteers. Wearing reflective orange vests, runners and walkers weave through the 840-acre park, carrying two-way radios and acting as additional "eyes and ears" for the Central Park police, reporting threats, attacks, and any suspicious activity. "Crime in the park is down twenty percent this year, and though we can't say that's because of us, that makes us feel very good," says Debbie King, safety director for the club. There are plans to expand the patrol to include cyclists, nannies, and other citizens who use the park.

Elsewhere, runners who seek safety are left to their own devices. Some carry Mace, but Mace is illegal in many states, and other states require certification. Gadgets include the Shriek Alarm, a hand-held device that emits a deafening sound at the push of a button, and D-Ter, a foul-smelling chemical a woman pours over herself to become an instant skunk. Police nightsticks, car keys, rocks, and knives are other companions. Rosalie Ratcliffe, a runner in Waldick, New Jersey, wears a T-shirt that reads "Police Officers' Running Club."[9]

Dogs are popular partners. Because not everyone owns a suitably aerobic or protective pooch, Shelley Reecher, of Eugene, Oregon, trains Doberman pinschers and other recognized protection breeds to escort women runners. Since its inception in 1981, Project Safe Run, Reecher's nonprofit service, has recorded more than 8,000 assault-free runs by women in Eugene. Reecher, who was once raped in an incident not related to running, was motivated to start the project because she "got sick of being hassled" during her runs. "I had men pinching me on my rear end, making very personal remarks, then streaking off when they knew I couldn't catch them. When I run with the dogs, the comments are generic, like, 'Nice dog you got there,' or, 'Nice day for running.' If I don't have to get upset about some jerk, my run is that much more enjoyable." Interestingly, these are not attack dogs. They are "defense dogs," trained to attack only if a companion is threatened. Project Safe Run now has thirteen chapters, most in the Pacific Northwest, and four corporate sponsors.[10] "It's so much better than saying to women, 'Don't run alone,' 'Don't run after dark.'" says Reecher. "I've never known a rapist to look at his watch and wait for nighttime."

Of all the safeguards, dogs and other human beings provide the best deterrent, police say. Weapons and protective agents of any kind can be difficult to use when the runner is surprised or overpowered, and few women carry them.

Catharine MacKinnon writes, "If you ask, not why do women and men do different physical activities, but why has femininity *meant* weakness, you notice that someone who is physically weak is more easily able to be raped, available to be molested, open to sexual harassment. Feminine means violable."[11]

I'd like to think that women athletes are less violable, less vulnerable, than nonathletes. Athletes are stronger, generally. Athleticism builds self-esteem as well as muscles, so athletes may be better prepared than other women to think on their feet and, when wise, fight back. They walk and run with a pride that could deter attack.

But in fact, most rape victims (84.6 percent) report that they fought back or tried to protect themselves in some way.[12] In fact, runners may be just as vulnerable as other women. Even strong, athletic women tend to be less experienced than men in wrestling and fighting, and many are intimidated by men.

Many women, even athletes, come to accept a seemingly benign male prerogative to physically control women. In *Body Politics*, Nancy Henley gives this example: "In a way so accepted and so subtle as to be unnoticed even by its practitioners and recipients, males in [mixed] couples will often literally push a woman everywhere she is to go—the arm

129

from behind, steering around corners, through doorways, into elevators, onto escalators, darting out in front when crossing the street."[13]

Adds Susan Brownmiller in *Femininity:* "Women who customarily expect to have their physical movements directed by others are poorly prepared by their feminine training to resist unwanted interference or violent assault. Fear of being judged impolite has more immediate reality for many women than the terror of physical violence."[14]

I can imagine a woman, even an athletic one, being reluctant to inflict harm. Since childhood, women have been taught to be gentle and kind.

Girls also rehearse running away, getting caught by boys. Yet just as children who play war neither understand the actual horrors of war nor expect to be wounded during play, the girl who squeals and runs does not think of rape, does not expect to be injured, then or in her adulthood. Just as war games do not prepare children for battle, boy-chases-girl games do not prepare women for assault.

Yet sports do train men for violence.[15] Andra's assailant sprinted toward her, then "body-slammed" her to the ground. Raleigh Mayer, editor of *New York Running News,* writes that the man who raped her in 1982 lunged for her football tackle style, and wrestled her into a stranglehold.[16] In a 1986 survey of 350 colleges, the *Philadelphia Daily News* found that male football and basketball players were 38 percent more likely to be implicated in sexual assaults than was the average male college student.[17]

If large numbers of women are not attracted to tackle football; if women do not think of sports in terms of dominance, power-over, and victors and victims (Barbara Logan's "snotty" feeling of "Got you!" notwithstanding), perhaps it is because they are aware of their own fragility. Perhaps they have empathy for the football player who lies motionless on the field, too stunned or injured to move. Perhaps they have been tackled and know that it hurts. Perhaps they fear being overpowered by men who somewhere along the line learned to use sports skills to inflict pain beyond the sporting arena.

So a woman goes for a run in the early morning, her favorite time of day, and ends up lying in the dirt, shirt pulled over her head, shorts in a bush. Another slips out of the hands of a half-naked man. Another's daily run becomes an obstacle course—around this bush, across this street, away from this car, that man. Yet another gets shot in the head. Surely, more women—particularly those who live in "dangerous neighborhoods"—would run if running were safer.

What's amazing, with the ubiquity of harassment, is that some 3.3 million American women run at least twice a week anyway.[18] They abandon the teasing wobble of girlhood games in favor of a cautious but aggressive gait. They share information and gather statistics, including success stories such as that of Kari Swenson, who competed in the biathlon world championship just six months after she was shot, and the brutalized investment banker, who began jogging—slowly—just two months after her assault. They are fearful and tense but they take self-defense classes, they run with others. They keep putting one foot in front of the other, drawing on an athletic courage that stems not from chosen, calculated risk, like the risk of mountain climbing, but from the unavoidable risk that comes, for women, from stepping out of the front door.

"I am afraid," says Henley Gibble. "But you take chances at everything. I'm not going to stop running."

A Silence So Loud
It Screams

Of course, I continued to question myself, especially when
the relationship became physical, which was soon enough.
I knew well enough that there were lesbians in tennis, and
I also knew well enough that some of the public tends to
assume that almost all female athletes are lesbians, but I
had certainly never dwelt on the subject of homosexuality
before. The gays and straights and bisexuals on tour coexist
wonderfully and it's no big deal.

—BILLIE JEAN KING[1]

*J*UST before she tees off, Angie Furey sees two women out
of the corner of her eye and frowns. Pairs of women are as
commonplace as visors at golf tournaments, but Angie, herself a lesbian, is disturbed because these particular women
are not thin, not wearing makeup, and not in any way trying
to appear straight. Angie will later describe them as "dykey
dykes—a motorcycle mama and a mud wrestler." They are
the sort of people Angie Furey does not want to associate with
and, more important, does not want the public to associate
with her. She waggles her club, draws the long driver slowly
back, hesitates, then whooshes the ball. Satisfied, she watches
the small sphere soar, bounce, roll, and come to rest in the

middle of the wide green fairway. Then she exchanges glances with her partner, Suzanne, who is standing among the several dozen people in Angie's gallery.

Suzanne's unstated message: Don't worry; I'll get rid of them. She saunters over to the troubling twosome and starts a whispered conversation. Somehow, she convinces them that they would be better off watching other members of the LPGA, the Ladies Professional Golf Association.

For Angie and Suzanne, this is all in a day's work. As a successful golfer on the pro tour, Angie has the job of hitting golf balls into little cups in as few strokes as possible. Suzanne's primary job, when she travels with Angie, is to preserve Angie's "het" (heterosexual) image—or at least to disguise her gayness—by any means possible. Her own relationship with Angie she obscures by befriending men or male-female couples and walking the course with them, rather than alone or with female friends. She also escorts spectators away, if such spectators "would give me a bad reputation," explains Angie.

In fact, Angie is frequently annoyed by both lesbians and straight men in her gallery. "A golf course isn't a bar," she says. "A lot of people go to sporting events to cruise. Women and men. It bothers me. I've spent many hours on a driving range developing this style. If there's somebody here witnessing it and enjoying it, and they're sincere, I'm glad they're here. But if you have a crowd of thirty women following you, giggling, saying, 'Isn't she cute?' or whatever, the other thirty people who aren't homosexuals can hear that. If men are only there to look at my boobs and butt, it makes me uncomfortable. Unfortunately, because of the way our society is set up, I worry more about the homosexuals. I'm concerned for the sponsor." By this she means: The sponsor may withdraw support from the tournament.

Yet in the case of the "motorcycle mama and mud wrestler," Angie later "felt bad. Turns out, [Suzanne] talked with the women, and one of them worked a twelve-hour day; then they drove seven hours to watch me play. And I didn't even acknowledge them, or thank them for coming, as I would a beer-bellied, beer-drinking man."

Such are the contradictions of lesbian professional athletes. They love women but resent "blatant" lesbians and in public often feel more comfortable with men. They know that lesbians are some of their most loyal, adoring fans, yet they avoid them, fearing that an indiscreet conversation overheard by a sponsor or reporter could cost them a contract or the respect of the media and straight fans. They come out to their parents, then insist their parents not tell anyone. They consult therapists in order to accept themselves more fully, but attend churches where ministers condemn homosexuality. They serve as role models for young girls, telling them in effect: Have the courage to do whatever you want—except be openly gay.

It is a life of fear, secrecy, and shame. It is also a life of love, support, passion, community, friendship, fun, pride, and in some cases wealth and fame—all of which seem to make the duplicity tolerable. But like the denial of physical pain, denial of affectional preference is a trade-off, an agreement to make a personal sacrifice in exchange for athletic reward. As happens when any minority group attempts to "pass," the silence, designed to protect reputations and purses, deprives those who are hiding of a sense of community and history, restricts their cultural and political affiliations, and engenders fear and even paranoia. In this instance it also exacerbates the homophobia of the men who own, organize, finance, and control women's sports.

There have been lesbian athletes for as long as there have been women athletes. Like other gay people, lesbian athletes have grown accustomed to dealing with persecution. They have learned to hide, and they have hidden from each other as well as from straight women and men.

Lately this hiding, this closetedness, has taken on a new aspect: protecting paychecks. Professional athletes are now

beholden to corporate sponsors, some of whom have threatened to withdraw support for individuals and tournaments if
women acknowledge that they are gay. It's food, automobile,
cigarette, and sporting-goods companies—or more specifically, their representatives—that lesbian pros are now hiding
from.

Straight women live in fear too, afraid a gay colleague will
come out and "ruin it for everybody." There is little resentment of the men who hold the purse strings; the golfers, in
fact, both gay and straight, often develop genuine friendships
with these men, who sincerely want to help women athletes.
Rather, athletes tend to focus on each other, criticizing the
less "feminine" women who give the tour a "bad name."

"Angie Furey" is a pseudonym for a golfer who told me her
story. Although some of the facts of her life have been altered
to protect her anonymity, her tale echoes the experiences of
many athletes, not just golfers and not just pros. Angie was
nervous about the interview, as was her lover, "Suzanne Rey-
nolds" (also a pseudonym).

"Are you sure this isn't going to turn into a Billie Jean King
thing?" Suzanne asked. A "Billie Jean King thing," tragically,
has come to mean a yank out of the closet, a situation in
which an athlete is revealed against her will to be gay.

I promised Angie and Suzanne I would disguise certain
facts so readers would not know Angie from other pro golfers. "But I can't guarantee you'll never be asked about gay
women in sports," I reminded Angie. "You've been asked
before, and you'll be asked again."

"I know that," she replied, nodding. She knows how to alter
certain facts too. She knows how to protect herself, how to
keep private an issue she desperately wishes were "no big
deal."

Angie has been playing golf for most of her twenty-five
years. She has been admiring women for about that long. As
a child, she says, she "played sports and chased girls."

She met Suzanne at a softball game in their junior year of

college. For two years, Angie says, "we thought we were the only ones." Suppression of information about lesbians is so successful that in an urban area, in the mid-1980s, these women reached college age with almost no information on the subject. They knew the names of no well-known lesbians, and it didn't occur to them that some of their classmates, teachers, doctors, friends, relatives, and political representatives were gay. When an acquaintance from Suzanne's office told them she was gay, Suzanne and Angie were shocked.

Gradually, they found lesbian and bisexual friends and began coming out to their straight friends. "At first, Suzanne was scared," Angie recalls. "But eventually she got excited. She saw that each time we did it, we had more people we could hold hands in front of."

Angie consulted a therapist "to help me see what I'd been socialized by my parents to think." She remembered: "They told me when I was seven years old that I didn't like 'niggers.' They told me when I was ten to be polite and quiet and shy. I learned how I really feel versus what I was told. That's when I realized that what I want in this world I've always found with women."

Suzanne and Angie were "married" in the Metropolitan Community Church, a Christian church with a special ministry to gay men and lesbians. Suzanne, a computer programmer, wears a gold band on her left ring finger; Angie lost hers on a driving range late one night. They own a house together in Dallas. Because Angie spends about nine months a year traveling from tournament to tournament in this country, England, and Japan, she is rarely home. Their phone bill exceeds what many people pay for rent.

Suzanne joins Angie for just one tournament each year. Her own work is demanding, and she is determined not to be a "wife," that is, not to give up her career to support Angie emotionally.

The arrangement works out well because Angie finds Suzanne's presence on the tour distracting. "I have a tendency to show off, to try to make her giggle, when I really shouldn't be doing that," says Angie. "I'll hit a bad shot and look over and go, 'See, I told you that wouldn't work.' I am emotionally involved with this person. Sometimes I look at my partner as, 'Oh, honey, you can make it better.' But I need to be strong and tough and very sure, and stay focused. I find that with her there, I just like to have fun. If we have had an unbelievable evening, I cannot get my mind on what I'm doing. In the morning I feel like, 'Oh, let's just go to the beach.' "

Angie's older brother, who first put a miniature club in her three-year-old hands, now acts as her agent, gathering big-name endorsements that decorate her visor, her bag, and her shirts. She also employs an accountant, a teaching pro, a sports psychologist, and a caddie. They are all men. In the gay lingo, none but her brother "knows."

The women in Angie's life—including many of the other two hundred women on the tour—do know. "Who is?" is a common question among young players curious about their colleagues. Although Angie would not dream of telling the men who double her already hefty earnings with endorsement money, or the avuncular, slap-on-the-back CEOs whose companies sponsor tournaments, or the eager male amateurs who compare their drives with hers in pretournament pro-ams and comment, "Gee, you hit that ball far for a little girl," or officials of the LPGA, she is comfortable with the fact that most of her competitors know. There is an unspoken honor code among female athletes at every level of competition: You almost never "come out" for anyone else—except trusted friends. Reporters have learned this the hard way, by badgering athletes for lists of names, only to come up dry.

But the fact that Angie and many of the other LPGA women are gay is of no great interest to most of the players. Once they have sorted out who's who, they choose friendships on the basis of other factors—a similar sense of humor, a mutual love of movies or horse races, shared political concerns. Angie's friends are gay, straight, and bisexual. "Some of my best friends are straight, and they love me as I am," she says. Most of the straight women on the tour "are mature about it."

In a Women's Sports Foundation survey of almost 1,700 athletic women, 76 percent of the women "agreed strongly" and another 17 percent "agreed somewhat" with the statement: "A woman athlete's sexual orientation is no one's business but her own."[2]

It's the tour's sponsors, promoters, administrators, and fans who, Angie fears, aren't mature about it; she also fears the media. She is afraid that the truth will mar the tour's image, and thus lead to fewer sponsorships, less or worse media coverage, and ultimately smaller paychecks.

History shows that she's justified in her fears. Homophobia and discrimination are rampant in the women's sports world. In 1983, a major corporate sponsor of "The New Agenda"—a national women's sports conference—threatened to pull out at the last minute if the word "lesbian" were used in conference materials. In 1989, a representative whose company sponsors women's golf tournaments told me, "Sponsors don't care about sexual orientation, but if you announce it, they'll be forced to say, 'We don't want our product associated with that.' "

Attorney and sports agent Leigh Steinberg confirms: "I deal with the marketing of athletes every day, and I know advertisers who use them to try to enhance sales are tremendously hesitant to become involved with controversy. Unless someone is trying to reach specifically into the gay community, using an avowed gay to market a product probably would be perceived as having not very many pluses and a lot of minuses."[3]

Angie is right; her secret—or the "secret" that many recreational, college, and professional athletes are gay—would not be safe in the hands of those who "support" women's sports. Corporate executives are for the most part cautious, conservative, older, white men. The LPGA, like all professional and increasing numbers of amateur and collegiate sports organizations, is beholden to these men, who donate money to improve the corporate image and who hire athletes to act as moving billboards for the company name. If written, the contract between players and sponsors would read, in part: "Players promise to be or act heterosexual in exchange for corporate sponsorship."

In fact, many of the contracts with sports agents—the people who negotiate for corporate endorsements—include a "morals clause" forbidding "conduct unbecoming a professional" or "any behavior bringing disrepute or bad publicity." These clauses, which, an agent explains, were most likely designed in response to male drinking or fighting, are now used against lesbians.

So players agree to "pass." The payoff is substantial: in 1989, the top 34 LPGA players each won more than $100,000, not including personal endorsements, and 103 players won at least $20,000.

How ironic that lesbians find themselves so dependent on male approval. Professional golfers are tightly reined in by male executives who run their show. In the forty-year history of the LPGA, women have never headed the organization. Not until 1989 did a woman serve on the LPGA board of directors.

Angie is comfortable with male control. When the commissioner of the LPGA, John Laupheimer, resigned in 1988 and various candidates, both male and female, were nominated to replace him, Angie said she preferred a male commissioner "because he can gain the respect of the male corporate executives he's going to be dealing with." (Bill Blue became the new commissioner.)

Sponsors, LPGA staff, and players attempt to eradicate what they delicately call their "image problem" by publicly denying the existence of lesbians on the tour. To this end they play up marriages and mothers, employ an "image consultant" to serve as hairstylist and makeup artist (people so frequently confuse a traditional feminine image with heterosexuality that hairdos and mascara still serve as effective camouflage), and maintain what San Francisco State University professor Roberta Bennett has called "a silence so loud it screams."

Even Angie, eager though she is to protect the image of the

LPGA, detests the "ladies first" marketing strategy. "I resent the tour playing on the femininity act all the time," she says. "This is the 1990s. Men and women both go to work, do dishes, vacuum the floor. What are [the LPGA administrators] thinking about? I don't deny what sex I was born into, but it doesn't make any difference in who I am."

Asked why she wears makeup during tournaments, she says, "I don't wear makeup because it makes me look feminine. I wear makeup because it makes me look better. I don't wear skirts, because they're not comfortable. I try to be a good person—to be fair, take time out for other people, appreciate all of our humanness. I think that's the most important thing. I guess the other stuff sells newspapers, but the priorities are nuts."

Some players seem happy to perform the femininity act. In 1989, five players posed in bathing suits for *Fairways*, the official LPGA magazine. *USA Today* and *Sports Illustrated* reprinted the photo.

But golfers aren't safe with their current stance. The sponsors aren't happy because the women don't draw as much attention as male pro golfers. This is most often attributed to the "image problem" or to the fact that the average female pro golfer doesn't drive the ball as far as the average male pro does. (Conversely, women's driving ability is also used to explain the success of the women's tour: male and female spectators can relate better to the women than to extraordinarily long-hitting pro men.)

What is the human cost of keeping golf's "secret"? How far could men drive golf balls (and how would they fare on nerve-racking three-foot putts) if they had to fend off questions about their sexuality between rounds? It would be interesting to see just how much attention women golfers might gain— and how their skills and personalities might change—if homophobia became extinct.

Some lesbian players are tense at postmatch interviews— and boring. By contrast, straight players tend to be relaxed, entertaining reporters with stories of their boyfriends, husbands, and children. Julie Inkster announced her pregnancy in June 1989 by saying, "I guess we're going to have another little bambino around here," and added, "I think this pregnancy was part of the victory celebration at the Crestar Classic," a tournament she'd won the month before.

Not only don't lesbians feel free to make such allusions to their sex lives, they don't feel comfortable naming or giving credit to their most cherished friends. They don't feel comfortable, period, and such unease creates the impression that they lack sparkle or passion. Reviewing some old film clips from sporting events of the 1930s and 1940s, I was shocked to see how friendly the athletes seemed with each other, holding hands, tossing arms around each other, giggling together. Such spontaneous affection has been squelched by modern-day homophobia, not a new phenomenon but one that seems to have increased in direct proportion to women athletes' increased visibility and opportunity.

Angie recalls a tournament in which she was leading after the first three rounds. She felt confident, lighthearted, and well loved as she approached the final eighteen holes on Sunday afternoon. Suzanne had not come along on that trip, but the two of them had stayed in close touch by phone. "I'd gotten a lot of encouragement, and Suzanne had said a lot of funny things to me," Angie remembers. But when reporters asked, "Why do you think you're playing well right now?" Angie answered flatly, "Well, golly, I'm just so happy." She complains: "You just can't discuss [your loved one] the way Nancy [Lopez] can say, 'I've got [daughters] Ashley and Erinn.' That makes her a personality, and it lets the world know she's a loving, compassionate person. Well, so am I."

Homophobia can create bonds, as women find allies and unite to offer support or advice. But it can also erode bonds. Some lesbians resent straight athletes for the media attention they receive. Straight women sometimes avoid lesbians for fear of being contaminated by the "lesbian" label. Even lesbians avoid lesbians—as in the case of Angie and the "dykey dykes."

The deception has devastating effects on self-esteem. Despite the support she has received from a therapist, Angie says, "I could be damned to hell for being gay. I'm not sure. I've prayed about it. I've tried to be a good person."

"While some advocates for women's sports boast of the progress in expanding sport opportunities for women over the past fifteen years, whatever gains have been made must be viewed in the context of the moral compromises we've made," says Pat Griffin, associate professor of physical education at the University of Massachusetts, Amherst. "Women's athletics is, in fact, held hostage to fear of the 'L-word.' As long as women's athletics continues to deny that there are lesbians in sport . . . we will never control our sporting lives and will be forced to waste energy defending a counterfeit heterosexual-only image that we all know is a lie."[4]

Some people repress their sexuality altogether. Celibacy among women athletes seems common. Angie says, "A lot of players would be gay, but they can't be. They're asexual." Having struggled with religious dogma herself, she adds, "I respect their obedience to their religious beliefs."

Perhaps most tragically, homophobia keeps some women and girls out of sports. "I receive more questions about the potential danger to a daughter's sexuality than anything else," says Bruce Ogilvie, a sports psychologist and former consultant to the U.S. Olympic team. " 'How can I protect my daughter from succumbing to the seduction of athletes?' parents ask."

"We need information to correct stereotypes," says Griffin, sighing. "What if a freshman softball player is dating a senior football player—is he preying on her, converting her to heterosexuality?"

Laurie Priest, president of the National Association for Girls and Women in Sport (NAGWS), tells the story of a basketball team on which three of the women were openly lesbian. She told the male coach, "Look, you are heterosexual, and you don't have any influence on these kids' sexuality whatsoever. But if you were a lesbian you'd be held responsible for this. If the parents found out, and wanted to make a stink, it could ruin it for you."

Many people are gay, so naturally, many athletes are gay. This is true for men as well as women. Glenn Burke, the man who delivered the first "high five" salutation, is gay; for six years he was an outfielder with the Los Angeles Dodgers. The late Tom Waddell, 1968 Olympic decathlete and creator of the Gay Games, was gay. Former Washington Redskin David Kopay is gay.

Bill Tilden, tennis champion of the 1920s and 1930s, never acknowledged he was gay but was convicted on a morals charge involving a teenage boy. Frank Deford wrote of Tilden: "The fact was that Big Bill was alone then, as he would be alone now, competitively dominating in a cruelly homophobic society that hated all he represented. He was forced to personally pretend to be something he was not, and publicly he was necessarily a non-person, without substance."[5]

Naming openly lesbian professional athletes is difficult. Two of the most influential women in modern tennis—Martina Navratilova and Billie Jean King—have had or are having intimate, sexual, committed relationships with women. Both prefer the word "bisexual."

At the recreational level, where corporate dollars and media coverage are not factors, lesbians are more visible, playing in thousands of softball, basketball, and other sports leagues. There are national and international gay bowling, softball, volleyball, rodeo, swimming and diving, and soccer organizations. More than 7,100 people from twenty-seven countries, about half of them women, participated in the Gay Games III in Vancouver in 1990.

According to conservative estimates, 10 percent of the U.S. population is gay. According to the National Golf Foundation, 10 percent of the population are golfers. Which means that there are about as many gay people in this country—about 25 million—as there are golfers. Some people, of course, are both.

Angie Furey declines to estimate what percentage of the players in the LPGA are lesbians. When I say, "More than ten percent, certainly?" she laughs.

Other golfers have offered estimates, but they vary so widely they become meaningless. Few female athletes would deny that many of their teammates and competitors are gay. Both Billie Jean King (*Billie Jean*) and Grace Lichtenstein (*A Long Way, Baby*) have published books acknowledging that there are many lesbians in professional tennis. Other books discuss the influence of homophobia in women's sports, and scholars have addressed the topic in numerous journal articles over the past decade.

Still, numbers are difficult to come by, and the attempt to quantify is controversial. A common refrain: "If they find out how many lesbians are in sport, they'll ———." Fill in the blank: hate us, ostracize us, freak out, not let us coach, not let their daughters play, stop funding our tournaments, give us a bad name.

How many football players are gay? Glenn Burke and David Kopay contend that there are more than a few. How many synchronized swimmers are gay? No one cares. Only contact sports, team sports, and traditionally male-dominated sports are rumored to be lesbian havens. (Similarly, sports requiring grace and judged on beauty—such as diving, skating, and gymnastics—are rumored to be populated by gay men.) Female athletes in traditionally masculine sports challenge social dictates about proper behavior for females; therefore, the reasoning goes, there must be something wrong with them. Golf, like tennis, swimming, and ice skating, has traditionally been considered a suitably feminine sport for women, yet at the professional level, golf and tennis players are also randomly accused of lesbianism. This seems a reaction to their professional status. The reasoning in this case: Any woman who takes sports seriously, who devotes her life to sports, must be gay.

Of course, the "all female athletes are dykes" slander does not stem from curiosity, fear, and ignorance alone. Don Sabo says, "Many so-called gay issues are really sex-equity issues. Homophobia doesn't pertain to genitals but to jobs. It doesn't pertain to preference as much as it does to opportunity. Homophobia in sport perpetuates male dominance and the male monopoly of existing resources."

Jackie Joyner-Kersee puts it more simply: "It used to be, you couldn't play basketball or any sport without, 'Oh, she's a lesbian.' Now it's a little better. But it's something they do to keep you from playing sports. That's all it's about."

Homophobia in sports serves as a way to control women, both gay and straight, and it reflects a gross misunderstanding of who women are as physical and sexual beings. But why *does* there seem to be a disproportionate percentage of lesbians in sports? Do lesbians choose sports, or might there be some truth to the notion that sports create lesbians?

First, one must consider why heterosexual women have avoided sports. With the advent of aerobics and the fitness boom of the seventies and eighties, more women than ever are working out, running, racing, and joining teams. Many of these are straight women; nowadays women often begin lifting weights or riding bikes or playing tennis to spend time with their husbands. As sports become increasingly socially acceptable for women, and the number of women increases, the percentage of straight women seems to be increasing. Surely the percentage of straight women in sports now is higher than in the past, when only the most audacious women dared play.

Still, no one estimates that 90 percent of today's participants are straight. There are numerous reasons for the relative absence of heterosexual women: lack of opportunity, lack of encouragement, lack of interest, concern with personal appearance. The femininity mandate—the concept that only certain behaviors are appropriate for women—remains pervasive.

Femininity training includes crucial information on how to please men. Girls still learn at a very young age to avoid things—including sports achievements—that would render them unattractive to boys. In a 1988 survey, 36 percent of female respondents aged seven to eighteen reported that boys make fun of girls who play sports.[6]

It is, therefore, lesbians who feel free to play. As Pat Griffin says, "Lesbians are not stupid. They know to go where there are other lesbians. Sports arenas have been a place where there are women who are strong and independent."

So the young lesbian learns that boys won't like her if she outraces or outplays them, and she continues to compete anyway, consciously or unconsciously knowing that such threats hold less meaning for her than for her heterosexual peers (although no one likes disapproval, whatever the source).

In addition, a girl or woman who knows she's a lesbian or senses that she's "different" may be less reticent than others to explore nontraditional paths. Already shoved outside the social fold, she may feel freer to make her way, to write her own rules, and to follow the pursuits that interest her.

But the subject is complex. Many of today's female athletes—the majority, certainly—are heterosexual; they somehow find the courage to participate in sports despite the social stigma. In addition, human sexuality is not static; it ebbs and flows over the course of individual lifetimes and is influenced by culture and circumstance. Some people who once defined themselves as gay now call themselves straight. Many lesbians once thought they were heterosexual, and bisexuality is much more prevalent than one would guess from its absence in most gay-straight discussions.

Like many lesbians, Angie Furey had a "het" phase. Confused by her feelings for women and desperately wanting to fit in, she dated men in college. They liked her; one asked her to marry him. But she prefers women. "I find women attractive," Angie says simply. "I think a woman is a really beautiful being. I like a kind, gentle person who listens and shares, and I've found women to be more that way."

As a professional athlete, Angie deems this gentleness essential. The media, she says, constantly grade her and her peers: "Well, this is the next superstar, no, maybe that's the next superstar. Well, you did good today, what was wrong with you yesterday?" In this environment it's necessary, she says, "for someone to be kind to you." A woman has "an ability, almost an innate sensitivity to comprehend the need for that. It appears to me that by nature, women are more forgiving and accepting than men." When Angie calls home during a tournament, Suzanne will say, "Honey, just remember who you are out there, know that you can do it, I'm here thinking about you, and pulling for you; let that be a strength."

What Angie is describing is a bond based primarily not on sexual attraction but on affection, support, respect, and love. Virtually all women, not just lesbians and not just athletes, know this sort of female bonding from personal experience. Women love each other, receive joy and sustenance from each other, and frequently choose each other's company.

Adds Angie: "I'm not sure that the love affair you have for your sport doesn't get caught up in the love affair you might have for someone who is good at your sport. There's a mutual admiration society, a real deep understanding. And not just with women. How about the guys in the NFL? People are attracted to people who are good at what they do and are successful. They want to learn from them; they admire them. If you're in the same profession, you know the grind and struggle of it, and you appreciate it more than the outsider would."

In every myth there is a grain of truth. That's what makes myths powerful. In the myth that black people can't swim, for instance, is this grain of truth: Many black people grew up without access to public or private pools, and never learned to swim. But some black people can swim very well, as top college swimmers Sybil Smith, Anthony Nesty, and Matt Twillie have recently proved. So the statement that black people can't swim is a myth, but there is truth in it.[7]

Similarly, there seems to be truth in these two myths: that all women athletes are gay; and that sports make girls gay.

The first I have already discussed. *Many* women athletes are gay, but the myth is false, because *most* women athletes are not gay.

The second, that sports make girls gay, is likewise false but also contains a grain of truth. Athletes, teachers, coaches, and sports psychologists have tried for decades to prove (in particular to convince nervous parents) that sexuality is a matter determined by forces beyond our control, and that participation in sports is unrelated to sexual expression.

"It's a phobia without foundation," says Bruce Ogilvie. "If a person's orientation is uniquely heterosexual, then the 'threat' of the sports environment changing that is no different than anywhere else in society."

He's right. Sports do not create lesbians or gay men but they may, like other liberating experiences, create opportunities. A sporting experience, by developing a woman's body and mind, may give her the courage to act on feelings of attraction—sexual, emotional, intellectual—toward other women.

"Many women say it's a choice," reports therapist and sex educator JoAnn Loulan. "They have chosen lesbianism because of positive experiences with women."[8]

This is the fear: that women will take to the tracks and sprint headlong into love affairs with each other. Sometimes it happens. It happens among male athletes too.

But love is not the problem. Hate, fear, and discrimination are the problem. Denial has not been effective. Secrecy—particularly in combination with oppression—leads to shame. As long as women refuse to acknowledge the presence of lesbians, the accusation "Dyke!" will remain potent. Fortunately, sportswomen are now trying another approach: coming out.

Women's golf tournaments attract three types of people, a friend of mine noted. First, there are the old people: white-haired women and basketball-bellied men. Second, there are the lesbians, often in pairs, wearing hers and hers polo shirts, shorts, and sneakers. Third, there are the Japanese photographers. Faces obscured behind the long black lenses, they swarm from tee to fairway to green to tee, snapping countless pictures of Japan's superstar, Ayako Okamoto.

Some of the old people are no doubt gay, and some of the Japanese photographers are no doubt gay. But the pairs of women are the ones who make players and sponsors nervous. The rule in women's golf, as in most women's sports, is not so much that one shouldn't be gay, but that one shouldn't be *openly* gay.

Which is why Martina Navratilova's refusal to hide or disguise her partner shocked the sports community. That Martina had chosen a female lover was not surprising, but she didn't even deny it!

Martina Navratilova does have fewer endorsements than Chris Evert did, and fewer than one would expect of a woman of her stature. Yet the companies that do choose to sponsor her seem to have no qualms about it. "No one but you has ever raised a question about it before," Dick Rossi, a spokesman for the DHL delivery company told the *San Francisco Examiner*. "She's a gigantic star. Everybody loves her."[9]

Martina, however, has been hurt by the rejections. "I've lost so many endorsements," she told Michele Kort in a *Ms.* magazine interview.[10] "It's sad. It gets to the highest level, and then it's: Oh, isn't she gay? Or, hasn't she had relationships with women? Or, isn't she living with a woman? The president of a corporation may be my best friend, but he still won't take that chance because of the public. He might get five bad letters and a hundred good ones, but the five bad ones are the ones that matter. I know also why sometimes I get boos on the tennis court from some people. They're booing my lifestyle, rather than me as a human being."

Because she is financially untouchable, Martina had nothing to lose except fans and friends. Despite her sensitivity about boos from the crowd, she remains immensely popular. By quietly acknowledging her long-term relationship, she has

149

forced sportswriters and sportscasters to be equally nonchalant about it. It would be as ludicrous to "accuse" her of lesbianism as it would to accuse Nancy Lopez of being Hispanic or Jackie Joyner-Kersee of being black. *Boston Globe* columnist and NBC tennis commentator Bud Collins recently praised Martina as a "very brave person" who dared to defect from Czechoslovakia, dared to lift weights to improve the level of her game, and dared to be open about her life-style. She has gained his respect in part *because* of her openness.

Yet to Angie Furey, a devout Republican, Martina is "militant." In Angie's view, Martina is "fighting for people to accept her sexuality. 'Accept me. Accept my sexuality.' That's like asking someone to drive a Cadillac if they want to drive a 'Vette. I mean, what for? To me there's no purpose in that. If they're the type of people who can't accept me, I'm not going to dislike them for it. I just won't get close to them. I'm not going to be the one to crusade for gay rights. I'm not going to march in the streets."

When I point out that vocal women, both gay and straight, "crusaded" and marched in the streets to gain equal rights for women in this country, including the right of women to make money as professional golfers, Angie says, "You've got a good point."

Angie and most of the other gay professional golfers I know have no intention of coming out. One said she envisions herself coming out "after I make it big, after I win some big tournament or something." In fact she has won big tournaments since that time, and still no announcements. The more she wins, the less likely it seems that she will come out, since among athletes, financial success is inversely proportional to being openly gay. In other words, recreational athletes are much more likely to be openly gay than Olympic or professional ones.

I asked Angie how she would respond if a reporter asked her directly if she were gay.

"I might say, 'Do you jack off? Are you impotent?' " she

responded angrily. "Or I would say, 'Why are you asking me that? Why do you want to know?'"

"If someone found out, then confronted you, what might you say then?" I asked.

"I'd say, 'Okay, what do you want to do, put me in front of a firing squad and shoot me? Have I fucked up your kids any more than you have?'"

The subject is a painful one for her, obviously. But in my discussions with other women, I found, to my surprise, that plenty has changed in the years since Billie Jean King came out. Sports scholars are addressing homophobia in their research. Women's sports leaders are publicly insisting that discrimination against lesbians be eradicated. These events mark an extraordinary break from the legacy of silence. Even more remarkable is the fact that although professors and coaches still lose their jobs because of their preference or their politics, several professors are publicly coming out as lesbians—and many more leaders are publicly coming out as lesbian advocates—with few negative repercussions.

"What bad things happened to you when you came out?" I asked Pat Griffin.

"Nothing," she said.

A former national sports champion, writing anonymously to "protect" other stars, says in *Long Time Passing* that for her, "aging has produced freedom from those awful 'What if's?' of my years of stardom. What if my business manager learned the rumors about me were true? What if my fans found out? What if my respected coach learned the truth about my sexual orientation? What if the parents of the junior athletes I coached knew?" (When she came out she was delighted to learn, she adds, that her business manager was gay, some of her allegedly straight fans were gay, and some of the mothers of her young protégés had crushes on her.)[11]

The North American Society for the Sociology of Sport discussed homophobia at its annual convention in 1989—a significant first. The Women's Sports Foundation; the American Alliance for Health, Physical Education, Recreation and

Dance; and the Canadian Association for the Advancement of Women and Sport have all addressed homophobia at recent meetings. NAGWS president Laurie Priest speaks out publicly against homophobia. So does Donna Lopiano, the women's athletic director for the University of Texas at Austin, which has one of the best women's sports programs in the nation.

Says Bettye Jaynes, executive director of the Women Basketball Coaches Association: "We're losing women in coaching because they're afraid of being labeled lesbians. We've got to find a way to stop it."

Pat Griffin is the Mikhail Gorbachev of the recent women's sports *glasnost;* she has urged other gay and bisexual people to come out and has solicited the support of straight sportswomen. Since 1987, in collaboration with straight men and women, Griffin has been offering workshops on how to deal with homophobia for numerous sports organizations and at many women's sports conferences. "Every time, we're filled beyond capacity," she says. "People are eager to break the long silence."

As women's sports leaders gradually, painstakingly come out and come out against discrimination, lesbian athletes are also creating thousands of gay sports teams at the grass-roots level. Brenda Pitts, a sports administration professor at the University of Louisville, surveyed 132 gay sports organizations nationwide and found that a primary reason for creating the leagues was to escape the homophobia of nongay sports leagues.[12]

Once involved, gay women enjoy their sports experience as more than an avoidance of homophobia. Women's softball leagues form the backbone of the gay community in many cities and towns. "To most lesbians, softball is more than just a game," writes Yvonne Zipter in *Diamonds Are a Dyke's Best Friend.* "It is a social event. It is a test of endurance and skill. It is the incubator for the extended family. It is a way of fitting in, of making friends. It is a statement of independence, of courage, of commitment. It is the sheer joy of outdoor physical activity. In short, it is the beauty of distinctly different parts coming together to form a whole; for some it is almost a mystical experience."[13]

The most visible—most publicized by the media—of all gay sporting events is the Gay Games, a multisport festival that has taken place every four years since 1982. It is deliberately inclusive: people of all ages, skill levels, and sexual orientations are invited to participate; and deliberately supportive: athletes take an oath promising to encourage all other athletes, regardless of their relative success or failure.

I had the pleasure of competing in the Gay Games in San Francisco the first year they were held. I'll never forget marching into Kezar Stadium for the balloon-filled opening ceremonies, some 1,300 athletes from around the world marching with me. I felt a little silly at first, and waved to the hordes of people in the stands sheepishly. But the roar of their approval enveloped me and their clapping and cheering overwhelmed me; for the first time in my life, I was cheered not for swimming fast or putting a ball through a hoop but for being both athletic and honest.

I was competing in masters swim meets in those days, so I entered four freestyle swimming events. The races were competitive in the best sense of the word: everyone tried as hard as he or she could, then afterward all wholeheartedly congratulated each other. Medals dangled on proud chests; I brought home two silvers and two golds myself. But what made the experience euphoric was the sense of freedom. In high school, college, and professional athletic contests I'd participated in, the fear of being thought gay had restricted even spontaneous expressions of emotion; at the Gay Games, in contrast, women gave each other loving, unhurried hugs after triumph or disappointment or simply out of affection. Men held hands. The lack of homophobia was like a welcome blast of fresh air—or like nitrous oxide, making everyone giddily happy. It was a taste of what could be: a gathering at which everyone, regardless of skill, could pursue excellence, where competitors could encourage each other, and where athletes could be caring and demonstrative without hesitation.

Back at the driving range, I asked Angie Furey why she agreed to be interviewed. "It gives me a chance to speak out," she said. She paused, as if formulating a sound bite, her last chance to comment on a perplexing, endlessly frustrating problem. "It's okay with me if people know that there are gay women in sports. We're slandered. I don't think that's right. We're all in this together. We're all people. Let us be people."

Who's Running
the Show?

She was a big, tough woman,
The first to come along
That showed me being female meant you still could be strong.
And though graduation meant that we had to part,
She'll always be a player on the ball field of my heart.
—MEG CHRISTIAN "Ode to a Gym Teacher"

*J*ACKIE JOYNER-KERSEE, considered by many the world's greatest female athlete, is teasing her coach, accusing him of "coach abuse," by which she means to imply that he is being cruel to sprinter Gail Devers. Bob Kersee, Jackie's husband as well as coach, is guiding Jackie and Gail through individualized workouts on the brick-red track of Drake Stadium at the University of California, Los Angeles. It is a bright blue January day, a clear day that asks, What smog?

Joggers plod past, unaware of or unconcerned about the world-class athlete in their midst. Bob Kersee's instrument of torture is a rubber cord he holds by both ends, his hands extended as if grasping reins. The rest of the cord stretches taut through a shoulder and waist harness strapped onto twenty-two-year-old Gail Devers, a petite and powerful runner who stands about twenty feet away. Devers, Kersee's brightest star on the UCLA track team, crouches into a starting position, and the cord yanks her forward. She laughs nervously and crouches again, this time more slowly.

"You ought to get her a face mask," kids Jackie, but she does sympathize with Gail. While practicing for and competing in the seven running, jumping, and throwing events that make up the heptathlon, which has earned her the "world's greatest female athlete" epithet, Jackie has leapt over the high bar and missed the padded pit, banged her legs and feet on the hurdles, fallen face-first on gravel tracks. She has fallen while sprinting downhill, another speed-building technique. "I've fallen going over the hurdles, even coming out of the blocks," she readily admits. "You can feel the gravity under you, and you fall. It's scary." Track and field is not a contact sport and is not considered dangerous, but its athletes must become acquainted with fear and inured to pain.

"Women handle it better," Jackie offers, "because we're not afraid to say we're afraid. The men won't admit it. And you have to admit it first, to get over it."

Gail, admittedly, is afraid of falling on her face. Bob is trying to help her become less afraid, and faster, by slingshotting her forward with the cord. Ironically, this makes it more likely that she will fall, but it also helps her experience running fast. "Running is falling," Bob calls to Gail, as if to paraphrase a Laurie Anderson song. "But anytime you get into that zone, you spread your wings to catch yourself. As soon as you feel yourself starting to fall, shoot your head straight out, pump your arms. Your feet will recover faster than you think they can."

He adds with feigned generosity: "If you fall, I won't drag you."

Gail doesn't fall, and she does run fast, faster than Bob expected. She is, after all, the second fastest female sprinter in the United States, cordless, and seventh in the world. Bob has to step out of her way at the last moment so he doesn't get run over. He reattaches the cord to her harness and repeats the drill, this time stretching the human slingshot even tighter by standing a few feet farther away.

Soon it is Jackie's turn, not for the rubber cord but for the hurdles. The 400-meter hurdles is one of Jackie's best events, and she plans to get even better, not just good enough to continue to dominate the heptathlon in these post–1988 Olympics years but also good enough to win hurdles events.

Jackie agrees to run the hurdles "at eighty-five percent" effort. Her long legs snug in hot-pink tights, she meanders to the starting line and halfheartedly crouches. On her T-shirt, two black men are reaching for a rebound. "Do I have to come out hard?"

"No," says Bob, watching from the infield.

She sprints forward, legs pounding the track, then skims barely over the top of the first hurdle, right leg bent backward, left extended. Jackie is tall, five-ten, and her form in this difficult running-and-jumping event is nearly perfect, so the white barricades require only a momentary adjustment in her gait, a scissors kick sneaked into the middle of a sprint. Her pink tights flash open, then shut, and then it's over, she's back on the ground, running. She nicks the third hurdle with the tip of her shoe, but it doesn't fall and she ignores it. After the last hurdle she walks proudly and a bit defiantly toward the starting line, past Bob. Later she tells me, "The key to the hurdles is being able to sprint through them. But you saw me hit one today. Imagine hitting one twenty times in a practice. You'd better believe it hurts. After a while you just want to leap up and over."

Bob says to her, "Your toe was down."

"My feet hurt," Jackie complains. "Maybe my shoes are too small."

"Maybe your feet are too big," Bob retorts.

Bob Kersee has coached Olympians Florence Griffith Joyner, Valerie Brisco, Jeanette Bolden, Alice Brown, Sherri Howard, Greg Foster, and Andre Phillips. Each individual is different, he says. "I don't see a man or a woman. I see an athlete. As a coach I ask myself, 'What does this athlete need?' "

What Jackie needs, besides not to be coddled, not to be *treated* like the greatest athlete in the world, is goals. When Bob claimed that Jackie could break the 6,700-point mark in the heptathlon, track and field writers laughed at him. Even Bob was surprised when she became the first woman to break 7,000, with a world heptathlon record of 7,148 points in July 1986, at the Moscow Goodwill Games. That summer, she also broke her own record at the U.S. Olympic Festival in Houston. In 1988, she broke her own record twice more, and peaked with a 7,291-point performance in the Olympics. No other woman has approached 7,000 points. Jackie also co-owns the long-jump world record of 24 feet, 5½ inches. And now she's trying the hurdles. "She'll probably break an American record this weekend," says Bob, laughing. "She keeps amazing me."

After a brief series of hurdles, Jackie asks Bob, "Are we finished?"

"You never got started."

"You sure got a smart mouth," says Jackie.

"Nothing you can call me I haven't been called before," Bob says, and the banter continues as the two of them and Gail walk slowly off the field.

Name an outstanding female athlete, and chances are, she has a male coach. Swimmer Janet Evans. Tennis pros Martina Navratilova, Zina Garrison, and Jennifer Capriati. Diver Michele Mitchell. Golfer Betsy King. The best U.S. women's college soccer team, the University of North Carolina, has a male coach, as do the four top college women's volleyball teams. All female winners, all male coaches. All of which makes female coaches and administrators furious.

Throughout most of the 1900s, women's sports had women coaches. There were occasional exceptions: at its peak in 1948, the All-American Girls' Baseball League had ten teams, all with men coaches.[1] The legendary Ed Temple has coached most of America's best female track and field athletes to Olympic success. Wilma Rudolph, Madeline Manning, Edith McGuire, Wyomia Tyus, Willye White, and more recently Chandra Cheeseborough have all been Temple's "Tigerbelles" at Tennessee State University, a historically black college.

But in general, as long as most women's sports stayed amateur, nonscholarship, and unnoticed by the media, most coaches were female. In 1972, not even 10 percent of women's college coaches were male.[2]

In the mid-seventies Congress enacted Title IX, and suddenly colleges weren't allowed to give women shoddy facilities and graduate-student coaches anymore. Among other things, they had to provide uniforms and start paying coaches. Suddenly the idea of coaching female athletes became appealing to men.

Before Title IX, most colleges and universities had two athletic departments, one headed by a woman, one headed by a man. After Title IX, male administrators were appointed to head the new combined departments that most colleges established. By 1990, 84.1 percent of women's intercollegiate programs were headed by men. More than 30 percent of women's programs had no women at all involved in the administrative structure.[3]

Guess whom these male administrators hired? Almost 53 percent of the people coaching college and high school women are men. Men still coach more than 99 percent of all college men's teams.[4]

Nor do women have equal representation in other sports-related jobs. In a recent survey of the Olympic movement, sports media, and intercollegiate and major professional sports in the United States, the Amateur Athletic Foundation of Los Angeles found that at the end of 1988, only 5 percent of the 12,735 positions available were held by women.[5]

C. Vivian Stringer, head basketball coach at the University of Iowa, says of these statistics, "You think there are low numbers of women now, just wait. It's going to get worse." As a black female coach she is a rarity, especially in Iowa. But it's female coaches in general she's worried about.

Like environmentalists desperate to save an endangered species, Stringer and dozens of other women are searching for ways to return women to what used to be a woman's world. They're dedicating themselves to training, promoting, and—for the few who have the power—hiring women. In small ways, in certain states, they're succeeding.

Consider what would happen if the situation were reversed: What if women continued to hold virtually all the jobs coaching women and girls, and also took over more than half the positions coaching boys and men? What if women were the athletic directors in 84.1 percent of the men's programs? Men would surely complain, if not sue. "Something is wrong here!" they would say. "We want our coaching jobs! And boys need male role models! Women might teach them wimpy stuff!"

That's how women feel. They want their jobs back, they want control of the programs, and they are afraid men are teaching girls and women the wrong sorts of attitudes about sports. If women's sports is in its infancy, it's *women* who gave birth to it. Women were the ones who coached when coaches were rewarded only with postseason thank-you cards from the players. Women (and a few men, including Bob Kersee) were the ones who fought for Title IX and, several years later, for the Civil Rights Restoration Act of 1988, which restored Title IX to its full power after it was temporarily dismantled in 1984 by the Supreme Court in *Grove City v. Bell.* The National Collegiate Athletic Association opposed Title IX.

To have men take control of the game now, when the hard labor is over, feels to many coaches like having a child kidnapped. This is true even though male coaches usually do a fine job with women's teams.

Do women coaches offer a style or substance that men can't? How did all those Olympians and pros get to be so good with male coaches? Why don't more women coach men?

As I traveled from Los Angeles to the Iowa cornfields and then to the East, I listened to dozens of coaches and administrators at numerous conferences. The dearth of female leaders is the most talked-about issue in women's sports today.

First, let's consider what athletes say. Jackie Joyner-Kersee is happy with her coach, obviously; she married him. Before Bob, Jackie had a series of nonsupportive boyfriends. "They took my success as their loss," she says. "They were jealous. They kept trying to hold me back. Bob is incredible. We go places and people recognize me, and he's just my husband. He doesn't mind at all. He has no ego. It's great."

It seems that when heterosexual women athletes finally find men who are truly supportive and helpful, those men tend to be their coaches, and they often marry them. I ask Jackie if this rings true for her.

"Yes!" she says. "I think the same is true of Florence."

Florence is Florence Griffith Joyner, Flo-Jo, the world record holder in the 100 and 200 meters, the one with the audacious fingernails and one-legged suits. Florence didn't actually marry her coach; she married another Olympian, Al Joyner, who as Jackie's brother was accustomed to female strength. Later, after Al and Florence were married, Al became Florence's coach, taking over Bob Kersee's job. (Hence much confusion among the public, who still ask, Is Jackie the one with the fingernails?)

Bob and Jackie met in 1981, on the same Drake Stadium track they now train on. He was the assistant track coach and she was a basketball player and budding track and field star. After she graduated from UCLA, he proposed. They were at a pro baseball game, and the way Jackie tells the story, Bob turned to her and said, "I'd like to get married."

"That's a good idea," said Jackie. "You're a nice guy."

Bob said, "You don't get it. I'd like to marry you."

"Oh," said Jackie. "Okay."

Bob has something he calls a "49–49 philosophy," which means that he and his athletes each hold almost fifty percent of the decision-making power. "But if it comes down to where we can't agree, somebody's got to make a decision, and I can take that two percent off the shelf."

The trouble comes when Bob applies his neat 49–49 philosophy to his marriage. "At home, it's for religious reasons," Bob explains. "I'm a Christian, and I believe it's my responsibility to take care of my family and make the tough decisions."

How does that go over with Jackie?

"It doesn't go over too well," he admits, laughing.

"He tries, but it never works," says Jackie, also laughing.

Yet their relationship seems to work; certainly their athlete-coach relationship works. As far as I can tell, Bob Kersee is guilty of no form of coach abuse.

Jackie's contentment with her male coach seems typical. She would not prefer a woman. Nor would most female athletes. In fact, a 1986 survey found that female athletes respond negatively to hypothetical female coaches compared with similar hypothetical male coaches.[6] In another study, 49 percent of college athletes reported no preference for female or male coaches.[7] Those who did express a preference were generally happy with their current coaches, male or female.

The study most in support of female coaches showed that high school and college athletes discerned no gender differences in coaching abilities in four of six categories (such as "produces winners" and "is a good role model"). The athletes did, however, report that female coaches were better at "relating well to athletes" and "understanding athletes' feelings."[8]

This is the contention of women coaches and administrators. They lobby for equal job opportunity and argue that women make better coaches precisely because they are better at relating to athletes and understanding their feelings.

"A jump shot is a jump shot," Vivian Stringer begins, "and the technical aspects of the game—the X's and O's—have to do with your mind, your brain. There's nothing male or female there. But the playing of a game has to do with your feelings, your emotions, how you care about the people you're involved with."

She tells the story of a young woman who was learning low-post moves from a male basketball coach. "She didn't want to be a center. She didn't want to be tall. As a woman, I understand what her concerns are. She's wondering, 'Who's going to date me,' all that.

"I watched this guy instructing her, telling her how to post, using words like, 'You've got to get your big ass over here.' It was just a little thing, but I thought, That's really not the way. It's insulting.

"A bunch of guys were standing around. She was embarrassed. I pulled the coach off her and tried to explain: She didn't want to hear, 'You gotta be mean, you gotta have a big ass.' "

Vivian told the young woman, "You need to make yourself wide and block out because everyone has a role, and that's your role." Vivian gave respect to the center position, but not in the same "aggressive, 'break somebody's teeth, get your ass over there' sort of way."

Franthea Price, one of the most hotly recruited high school forwards in the nation in 1986, chose Iowa "because Coach Stringer asked about me. She didn't lie to me. She didn't promise me I would start. She told me I would contribute. She cared about me." Price, who was named All-America her senior year, raves about Vivian. "She treats us as equals. She doesn't talk down to us or yell at us like some coaches. She loves us."

"We function on respect and loving," Vivian says. "It's down-to-earth. It's simple. I'm an emotional person, and I want my players to care just as much as I do."

Lisa Rubarth, editor of the newsletter *Women and Sport* and a founding member of the Coaches Advisory Roundtable of the Women's Sports Foundation, claims women have a better concept of teamwork. "Whereas men will say, 'We've got this star player and we'll go with her even though the rest of the team can't keep up,' women will develop the group as a whole," says Rubarth. "It's the way we've been socialized—to think of the good of everyone."

When asked how this "good for the whole" approach affects win-loss records, Rubarth replies, "We need to ask ourselves, 'At what price success?' Do we pamper the number-one athletes, give them money, make sure they have drugs, give them an inflated view of themselves, and forget about the other athletes? We're going to see more problems in women's sports that we're seeing right now on the men's side. There'll be such a premium on success that all the wonderful qualities that sport supposedly teaches will be lost. That's why we need more women in coaching."

Some men agree. "In many ways, women are more sensitive to the needs of children," says Michael Pfahl, executive director of the National Youth Sport Coaches Association.

Jamie Gordon, head coach at the Florida Rowing Center, says he deliberately hires female coaches to work with women. "I'm six-four and two hundred pounds. I'm the nicest guy in the world, but we get women here who have never seen a boat before. They relate better to a woman."

Bob Kersee says simply, "Male coaches hold women back. Their egos are threatened."

Despite his own sixteen years of experience coaching women (he was one of the few male volunteers in the seventies), Kersee says, "I don't think a male can coach a female without getting another female's opinion. I don't care if you've been coaching females for a hundred years. There are things that females can tell you that you wouldn't think of yourself."

All three of Bob's UCLA assistants are men, so it is Jackie who reminds him, for instance, that women often have to contend with jealous boyfriends. "It wouldn't occur to me that that might be affecting an athlete," he admits.

One time, an athlete knocked her knee going over a hurdle, then wanted to quit. "I couldn't understand it. She was a good athlete," recalls Bob. "Jackie had said, 'I bet there's some man in her life who is afraid of her getting scars on her knees.' Turns out her father didn't want her to get scars on her knees. Jackie opens my eyes."

Do women and men really have different coaching styles? Apparently they do. Numerous studies support the theory that female leaders tend to be less autocratic than male leaders.[9] Summarizing her own research and that of others on gender differences among school administrators, Charol Shakeshaft, an associate professor of administration and policy studies at Hofstra University, concludes that female administrators "spend more time with people, communicate more, care more about individual differences, are more concerned with other teachers and with marginal students, and are better motivators than men."[10]

Women have been told that in order to succeed, they should apply the sports lessons they learn from men to their dealings in the business world. But women in the business world—which includes college coaching—don't seem to want to operate by the military model. Colorado sex-equity consultant Susan Schafer says women are hungry for a more caring leadership model. "I gave a speech to the Women's Basketball Coaches Association recently; the topic was 'How to Make It in the Real World.' I used a lot of stuff from *Games Mother Never Taught You,* by Betty Harragan. The women didn't like it. They came up to me and said, 'Don't you have a different vision?' "

Some men too seek a different path. Katie Donovan, director of the American Coaching Effectiveness Program (ACEP), has introduced her program to more than 100,000 coaches and administrators nationwide, most of them male. Although resistant at first, many men eventually resonate with the "Athletes first, winning second" motto, she says. "Men know in their hearts that something is terribly wrong with the sports system." In seventeen years of coaching, Donovan's winning record was well over .800, but she says, "I'm not proud of how I did that," citing insensitivity to the players' needs. After listening to Katie's own confession and her description of the ACEP philosophy and practice, "men get very emotional," she says. "They come up to me afterward and say, 'I've been doing it all wrong, I've been harming my kids.' "[11]

. . .

If women's leadership style is so great, how come there aren't more women coaching? In a nationwide survey of athletic administrators, Brooklyn College professors Vivian Acosta and Linda Carpenter found that women and men offered different reasons.[12] Women cited the success of the old-boy network and the failure of the old-girl network. Men blamed it on a lack of qualified women coaches and the failure of women to apply for jobs.

The women are right: the old-boy network is vast and so-phisticated. "I have men apply for jobs, and everybody and their mother calls me," says Mount Holyoke College athletic director Laurie Priest. "Officials, athletic directors, col-leagues—everybody calls out of the blue to say how great this guy is. When women apply, no one calls. These are the kinds of things women need to share with each other, so we know how to play that game."

The men are also right: women don't seek jobs. "They didn't apply!" is a popular refrain among both female and male athletic directors in response to queries about women coaches.

And men are partially right about lack of qualifications: women's programs developed so rapidly in the seventies that they outgrew some female coaches who had no familiarity with the more demanding modern style of competition, which at the college level involves media and marketing savvy and aggressive recruiting skills. In sports such as soc-cer, which most colleges started offering to women only re-cently, qualified women coaches are particularly hard to find.

But in general, women coaches are at least as qualified as the men, often more so. A recent study shows that female college coaches are *more* likely than their male peers to have played college varsity sports. They are as qualified academ-ically as their male counterparts. Their win-loss records are identical.[13]

A more important factor limiting women's professional development in sports is the familiar "family or career?" dichotomy. The majority of male college coaches are married (93 percent) and have children (80 percent), while only 35 percent of female coaches are married and only 16 percent have children. Female coaches who are married work on the average twenty-seven more hours a week than do married male coaches; most of this is child care and housework.[14]

Married women are further constrained by husbands who successfully pull that two percent of extra decision-making off the shelf. "If you're married, you usually can't say, 'I just got an offer at this university, so we're moving,'" notes Susan True, assistant to the director of the National Federation of State High School Associations. "Even today's women don't have the mobility men do."

"Men don't seem to be able to cope with their wives as head coaches," concurs Chris Grant, women's athletic director at the University of Iowa. "Our divorce rate in this department is very bad."

Vivian Stringer is at her University of Iowa office by nine-thirty in the morning, and often lingers until well after dark. After arriving home, she may stay up until two or three in the morning watching game films.

It's her husband, Bill, who picks up their three children (including a severely disabled daughter) after school, Bill who cooks dinner, Bill who puts the kids to bed, Bill who wakes them in the morning, feeds them, and drives them to school. Bill also has a full-time job—as exercise kinesiologist for the university's women athletes—but in a classic role reversal, he does most of the housework and child care.

Vivian is amazed and grateful about a state of affairs men often take for granted. "If he weren't making me feel comfortable with the kids, it would be impossible," she says.

Women without kids or husbands can have different problems. Vivian says that on about one out of every three visits to a recruit's home, her parents ask about lesbians in sports. She doesn't know any, Vivian tells the parents. There have never been any problems. But an unmarried coach, whether lesbian or not, would likely feel uncomfortable with the question.

In 1988, female coaches across the country were upset about an anonymous list reportedly being sent to some of the nation's best high school basketball players. Under the heading "Straight Coaches" were the names of some of the top women in the country. Under the heading "Gay Coaches" were the names of other top women. Some of the designations were wrong.

No one I talked to actually saw this list, but the rumor raced through the women's sports community, accompanied by intense fear and anger. Virtually all women coaches seem to feel threatened by it. "The extent of discrimination in hiring practices, especially at the high school level, is incredible," says University of Texas women's athletic director Donna Lopiano. "I'm talking about basic violations of equal-opportunity employment rules."

Even Vivian Stringer is uncomfortable discussing it. "It's a terrible thing to say, just because you're not married you're gay. Or just because you're married you're not gay. It's a sick thing. I don't go out of my way to find out. I don't want to know. I do take offense to someone suggesting, 'So many of them are gay anyhow.' Wow. I don't want anything negative associated with my profession. But it's really none of my business."

From Vivian Stringer's perspective, female coaches are desperately needed, primarily as role models, to show young women that there are "big, tough women"—or little tough women—to emulate. "Who better than a woman can tell women not only how to play basketball but how to get along in a male-dominated society?" she asks. "Who better can show young women you can be a leader and also a mom?

"It doesn't matter to me, because Vivian is established," she continues. "I've got mine. My daughter is not going to be a basketball coach. My two sons will be going into the men's world. But young women keep seeing women as assistants, always taking orders, not being in charge. Then they assume that posture with whatever else they may do. There's nothing wrong with nurses, but these players of mine, I want them to be doctors. I want them to know they can be whoever they want to be."

Chances are, they won't be coaches. Despite Vivian's support, role models are rare. Of her fourteen players, eleven had male head coaches in high school. Most of the coaches they compete against are men. Division I women coaches earn less than men: women's mean salary is $26,281; men's is $32,180. Women are also more likely than men to feel discriminated against.[15] Athletes notice these things.

Young women may also be reluctant to coach because of the larger game that now dominates women's as well as men's college sports: cutthroat competition and a trend toward athletic elitism, away from participation by masses of students. The win-loss record, the most tangible evaluation of performance available, can be intimidating or distasteful to women who understand the arithmetic involved: 50 percent of teams lose at least 50 percent of the time. Regardless of their personal sports ethic and regardless of how humane and educational their leadership styles may be, college coaches are forced to play the "win or lose your job" game.

"The system doesn't appeal to women," says Katie Donovan. "Frankly, I think women are too smart to go into coaching. I don't blame them."

Vivian Stringer has three female assistants. She carefully explains: "If a male and a female are coaching together, it is often assumed that he must be the brains, so to speak—the one who gives technical expertise—and that she is the one who gives emotional support to the athletes. Even if she is the head coach, this is assumed. It is extremely important that young women and society see that women can be very capable leaders. Because of this, if I had an opportunity to work with a male or female assistant of comparable skills and backgrounds, I would hire the female. Even if she were a little less qualified, I would still give her the opportunity. Often she *would* be less qualified, because she hasn't had the opportunity to participate in organized sports since the third or fourth grade like men have."

Of the ten women's sports at Iowa, eight are coached by women. This is a much higher percentage of women than the national average, but Chris Grant is apologetic about not having an all-female staff. If she had known about the impending decline in numbers of coaches nationwide, Grant says, she would not have hired those two men.

"You see, I anticipated very naively that the coaching positions in men's athletics would open up to women," says Grant. "I knew it would take some time, but it never happened." To begin to return women to positions of power, and to support women currently in power, Grant recently created the Council of Collegiate Women Athletic Administrators (CCWAA).

Foremost among many activists supporting female sports leaders is Susan Schafer, whose employer, the Colorado Department of Education, boasts the country's most progressive training program for women coaches. After conducting a survey and concluding that the proportion of women high school coaches in her state had declined from 89 to 38 percent between 1973 and 1983, Schafer created Sports Need You, the first model program designed to return women to sports leadership positions. In just five years, the proportion of women coaching in Colorado has risen to 41 percent, and the numbers of women head coaches increased by an average of twenty-five per year. Similar programs exist in Idaho, Iowa, Kentucky, Louisiana, Massachusetts, Michigan, Missouri, New York, Oregon, Pennsylvania, Texas, and Wisconsin.

To men, the women's motives are not always clear. Vivian Stringer is asked about her policy all the time. "Vivian, how come you've never hired a man? Wouldn't you, even if he were qualified? What if he were more qualified than the women?" The questioners are usually male coaches.

"Why don't you hire women?" Vivian could answer. But she is more diplomatic than that. To one coach of a men's basketball team, she said, "Don't you think that if your daughter is looking at a woman, she's more likely to realize that she can be a coach, or a leader of any sort?"

Vivian is careful not to offend, but offense is sometimes taken anyway, and she finds herself apologizing, backtracking. "I always have to explain myself," she says, aware of her role as an ambassador for the university and a symbol of all women's sports leaders. She mustn't sound too angry, too shrill.

"Men would like to keep women 'in their place,'" she says. "If you start to move beyond that, you get a lot of criticism, a lot of barriers: 'She's too aggressive, she's too bossy. She's trying to act like a male.'"

Individually, women are not necessarily the best coaches. No women's coaches have yet been compared to the University of Indiana's Bobby Knight, but they're not all gentle Vivian Stringers either. Women can be too forgiving when what a player needs is a figurative kick in the pants; they can have expectations that are too low, based on memories of their own playing days. Women can be too harsh or demanding or uninformed or unethical; they can and do fail in all the ways human beings fail.

I have seen women verbally brutalize players. I've seen lesbian coaches who, trying to be wholesome, noncontroversial role models, inadvertently convey to their young charges their own shame.

But overall, women are as qualified as men: as educated, as experienced, as effective. They may be more sensitive and communicative, but they shouldn't have to be better than men in order to work as peers in the same profession. It seems to me that women should stop claiming they are uniquely qualified to coach females and assert that they are equally qualified to coach anyone. In other words, women should start coaching men.

171

.   .   .

In 1989, the University of Tennessee, led by Pat Summitt, defeated Auburn University for the national women's college basketball title. Immediately after the game, television announcer Tim Brant asked Summitt if she'd be interested in coaching the Tennessee men. It was inappropriate as the sole question for the quick postgame interview, especially since Summitt had already said she was not interested. She declined again, graciously switching the subject back to the championship.

But as long as Pat and other top women stay committed to women, men's sports will keep being the domain of men, while women's sports will probably remain heterogeneous. Vivian Stringer, Christ Grant, and their colleagues may be playing a game they can't win. What if stewardesses, who once held virtually all flight attendant jobs, tried to win back those positions for women? It wouldn't work. If women want half of all airline-related employment, they must apply for jobs as mechanics, baggage handlers, pilots, and air traffic controllers, as well as flight attendants and ticket agents. Similarly, women must start applying for jobs coaching and officiating men and boys, and must assert their right to "fly the planes"—to serve as athletic directors not only in women's departments but in men's and coed departments as well.

Male athletic directors are not exactly eager to step aside and have women fill their positions; nor are they, as their records show, eager to hire women to coach men. "They'd have the boosters on the phone so fast," says Susan Schafer, speculating on what would happen if Tennessee hired Pat Summitt to coach the men's team. "They'd say, 'Sure, Pat's a great gal, but we have real men down here.'"

Women may be reluctant to coach and officiate men because they anticipate sexist attitudes from male players, coaches, and administrators. Many women simply prefer the company of women and girls.

But people such as Little League coach Pat Elkins, University of Pennsylvania swim coach Kathy Lawlor-Gilbert, Air Force Academy diving coach Micki King Hogue, and high school basketball coach Wanda Oates—all of whom coach men—could be in the forefront of a transformation in sports leadership.

A registered nurse and the mother of thirteen, Pat Elkins coaches mostly male Little League teams in Danville, Virginia. "When I first started out, I found myself being a mother to all the kids," says Elkins. "I thought, Is this the right role model? And I realized that it is. Men want to make the kids little adults. I've seen men hit, kick, swear at, and spit at kids—whereas women know what it's like to cry and perhaps to have a difficult experience with sports at a young age. Women think more about how they felt and about how the kids feel."

Wanda Oates, head coach of the boys' basketball team at Frank Ballou High School in Washington, D.C., led a girls' softball team to a league championship and a girls' basketball team to ten league championships before switching to coaching boys. Oates says that because boys' sports carry more social status than girls', a league championship with her boys' team would mean more to her.

Indeed, women coaches will probably never achieve the fame or fortune of their male counterparts—nor can they hope to overcome male dominance in sport—until they start coaching the high-status games: men's and boys' games. If a men's or boys' team is glorified and a woman is at the helm, she may share the glory. If women were to gain half of the control of sports in general by claiming half the jobs coaching males, what role models they would provide then!

Says Katie Donovan, "Women are coaching in nontraditional ways. Male players and male coaches need to see that. The notion that only women are being hurt by women not being in coaching is nearsighted. Men are being hurt just as much. They may not recognize it as a loss, but it is. Whenever women are held down, men lose too."

. . .

When Kathy Lawlor-Gilbert arrived at the University of Pennsylvania as the women's swim coach in 1974, the men's team called the women's team the Sea Hogs. "They even had a chant they did about it," she says. "That had to go immediately." Lawlor-Gilbert forbids all sexist remarks. "I can't stand comments regarding women's bodies. I kicked one guy out of practice for a comment he made, and that was before I was the men's coach. They learn. Now the guys are respectful of the women's team."

Former Olympic diving champion Micki King Hogue is nonchalant about her role as diving coach at the Air Force Academy. "When I arrived, people thought I was going to paint the diving boards pink. But there's nothing new about coaching men. I've been coaching my teammates all my life."

Wanda Oates seems to enjoy shaking up the patriarchal system. Oates, who once sued, unsuccessfully, for the right to coach high school football, still plans to do it one day. "The men are really having a difficult time losing to me in basketball," she says happily. "If I start whipping them in football, they might never recover."[16]

If some men are qualified to coach women, as clearly they are, there's no reason why some women aren't qualified to coach men. The only difference between coaching women and men, says Lawlor-Gilbert, is that women athletes worry more about their weight.

The struggle over who coaches whom is not about sports but about power. "Start coaching men?" one woman responded when I asked her about the possibility. "They won't even let us coach women." Well, no, often "they" won't. Then women must become the "they"—the athletic directors, university presidents, United States Olympic Committee members—who make such decisions. In Jackie Joyner-Kersee's words: *The key to the hurdles is being able to sprint through them.* The example of female leadership—the televised, public sight of women strolling along sidelines, yelling at or gently coaxing male athletes—has the power to change the way all of us think about women, and about sports.

New Wave:
Partnership in Action

> Throughout the cosmos they found intelligent life
> forms that play to play. We are the only ones that
> play to win. Explains why we have more than our
> share of losers.
>
> —JANE WAGNER, *The Search for
> Signs of Intelligent Life in
> the Universe*

*T*HE September air in northern California is chilly. The
women at Sunny Cove Beach remove their clothes anyway.
One snatches off a wool hat and stuffs her hair under a snug
neoprene bonnet. Another slips out of jeans and stands shivering, clad only in a Speedo, before sneaking one limb at a
time into a stubborn black wetsuit. A few yards away, the sea
puffs up like a strutting bird, collapses on itself, and dissolves
into a thin line of white foam that flattens toward the women,
then recedes.

Lauren Crux, leader of the bodysurfing workshop about to
take place, is already wearing her wetsuit, a $200 custom-made black skin inlaid with strips of neon fuchsia. At almost
five-ten, Lauren is taller than the other women on the beach,
and in her proud, flashy outfit she looks majestic. If it weren't

175

for the gray bangs, she could be a surf-shop model come to life.

A lifelong athlete, Lauren has been offering free bodysurfing workshops in Santa Cruz for seven years. She also teaches cycling, hiking, wrestling, or whatever else she feels like having some company for. Her style is inclusive, gentle, and empowering; she also trains women to compete. She sees no contradiction there. She uses the partnership model ("Yes, that's exactly what I'm doing," she says enthusiastically when I describe it), and because she operates outside of municipal, educational, and professional sports systems, she is free to teach and practice sports as she sees fit, unencumbered by win-loss records. Unlike many athletes, for whom the partnership model is intuitive or undeveloped, Lauren deliberately creates an alternative to the military model, which she calls "violent and degrading."

For Lauren, partnership works better when exclusively female. Although she occasionally invites men to help her teach, she prefers a for-women, by-women environment where men will not intimidate, compete against, or even assist the women.

She calls her organization Wild Women in Free Places. Or she calls it Free Women in Wild Places. Or Wild Women in Weird Places, or Weird Women . . . She keeps changing it.

Lauren Crux loves sports. She loves introducing women to sports the way some people love introducing friends from different social circles: I just know you two are going to enjoy each other.

Lauren was introduced to bodysurfing, now her favorite sport, on a Santa Cruz beach early one morning in 1982, when she was thirty-five. She was strolling on the beach alone, relaxing before a day's work in her therapy office. Through a dense fog she saw a man bodysurfing, "cutting along the glassy wave the way boardsurfers do," remembers Lauren, "riding in the tube."

Having spent much of her childhood in southern California, Lauren knew how to churn her arms, be swept up by a wave, and bump along, chest out, until smashing into the sand face-first. Any coast-dweller knows that. But good body-surfers—real bodysurfers, they call themselves—add control, flair, and daring, whisking through water with the finesse of skillful downhill skiers.

Lauren watched, transfixed. When the bodysurfer emerged from the water, she hurried over. "I want to learn to do what you do," she said. "Will you teach me?"

"No," he answered, and continued walking.

Just as she was turning away, he called to her. "Do you have fins?" Fins are flippers, as scuba divers wear, only lighter and more maneuverable.

She didn't have fins. She thought real bodysurfers didn't use fins.

"Go buy fins," he said, "and show up tomorrow morning at the same time."

Lauren fell in love with bodysurfing. "For a lark," she started entering competitions. She now has a closet full of fins—the usual prizes—but she's not particularly competitive and she has trouble remembering exactly what she's won. "I think I was fourth in California one year," she says. "I've come in second or third in northern California a few times." When categories are divided according to age, she always wins. "Of course," she adds with a laugh, "usually I'm the only woman in my age group."

More fun than competition is the feeling of bodysurfing. Lauren likes twelve-foot swells. She likes Steamer Lane, a few miles north of Sunny Cove, where the waves crash in water twenty feet deep, so that even after the ride, you float in what feels like the middle of the ocean. When Lauren surfs at Steamer Lane, one of the nation's best boardsurfing spots, she is usually the only bodysurfer, and the only woman. People tell her she's crazy to surf there without a board. She loves it. "Sometimes the water goes so fast beneath you it seems it will tear your wetsuit right off," she says. "You can feel the whole ocean rushing along your belly. Nothing matters—work, outside pressures—everything goes away, and all that's left is a sense of peace. It's a profound, relaxed, deeply erotic, and sensual feeling. When I step out of the ocean, I've been transformed."

Latecomers struggle into caps, booties, earplugs, and head-to-toe neoprene—cumbersome gear that they pray will keep them warm in the fifty-five-degree water. Tomorrow, Monday, most of the women will return to work. Tish Denevan, one of Lauren's assistants, is a sales manager at Casa del Rey, one of many retirement villages in Santa Cruz. ("One of these days I'm going to hold a bodysurfing clinic for ninety-five-year-olds," she jokes.) Others work in the computer industry, which is inching its way south from San Jose's extended Silicon Valley, thirty minutes north of here. A few will return to classes at the University of California, Santa Cruz, the redwood-encircled school that a few years ago, much to the chagrin of its administration, named as its school mascot the banana slug.

In the summer, beach-comers from San Jose and the San Francisco Bay Area convert windy Highway 17, the road that twists through the Santa Cruz Mountains, into a snakelike caravan of convertibles, sunglasses, and cases of beer. In the winter, Santa Cruz is quiet but not deserted. There is a large, active feminist community and a respect for counterculture ideas and activities that has not abated in recent times.

Women own banks here but not necessarily bras or skirts. Several of the women changing clothes on the beach today are hairy by most standards; shaving remains optional. Soon after my visit Santa Cruz would make national headlines for being near the epicenter of the misnamed San Francisco earthquake, but for now the quaint old buildings are intact and the small town is best known as an offbeat place, and a surfer's paradise.

Fifteen women are here now, and the workshop begins. Before she will let them clomp into the surf, Lauren lectures about safety: how to read the waves, how to identify undertow and riptides. She leads the women through warm-up exercises to stretch and strengthen backs and necks, the parts of the body that, she warns, are particularly vulnerable to injury in this sport.

Tish Denevan eases into the water, strokes away from the beach, and waits. Tish grew up in San Jose and spent summers in Santa Cruz, boardsurfing and bodysurfing with eight brothers. In 1989 she placed second in the world bodysurfing championships. "She'll take this one," Lauren says to her assembled students as a wave gathers momentum and Tish starts paddling. "Watch how her head stays up, and see her right arm extended out front? You have better control with one arm. You're riding on your chest," she adds. "You have to make it stiff, like a board."

"Mine's already like a board," one of the women jokes.

Tish also demonstrates a no-arm ride and shows how to exit a wave (drop a shoulder and turn) before it forces you to kiss the beach. On her last ride, Tish flings both arms out, airplane style, and twirls twice mid-ride in a move called a spinner.

"Oh, now Tish had to go and show off," Lauren teases.

Finally, Tish shows the women an underwater takeoff, whereby she avoids all that frantic paddling. Instead, she submerges and waits for the wave to lift her into the crest. "The power of the wave throws you out," Lauren says.

One young woman stares at Tish, awed. "Wow," she says.

Lauren laughs. "Wow. That's how I feel about it. Wow."

The women divide themselves into three groups: beginner, intermediate, and advanced intermediate. Tish and Mary O'Neill, another friend of Lauren's, each take one group into the water. Lauren has the beginners, and at first they stay close to shore.

Lauren spent her first years in Vancouver, British Columbia, where she excelled at badminton, a popular Canadian sport, as well as golf, baseball, and tennis. Her father was a former boxer, her mother, a dancer; and Lauren wrestled and shot rifles with Dad and rode horses with Mom.

179

But the family moved to Palm Desert, California, in 1955, when Lauren (then called Candy) was eight, and she was appalled at the lack of organized sports for girls. Boys raced quarter-midget cars, but girls were not allowed. Boys had baseball competitions, but girls were not allowed. Girls' basketball had the three-bounce rule.

When Lauren was in sixth grade, her teacher made an exception and let her play in a boys' baseball game but put her in the outfield, where she'd never played before. When her one chance came to catch a ball, she dropped it and felt humiliated.

"I knew that it was absurd," says Lauren. "I remember sitting down on my bed with my girlfriend and saying, 'There's something wrong here. Why is this happening to girls and not to boys?' "

In her senior year of high school, Lauren decided she wanted to be a physical education teacher. "I was wildly in love with sports, wildly in love with my PE teacher, and it was very clear to me that sports were making life worth living," she says.

Her father said, "That's not good enough for you."

So Lauren chose a more respectable profession: high school English teacher. Later she became a psychotherapist, photographer, and writer.

But she also teaches PE here on the edge of the continent. "Teaching women to bodysurf is one way of making up for what happened to me as a kid," she admits. "You don't get a minority population to do something that a majority has dominated simply by saying 'Try harder.' You have to recruit; then, when you recruit, you have to train. So I'm intentionally populating the ocean with women, teaching them, This is how you do it."

Fifty yards out, the ocean is a colorful playground, abob with bright buoyed heads. Each time the sea rears back and sneezes out a white foam shelf, intermediates and advanced intermediates *whee* along for the ride. Laughter bounces off the waves and back to shore, where a lone mutt paces and sniffs the water's moving edge.

But one beginner in Lauren's group stands chest-deep, trembling. Poised like a sprinter, she prepares to outrun a wave. Lauren has told her to look out to sea, to watch waves coming, then to duck, but each time one approaches she panics and races to shore. Waves overtake her, knocking her down. Lauren coaxes her back out, explains again how to dive under the wave, demonstrates.

"I've never done this before. It's scary," pleads the woman, her voice a hoarse shout over the roar. "How do you know when it's going to break?"

"I'll tell you," says Lauren patiently, "and you'll learn." Lauren holds the woman by the hand. "Stand with me. I won't let a wave hurt you. Okay, we're going to duck under. Now!" They disappear. When their heads emerge, the woman is still trembling.

"I'm still scared," she says.

"That's okay," says Lauren. "I want you to keep trying this."

After a while, Lauren and the beginners wade close to shore. "Tumble," says Lauren. "Roll around. It's safe here." She flops into the water like a sea lion, sinks for a moment, then buoys up and lets a wave roll her onto the sand. There she sits, baby waves tugging at her knees. "Just float around," she tells her frightened crew. "Feel the water under you. This is the fun part." She grabs her ankles and tips like a child's spill-proof cup. "Feel how this wave can't hurt you this close to shore. If you let your body go, it carries you in, and it's fun."

Later I ask Lauren why women who are so scared come to her workshops. "Women are not stupid," she says. "They love water, or they suspect they might love water, and the human spirit will carry us past any obstacle if we give it the teensiest bit of encouragement. The excitement in life comes only in the risking. It doesn't come in being totally safe. So it makes sense to me that these women would say, 'I want to learn to do it, and I'm afraid.' Of course you'd want to learn this, it's great stuff. And of course you'd be afraid, because anytime you learn anything new, it's scary."

Other students, including courageous beginners who have promoted themselves to the more advanced groups, are merrily catching waves, practicing underwater takeoffs, cheering for each other. "Did you see that?" they say, and "Go for it!" and "Here comes one!" They are elated, oblivious to the cold water, to their odd outfits, and to the group of men floating on surfboards and bodyboards (Styrofoam half-surfboards) farther out, beyond a rocky cliff that defines the north side of Sunny Cove.

Santa Cruz is a small town, bodysurfing is a silly pursuit, and Lauren Crux will never be a giant in the world of women's sports. Lauren's body—long, strong, and the envy of any forty-three-year-old—will never be featured in national magazines, not even in the summer, in a bathing suit.

But something's happening here. Lauren is teaching a sport—remedial physical education, at first, but also competitive technique—without violence, one-upmanship, or unnecessary injuries. She encourages the women she'll compete against. She values excellence but is not particularly interested in victory. She has no killer instinct.

Lauren is not alone. Dissatisfaction with traditional sports and the search for alternatives are pervasive. Even beyond enigmatic Santa Cruz, across this country and in Canada, Norway, and other countries, in Girl Scout troops and parks-and-recreation departments, and at the professional and Olympic levels, women are saying, "We must do it differently." Whether the sport is bodysurfing or billiards, basketball or bowling, women are adapting sport—or trying to adapt it—to fit the needs and desires of women.

Many of the guidelines from the 1930s and 1940s—which held that sports should be inclusive, in balance with other aspects of life, educational in orientation, cooperative and social in spirit, safe and scientifically sound, and coached, officiated, and administered by women—are resurfacing. The partnership model seems a good way to frame the system that is being created, piecemeal, in this country and elsewhere. Observe a women's softball practice session and you may hear boisterous debates on topics ranging from coaching styles to the merits of rotating pitchers.

"Reconstructing sport is an ongoing process," says sports sociologist Cheryl Cole. "There is no road map. You try something, and it doesn't work, so you say, 'Okay, let's try something else next year.'"

Some participants make up their own rules, changing games to emphasize cooperation ("Let's see how many times we can hit the ball over the net"). Some rearrange teams partway through a game to make competition more fair.

Professors Susan Birrell and Diana Richter tell the story of an Iowa City softball player who hit a ball deep into center field, rounded first, then kept running toward the woman who caught the ball. Hugging her, she said, "I hit it so hard and you caught it and that's really good!"[1]

Leaders tend to be democratic. Violence is not glorified, and most players reject the "win at all costs" mentality. They speak of harmony and unity rather than battles and defeats. Few women play through pain. They respect nature.

Access to sports opportunities is an essential element of partnership since, surveys reveal, a major hindrance to women's participation in sports is lack of affordable equipment, clothing, and facilities.[2] By offering free workshops, Lauren Crux gives women who cannot afford to join health clubs and those who cannot find teammates or sponsorship for recreational leagues a chance to become Wild Women.

She also provides access to nonathletic women, shy women, and women who, under other circumstances, wouldn't be caught dead in a bathing suit. Swimming ability is essential, but beyond that, Lauren does not require sports skills. The women who attend her workshops—who are fat and thin, lesbian and heterosexual, brave and timid—know that they will be respected. They will not be forced to endure the humiliation of being chosen last or cut from a team. For women, many of whom were scarred by childhood athletic experiences, these assurances create a necessary sense of emotional safety.

Indeed, because of their childhood memories of exclusion from sport, partnership-model athletes welcome everyone. Susan Birrell's own softball league in Iowa City includes two women who weigh more than two hundred pounds. "There are certain body sizes you rarely see on a softball team, because if you can't run fast, you'll never get on base unless you hit the ball incredibly hard," notes Birrell. "But it's just as important for these women to play as for others."

Inclusion sounds simple, but its implications are complex. If, for instance, you invite a previously nonathletic thirty-eight-year-old to play on a recreational soccer team with you because she is your friend and you value the "sports for every-one" ethic, you will probably have fewer victories than if you had recruited only your most athletic friends. If you teach this woman, she will learn, but if she has spent her first thirty-eight years without the benefit of sports training, she may learn slowly.

Challenges will arise. You will be losing a game by one point, time will be running out, and this woman will material-ize, unguarded, in front of the goal. Do you pass to her, know-ing she will probably not be able to score? Which is more important, her experience of receiving a pass, taking a shot, and knowing you trusted her to do her best, or victory? These are the kinds of questions partnership-model athletes ask themselves.

Lauren and other partnership women also reject the "no pain, no gain" credo that is beginning to pollute women's college sports, particularly basketball. Cheryl Miller, Kamie Ethridge, Cindy Brown, Clarissa Davis, Terri Mann, Tonya Edwards, and Vickie Orr, some of the best basketball players of the past few years, have all had major knee surgery. "Maybe there's something, as coaches and players, that we're doing to encourage these injuries," admits the coach of the 1988 U.S. women's Olympic basketball team, Kay Yow.[3]

Lauren explains the dangers of the ocean, teaches women to judge the waves, and leads them through careful exercises, emphasizing bodily integrity. When, halfway through the workshop, the currents change and the waves become fierce and unpredictable, she calls the women from the ocean and cancels the workshop. "There's no sense in taking unnecessary risks," she says. "This surf is not safe for beginners."

We seem to have come full circle, from the days when men said, "Our games are too dangerous for you," and women argued, "No, they're not," to an era in which some women are saying, "We've tried your games, and you know what? They *are* too dangerous. From the looks of your mutilated bodies, they're too dangerous for you too. We're going to make up our own games, or alter your games so we can take care of ourselves."

Because they were taught to be fearful ("Don't climb up there, dear, you'll fall"), novice women athletes bring to sports their fear: fear of water, fear of falling, fear of movement, fear of failure, humiliation, pain. Fear of junior high PE class revisited.

Rather than, "You shouldn't be afraid," these women are now hearing, "It's okay to be afraid." Lauren Crux holds women's hands. "I won't let this wave hurt you," she says. "In bodysurfing, if you are timid, you will get hurt. You have to learn to deal with fear, because when the waves are big, it's scary out there. You have to go or not go; if you hesitate, you get mangled." Lauren tells the women, "Relax, keep your energy flowing." Later she explains, "I want them to be safe, but I also want them to be courageous."

Consider this passage from *The Art of Body Surfing,* by Robert Gardner: "Body surfing will always be the supreme test of man's age-old struggle to conquer his most ruthless, dangerous, and implacable enemy—the sea."[4]

Contrast that to Lauren Crux's description: "I deliberately

don't talk about managing, controlling, or dominating the ocean. I'm asking, How can I go *with* the ocean? If you learn to bodysurf well, the ocean is not a threat; it's an opportunity to be in harmony with nature, with godliness."

From spring through fall, Tish and Lauren bodysurf together almost every Tuesday night, then compete against each other on some weekends in between. They watch out for each other when one "gets dumped," applaud success, share new tricks. "Next to the bodysurfing itself, the camaraderie is the greatest joy," says Lauren. "The beginners will be there, and Tish and I will be there; the joy is having a group of women laughing and playing, truly thrilled. Occasionally a few men will join us, and it's the same way. There's enormous laughter."

Tish Denevan played basketball at Cabrillo College in Aptos, south of Santa Cruz, and her team won the state championship both years she was there. But Tish spent most of the time on the bench. She says, "In college sports, the reason you're there is to win games. Somebody always gets left out. Who starts and who doesn't? Right there, somebody is going to feel not as good." She still plays basketball, on a recreational team made up of many of the same players from the college team a decade ago. Now, though, no one stays on the bench for long.

Lisa Fraser, another bodysurfer in Lauren's class, switched from high school coaching to educational administration because "the girls would lose a volleyball game and come into school the next day devastated. The emphasis on winning was totally out of proportion. I used to wish someone would ask me not, 'Did you win?' but, 'Did your kids learn something about compassion or friendship?' "

These attitudes about partnership sports are not limited to women. Both women and men play Ultimate Frisbee—a team sport similar to field hockey but involving a Frisbee—without referees. Players abide by an honor code, calling their own fouls and violations. The immensely successful Special Olympics, founded by Eunice Kennedy Shriver in 1968, offer tournaments and league play to 750,000 mentally retarded children and adults worldwide; the program promotes skill, courage, sharing, and joy, along with physical development. The Senior Olympics operate on a similar model. The Gay Games too are based on the ethic of participation and fun for all. George Leonard *(The Ultimate Athlete)*, Andrew Fluegelman *(The New Games Book)*, Terry Orlick *(Winning Through Cooperation)*, W. Timothy Gallwey *(The Inner Game of Tennis)*, and other men are also exploring nonhierarchical approaches to sports and games.

Even football legend Vince Lombardi, credited with the infamous "Winning isn't everything, it's the only thing," didn't really mean that, according to James Michener in *Sport in America*. Lombardi retracted the statement shortly before he died. "I wish to hell I'd never said that damn thing," he told Jerry Izenberg. "I meant the effort. . . . I meant having a goal. . . . I sure as hell didn't mean for people to crush human values and morality."[5]

Still, women are in the forefront. Susan Birrell and Diana Richter offer the story of a game between two softball teams, one composed of beginners and the other in contention for the league title. "To make the game more competitive and more fun, the more skilled team decided not to play their usual positions but to try new ones. When the rookies actually pulled ahead, the skilled team remained true to their commitment—eventually losing the game and falling in the standings. But they were convinced they had created something more important than winning—an enjoyable, competitive game."[6]

Revised forms of sport do not come easily. I coached a women's recreational basketball team one year, and decided—with the team's approval—to give everyone equal playing time, regardless of skill level and regardless of the score of the game. This is not a novel idea. Nor is it necessarily a wise one, I muttered to myself when we lost our first game 75–12. But we talked it over, experimented, and came up with a system of play that included skill-building, fun, camaraderie, and teamwork, as well as an effort to win. This in itself is critical, I believe—this process of discussing, refining, and evaluating sport. We had a perfect season—0 and 10—and no regrets.

But when someone suggested we play in the same league the following year, I advised against it. We just didn't have the skill to create fair, evenly matched games, so to sign up knowingly to play "out of our league" would have been a disservice to other teams as well as ourselves.

Some of the same women and I joined a volleyball league the following autumn. In one game, the other team could not return any of my serves. Time after time, I served the ball and they failed to send it back over the net. Were this an Olympic competition, the tension created by unreturned serves could be exciting and challenging for both teams. But this was not the Olympics. I became concerned for my teammates and for the other team. Were we having fun yet? If the unreturned serves continued, we would win the match 15–0, and no one but me would have successfully hit the ball. I considered serving less hard, but I really have only one serve. Besides, would it be insulting to the other team if I eased up? Should I just keep giving them the opportunity to learn to return my serve? A lot of thoughts, none of which had to do with the thrill of victory, went through my head as I kept serving and serving. Eventually I hit the ball into the net by mistake and everyone seemed relieved.

Maybe, as someone suggested later, I could have tried practicing a new serve. That way I would still have challenged myself and not pampered the other team.

Even the pros hash these questions out. In her autobiography, Martina Navratilova explains how she and basketball star Nancy Lieberman differed. "Nancy felt I had to hate Chris [Evert] in order to reach the top, but I knew Chris wasn't taking anything away from me. Nancy also told me not to talk to the players or show them what I was eating or how I was working out. I could never understand that. I felt that

I could beat them and still go out to dinner with them afterward."[7]

Some recreational women's teams rotate coaching responsibilities in an effort to avoid giving one individual excessive decision-making power. Of course, not everyone has coaching skills, so this can be as disastrous as rotating parenting responsibilities among all members of a family.

Some softball players go so far as not to slide into base if they think they might injure the person covering that base. Cheryl Cole, a former water polo player and former coach of men's high school and college water polo teams, stopped playing the sport because of the roughness it demanded. "This is my personal dilemma," she admits. "The more politically conscious I became, the more careful I became, and the less athletic. In water polo, it was hard because part of being good meant being very aggressive. It's so easy to accidentally hit someone with an elbow. I had a hard time doing that to another woman."

I've heard of recreational teams that have deliberately not practiced. Why not? To practice would be to take sports seriously, the argument goes, and to take sports seriously would be to put excessive emphasis on winning.

Pretty soon, one begins to see that athletes struggling to avoid the military mentality can throw out the baby with the bathwater. If you don't practice, and don't slide into base, and don't lunge after the ball, and don't allow anyone to lead, the excitement and skill can be drained from the game. Players are deprived of the rich experience of playing the best they can, as hard as they can.

As Lauren Crux says, "There's no joy in mediocrity. We push each other to be good. We don't just flub around in the waves and go, 'That's wonderful you didn't catch that wave.' To hell with that."

. . .

Sculpting an effective partnership model is made more difficult by the presence of antagonistic men. Because men have viewed sports arenas—including parks, playgrounds, lakes, and even oceans—as male territory for so long, they are often unwilling to share the space with women.

Which brings us back to Lauren Crux, splashing around in the ocean. As Lauren coaxes her beginners to relax in the safe, shallow water, the other students are porpoising under waves and riding along with them, their heads protruding like ship figureheads.

Then a lone teenage bodyboarder catches a wave and swoops toward two women who are riding the same wave. I recognize him—earlier, he had struggled with the zipper in the back of his wetsuit and, alone with me on the beach, had approached me sheepishly, like a son embarrassed that he still needed help getting dressed. His young back was taut but not yet bulky, his neck a soft blushing pink.

One woman sees him out of the corner of her eye, turns sharply to exit the wave as she has been taught. The other, enjoying her ride, doesn't notice him until he is within inches of her head. At the last moment, he curves away from her and paddles back to his friends, laughing.

Other bodyboarders launch similar attacks.

Lauren, busy with her beginners, doesn't notice. Soon she calls all of the women from the water, and they huddle in a shivery circle. The waves are getting increasingly rough, and Lauren wants everyone to check in.

"How's it going out there?" she asks.

"Great!" says one.

"I'm scared," says another.

"I have a headache," says another, tugging at her ear.

"Here," says Lauren. "Your ears are probably freezing. Try my earplugs."

The next woman in the circle says, "Those guys are aiming for our heads."

"They are?" says Lauren. There is sadness in her voice, and no surprise. She has dealt with this problem before.

190

"Luckily, bodyboards are soft," someone contributes.

"Baloney," says Tish. "They hurt."

"Is it kosher to give them shit?" another woman asks—a uniquely female question.

"Tell them to get out of your face," says Lauren.

"What will they say?" asks the polite one. She has never had a fight with a teenage boy in an ocean and wants to be prepared.

Lauren answers, "They'll say, 'Fuck you, bitch, you're fucked, you fuckin' A.'" Everyone laughs. Then the women flock back into the ocean, tell the boys to get out of the way, and the teenagers respond exactly as Lauren predicted.

"How often does this happen?" I ask Lauren later.

"It always happens," she says. "I have to go out there and say, 'You mess with this class, I'm going to bust your head.'"

"Do you say it like that?"

"No. At first I'm very polite. I say, 'We're teaching a class. Now give us space.' If one of them continues to hassle us, I swim over to him and say, 'What you're doing is not okay, and I want you to stop it.'"

"Then they curse at you?"

"They always go, 'Fuck you, bitch, fuck blah blah blah.' I never react to any of that. I just look them in the eye and say, 'Don't do it anymore.' It took everything I had to learn to say that. But it's amazing what you can come up with if you see someone you love in trouble."

Lauren explains the hierarchical nature of surfer society this way: "The older surfers attack the younger ones—'You dickhead'—if they make a mistake. They ridicule them. If they get a good wave, they say nothing. They fight each other for the waves, they aim for each other.

"Then the young boys go for the younger boys. It goes straight down the hierarchy: older men to young boys, young boys to women. I am a forty-three-year-old woman, and I have had a ten-year-old boy paddle by me and go, 'Get the fuck out of my way, you fucking bitch.' It's so tragic. My heart aches."

What did she say to the ten-year-old?

"Nothing. I was too stunned."

To Tish Denevan, such behavior is not stunning. Her brothers taught her the ways of the waves. "If someone goes out in front of [my brothers] and wipes out their waves, they'll kick their boards into other people's backs and legs," she says. But Tish will drop out of that sort of competition. "Lauren will fight harder for a wave than I will," she says. "I'll just swim away."

Not all of the men are antagonistic, Lauren is quick to point out. Some of the older boardsurfers are the laid-back boys of summer—summer in the sixties—whom you'd expect to find in a coastal town such as Santa Cruz. "They're not just laid-back, they're cooperative, they welcome you," says Lauren.

Once, while waiting for a wave, a male surfer told her, "I'm glad to see you out here. You don't see too many middle-aged women out here." Lauren was shocked by the "middle-aged women" part—she had been feeling like an athlete, beyond age or gender—but his friendly intent was clear.

Bodysurfers, unlike boardsurfers, tend to be friendly. The Santa Cruz Bodysurfing Association, a mostly male organization, has given Lauren money to advertise, helped her teach classes, and run contests for women, supplying wetsuits as prizes.

In Hawaii, Lauren has found gracious male boardsurfers. "I've been welcomed by the Hawaiian men there," she says. "They were quite pleased to see me out there. But the minute white male Californians came out on their boards, everything changed. It became hostile, competitive."

There is surf etiquette, and part of the problem for Lauren and other women has been learning the ways of the waves. A rare female boardsurfer yelled at Lauren one time, using the usual profanities, and Lauren asked, "What are you so upset about?" It turned out that Lauren was paddling away from shore, and the woman, riding in on her board, didn't know that Lauren would duck under the wave at the appropriate time. "*I* know I'm going to go under them, it's not going to be a problem, but they don't know that," Lauren admits. "It's disorienting to them. So now I do my best not to get in their way."

Bart Davis, a twenty-five-year-old Santa Cruz native who surfs with and without boards, agrees that "the atmosphere is tense" and that boardsurfers are usually to blame. A male friend of his was once rammed by a boardsurfer and needed stitches in his head.

Most of the resentment is aimed toward beginners, male or female, says Davis. He says he and his friends welcome women, even if they are beginners who lack the control to stay out of the way. "I very rarely see a woman in the ocean. When I do, I'm happy to see her out there." In fact, he says, it could be worse. "If anything, I think women are given a little more slack. Other male beginners will get beat up, that sort of thing. They get into heavy verbal exchanges and maybe push each other and maybe throw a punch."

Lauren remains convinced that men are defending what they perceive to be male territory. "One time I was just walking down toward the water and this man who was coming out turned to me and started, 'You stupid bitch, cunt . . .'" Lauren's voice returns to its normal calm. "Just my presence is a violation."

So the boys are still saying, "You can't because you're a girl." Bart Davis surmises that, ironically, Lauren's confrontation style may make matters worse. "There's things that happen out there, and they need to get straightened out, but the way a male would do it is probably not so straightforward. There's a protocol, a way it's done. You're cool about it; you say, 'Hey, cool it, buddy.' The protocol is male-established, and maybe [men] freak out a little bit when Lauren confronts them. It's a different way of communicating."

Of course, Lauren cannot say "Hey, buddy" to the men, because they would not be able to say "Hey, buddy" back to her. She is not a buddy, and this is part of the problem: there is no place in the male hierarchical system for an athletic woman in her forties—or her students.

Lauren thinks she has learned a new way of asserting herself, a new skill. When grocery-shopping in her community co-op recently, she saw a man shoplifting. "I went right up to him and said, 'It's not okay what you're doing.' I never would have done that," she adds, "if I hadn't had to learn to do it bodysurfing."

What did he say?

" 'Fuck you!' Of course!" She laughs long and hard. "It was so predictable!"

Lauren Crux believes her strategy works, but men and boys continue to attack her and her students. The responses of these males hardly reflect the respect Lauren wishes she could command.

What could she do differently? I don't know. It's a pervasive problem: women trying to find space, either indoors or outdoors, where they can play sports without harassment from men. Tish's strategy—moving to a different location—seems no more effective in the long term than does a woman runner's strategy of running only in certain well-lit or populated areas. Ultimately, women are going to have to assert the right to move and play in the entire public domain, not only in the few corners men will grant them. Women have to learn, somehow, to claim space effectively, and men have to learn, somehow, to share it.

Meanwhile, Lauren Crux goes about populating the ocean with Free, Wild, Weird, ordinary women, teaching them how to develop strength, how to stand up for themselves, how to support each other and gentle men. Some enter competitions; some win. The ocean is not the enemy, and Lauren is not trying to conquer anything.

After the workshop, Lauren dries off and we drive to a natural fast-food restaurant called Dharma's (formerly McDharma's, until threatened with a lawsuit by McDonald's). Lauren orders vegetarian chili. I have a tofuburger.

"Some women will never bodysurf again [after the workshop]. It's not for them. That's fine," she comments between bites. "But there are women who develop a new sense of their bodies, a new sense of how to manage in the world. They are more courageous, safer, more playful."

Lauren breaks her rhythm for just a moment. "I'm not saying because of me they have all this. But there's a renewed sense of: 'I am somebody and my life matters and I can effect change in the world. I can be creative or a better parent or whatever.' That's my revolution. They're going to pass it on. In fact, I think that's how we're going to change the world. It's going to be little people in little towns doing their little thing and being insistent about it—and having fun."

Together at Last

We saw with satisfaction the great advantage in good fellowship and mutual understanding between men and women who take the road together, sharing its hardships and rejoicing in the poetry of motion.... We discoursed on the advantage to masculine character of comradeship with women who were as skilled and ingenious in the manipulation of the swift steed as they themselves. We contended that whatever diminishes the sense of superiority in men makes them more manly, brotherly, and pleasant to have about.

—FRANCES WILLARD, *A Wheel Within a Wheel;*
How I Learned to Ride the Bicycle (1895)

*Y*OU can't be a female athlete without addressing questions of femininity, sexuality, fear, power, freedom, and just how good you are compared with men. In the complex, contradictory world of women's sports, female athletes want a piece of the male pie one day and serve an all-female pudding the next. They wear crop-tops to look sexy for a bicycling date, then pedal home alone hoping not to attract heckling or worse. The paradoxes can be paralyzing, but they yield tenacious women who are dedicated not only to breaking athletic and cultural barriers but also to helping other women along the way.

Jacquie Phelan, three-time national champion of mountain biking, typically straddles two worlds, one foot on male turf, the other in a no-man's-land she tries to preserve for herself and other women. To meet Jacquie, I flew to Denver, crawled into an eight-person miniplane for a flight to Gunnison, Colorado, then drove forty miles until the paved road ended in Crested Butte, a town of fewer than 1,000 people at the base of a mountain by the same name. I then rented a fat-tire bike and pedaled from my inn to the A-frame where Jacquie and her husband were staying. Jacquie had come to Crested Butte from her home in Fairfax, California, to be inducted, along with nine men, into the Mountain Bike Hall of Fame, which was honoring the ten most influential people in the short history of mountain biking.

The history of bicycling itself is not short at all. Before Gertrude Ederle swam the English Channel, before Amelia Earhart flew solo across the Atlantic, before women secured the right to vote, before there were automobiles, and before the modern Olympics were first held, women rode bicycles. In the 1890s, a century ago, about 30,000 American women owned and rode bicycles.[1]

Some women were playing tennis before that, riding horses, running, golfing, and shooting rifles, but when the "safety bicycle" replaced the dangerous and difficult "high bicycle" with its huge front wheel, masses of women were given the opportunity to steer a new life course. Bloomers, popularized by Amelia Bloomer in 1851, became de rigueur in the gay nineties as upper-class women discarded cumbersome petticoats in favor of the infinitely more comfortable loose pants. Cheaper and lighter than carriages, bicycles enabled women to travel. Chaperones, reluctant to learn to handle the new machines, stayed home, thus freeing young women and men to explore the countryside or neighboring towns together, alone.[2] In 1892, the hit song was "A Bicycle Built for Two."[3]

Opponents of bicycling in general and women's bicycling in particular warned that the shape of the bike seat would produce sexual excitement, that wild cyclists would frighten horses off the road, that cycling would lead to immoral associations between women and men, and that the act of pedaling and sweating would produce all manner of diseases and disorders, from *kyphosis bicyclistarum* ("bicycle stoop") to "bicycle face" (the agonized expression of cyclists trying not to fall off).[4]

Cyclists counterclaimed that the sport could cure rheumatism, gout, liver trouble, depression, "nerves," and alcoholism (for how could one ride when drunk?). "Bicycle face," one writer asserted, was beautiful.[5]

Women raced as early as 1885, the year Frankie Nelson won the women's six-day race in Madison Square Garden in New York City. Another woman, Mrs. A. M. C. Allen, perhaps typified the determination of women to ride no matter what. In 1897, while she was setting a record for the most miles (21,026) pedaled in one year, "a ferocious dog fastened its teeth to her ankle." She promptly rid herself of the nuisance by drawing her revolver and shooting it, then pedaled another sixteen miles before seeking medical treatment.[6]

Jacquie Phelan identifies with that early bloomer brigade. She tells me that Frances Willard, the leader of the Women's Christian Temperance Union, learned at fifty-three to ride a bike she named Gladys. "It's so neat that bikes are related to feminism," says Jacquie. "You're in control, you're steering where you're going, you're moving yourself."

Jacquie has named her bike Otto. Charlie Cunningham, her husband and the owner of Wilderness Trail Bikes, designed and built it for her. Jacquie's and Charlie's bikes mean as much to them as Susan Butcher's huskies do to her; cycling is for them a life-style—a way to get from here to there, a source of income, a pleasing pastime, and a competitive outlet. "Cycling is a way to live lightly on the earth, and respectfully. At the same time, it makes you healthy and makes you feel good," says Charlie, a mellow mechanical whiz who has invented numerous now common mountain bike components, including Ground Control tires, named by Jacquie.

Jacquie says: "You feel the earth. It's not something you

turn on 91.8 FM to see what the hell's going on outside your envelope of steel and glass. It's happening right now, and you can talk with authority about the new Safeway burning down, because you can smell the smoke, or the fog rolling in, because you had to battle the headwind the fog makes. It's like being an animal, so all you care about is eating, sleeping, and making love. It does help boil things down to their essential components. Which I love because I'm so complicated and fragmented and scattered. It really does save me."

Jacquie is differently abled than her husband, forty-one, a longtime mountain biker, former top racer, and now renowned bike builder. Faster than 90 percent of the men she races with, Jacquie nevertheless is slower than Charlie. Despite their shared love of cycling, there are times when they can't figure out a way to enjoy their sport together, to accommodate the differences in ability levels. Here's Jacquie's explanation: "I get all bent out of shape about him not waiting for me. I just want him to behave the way I would if I were riding with someone lesser than me—I'd go in circles, I'd come back and ride together, then say, 'Well, see ya.' He never says, 'Well, see ya.' I get enraged. I'm terrible at it. He calls it psychodrama. He doesn't want to ride with that too much, if I can't keep a lid on my hate at myself for not being able to keep up with him."

To Charlie, the problem is simpler: he happens to be faster, and she makes things unnecessarily complicated by getting angry about it. "Riding together was one of the first things that bonded Jacquie and me," he says fondly. "She's quite strong. Lately we've been having great rides together every week. It's a real high. But yeah, there have been plenty of rides where we headed out together, and usually because I was going too fast up the hills she wouldn't be happy by the end of the ride."

Jacquie Phelan elbowed her way onto slippery hiking paths and fire trails back in 1980, when early mountain bikers were still steering one-speed clunkers. In the early 1990s, a decade later, an estimated 7.5 million people nationwide ride mountain bikes. But the mountains were empty in the early days, save for some intrepid backpackers. Though Jacquie recruited women everywhere she went, she spent most of her time with men.

On her first mountain ride, a twenty-five-mile Thanksgiving Day "appetite seminar" near San Francisco, a group of men tossed their bikes into the back of a pickup truck and drove to the top of Pine Mountain to begin the day's journey down. Jacquie, a "purist," didn't ask the men if she could pile her bike into the pickup too. Instead, she pedaled her five-speed Raleigh—complete with wicker basket—up the mountain. Then she slalomed down the mountain as skillfully and fearlessly as the best of the men.

Having enjoyed that taste of casual competition, she tried road racing, where there were more women and the bikes weren't old clunkers but sleek racing machines, so skinny-tired as to be almost two-dimensional. In 1981, she finished fourth at the United States Cycling Federation's National Time Trial Championships. With three more years' training, she might have qualified for the first women's Olympic cycling competition, in 1984.

But she didn't like the women in road racing. Too cliquish, she said. Jacquie Phelan is a true eccentric: clever, rebellious, voluble, yet insecure. The men in mountain biking—still bearded and long-haired, many of them, and rebels all—were more her speed, although she didn't really fit in with them either.

Along the way she alienated more than a few of them. She'd costume herself for races; for that first Thanksgiving ride she wore a helmet with a toy duck on top. Once, lacking a sponsor, she clipped a cereal boxtop and affixed it to her cap, calling herself "Team Flakes." She once sped across a finish line topless.

One night before a race in Redding, California, she and a group of male teammates, roaming the town with nothing to do, bought fluffy pink and blue bathrobes at a thrift shop.

Jacquie painted their fingernails and they clambered into stray shopping carts, wheeling each other past curious on-lookers and laughing like teenagers.

Soon afterward, the men kicked her off the team. "They were shocked by what they ended up doing," says Jacquie sadly. "Maybe they felt they had been bewitched. But can't the best woman racer in the country be tolerated a little bit? Or a lot?"

So despite her ability on a bike, she didn't earn the honor of being "one of the guys." Which only inspired more rebellion. "Anyone with an analytical bent would say I was acting out, seeking attention," she concedes. "It wasn't very professional. The thing was, it was okay if the guys goofed around, and not okay if I did. That pissed me off, and I did it even more."

Dr. and Mrs. Phelan, a psychoanalyst and a "frustrated house-wife," were dead set against Jacquie's and her sister's becoming athletes, Jacquie says. When Jacquie practiced gymnastics in school, her father admonished that he didn't want "a trained seal for a daughter."

Jacquie wrestled her four brothers anyway, and rode her bike the forty miles back and forth between their San Fernando Valley home and the Malibu beaches. She attended Middlebury College in Vermont, became fluent in French, Swedish, and German, and graduated with academic honors but no athletic education.

After college, Jacquie rediscovered cycling. She says it's the endorphin rush of riding fast down slippery slopes that saves her from depression, just as those early cyclists claimed. She has tried therapy too, but cycling, she says, is her main mood elevator, along with the foolish antics she has become infamous for. As the daughter of a psychoanalyst, she's given these things a lot of thought. "I think there will always be this low-level blues the clown is covering up," she says. "I can live with that."

. . .

Cycling requires quadriceps strength, strategy, and particularly in the mountain variety, guts. African-dance classes gave Jacquie a good start on leg strength, and some of her male teammates coached her on strategy. The guts she got from watching her mother, timid on roller skates and "cowardly" on a family rock-climbing expedition. "I never want to be like that when I'm older," Jacquie resolved.

Jacquie became known for her courage, especially on steep descents where, twisting over roots, around boulders, and between trees, any normal person would grip the brakes for dear life or hop off and walk. Jacquie, brow furrowed, eyes narrowed, skin contorted into a deliriously happy "bicycle face," never feels more alive.

Men hear her catching them, coming up from behind on the narrow mountain trails, and yell to their peers, "Jacquie's coming through!" If they don't yell, and don't move over, she squeezes by anyway, brushing their fancy bikes with her slim hips—not enough to make them fall, just enough to make them notice.

"I say, 'Here comes Jacquie, I'd better hurry up,'" admits Mark Slate, a business partner of Charlie Cunningham's who has come to Crested Butte for the annual Fat Tire Festival. Despite Jacquie's success and, more recently, that of other women riders, Slate still claims dominance, albeit of a shrunken empire. "If a woman beats me climbing, that's okay," he says. "Downhill, I won't let her."

In the early years, Jacquie loomed large in the tiny women's division of mountain biking, winning the National Off-Road Bicycle Association (NORBA) championships in 1983, 1984, and 1985, some of the same years her hero, Martina Navratilova, reigned supreme. But while Martina netted millions, Jacquie had to scramble through mud and muck for minimal prize money and a place in the fledgling racing circuit.

Among Jacquie's favorite accomplishments is finishing second in a 21-mile man-versus-horse-versus-bike race in Wales. Jacquie beat all the runners, all the cyclists (all male), and all but one horse-and-rider team (both female). "I beat the guys [on foot] and all the bike-riding men," she says proudly. "I didn't care if I didn't beat a horse."

When disgruntled men say she owes her victories to Otto, her $5,000 custom-built bicycle, Jacquie doesn't argue; that assumption helps Charlie Cunningham sell bikes. But she is troubled by male resentment. After all, these are her peers. One strategy to gain acceptance has been to create an alias, a persona Jacquie can blame for the rugged, aggressive style so necessary in mountain biking but so unbecoming a "lady." The person who races, then, is one Alice B. Toeclips. "Alice gets to thrash the guys; then Jacquie can be nice, and people will like her, won't they?" Jacquie's voice rises, almost pleading. "Come on, get it? There's two mes, and one is this gnarly animal who's bigger than life and goofy and has huge appetites. I really have a huge appetite for a lot of things, like sensation. I'm an endorphin junkie, you know?" She forgets to elaborate on that other me, the nice one she hopes people will like *even though* the "gnarly animal" can outride most male mountain bikers and has decidedly undainty appetites.

The *nom de pédale* doesn't fool many men. Jacquie's personality is too big, too intimidating. Although she's been pursued by plenty of men, on and off their bikes, she says her suitors have lacked a certain boldness. "How come I'm always sweeping the guys off their feet?" she asks wistfully.

Jacquie has a beautiful body, sculpted by thousands of miles of cycling—"hammering," or "pounding." Her calves are tight, ridged like a relief map, her thighs as sturdy as Otto's handlebars. But Jacquie is sensitive about being mistaken for a man and, at five-seven, 135 pounds, insecure about being "big, strong, and clumsy." Like virtually all women athletes, she must maneuver through murky questions about beauty and body image, but her response is to adorn herself with children's costume jewelry: dozens of plastic bracelets, bright earrings, fake braids. It's a parody of femininity, the kind of female impersonation a man might do. "That way," she taunts, "you can tell I'm a girl from the back."

Beneath the humor lie hurt and confusion. "I'm not too

sure about my femaleness, so I'll drape the externals on." She clarifies: "Femininity. I don't have any question about being a female. But being so brawny . . . I think I'm lithe, but I've been called stocky by guys who I guess don't know how to see."

Women's Sports and Fitness featured Jacquie in a stylized photograph a few years ago, and she was made to look glamorous in an athletic sort of way. When she came home after the photo session, still wearing makeup, Charlie said, "Wow, who's that sexy lady?"

What does "sexy" mean, absent weakness and vulnerability? "There's a part of sexuality that's very scary to me," Jacquie confesses. "I'm afraid of my own, in a way. I've never felt like I was very beautiful or sexy. I don't know if I am. How can I tell? In junior high and high school I was a dog. I wasn't the big-boobed cheerleader type. Skinny girls were cool too, as long as they slept with people, which I didn't do. I rode my bike." (As if to confirm the fears of those early opponents of biking, she adds: "It's a great way to get off.")

"If I were really sexy and beautiful, I'd just be too much," she concludes. "Way too threatening. I [feel fine] about the fact that I'm smart and strong. But if you threw in the magic third thing, everybody would hate me."

Jacquie relishes zipping past the men on the mountains, but she takes almost as much pleasure in charming them afterward. "I'm a natural flirt, I love jokes, I love lusty innuendos," Jacquie says. She has developed a reputation for being promiscuous; she denies the charge. She says it's born of rejection: men mad about not getting what they wanted, then saying they did. "I've had to endure strangers saying to me, 'You know what's being said about you? That you slept with half the pack.'"

Jacquie met Charlie in 1982, in the bike shop of her boyfriend at the time, Gary Fisher, another pioneer mountain biker. Charlie first's glimpse of Jacquie was of her back, bent over a bike. "She had just gotten back from a ride and had on a fairly skimpy thing—I don't know what it was, but it was skimpy," he recalls, adding with a laugh: "She was really sweaty and really sexy and I really liked her."

Jacquie liked the looks of him too; particularly that he wasn't too strong or too big. "I don't want to be with some-body I'm physically afraid of," she explains. "I'd rather be able to flail the guy weight for weight."

Her first impression of Charlie: He's a "nice, sensitive, soft-spoken, nonthreatening guy. He would never beat me up!

"It's a neat relationship," she now says. "He's my foil. We complement one another really well. He's the kind of guy no one can ever say anything nasty about. You always see a smile on his face. I'm the darker, brooding one."

Bicycling magazines, which promote the "wacky Jacquie" image that she admits to projecting, have reported that the odd couple live in a tree house at their "Offhand Manor" estate. In fact, Jacquie clarifies, they only *sleep* in a tree house. "We live in a normal house. Charlie threw up a tree house a hundred feet above the house, up a bunch of stairs and above the swimming pool, which is now a frog pond. It's a cliff dwelling [with] a bed-size platform, a roof, a solid deck floor, and a piss bucket and a chin-up bar for gymnastics and [for] holding the toilet paper. The roof comes up so you can look straight up at the stars. You hear all the birds and noise and neighborhood gossip."

Among women, Jacquie is marveled at for her mischief less than for her generosity. "What I like about Jacquie is that she's so unselfish," says Marilyn Price, founder of Trips for Kids, a mountain-biking program for inner-city youth based in Mill Valley, California. "She could be aloof, a big star, but she's not; she's always helping other people."

Even during the years when she was winning every compe-tition the sport had to offer, Jacquie spent her spare time recruiting women, egging on the best of them with a line she became known for: "You could beat me."

Carole Bauer, forty-three, remembers meeting Jacquie in

1984. They were racing to Crested Butte's Gunnison Pass, which ascends to 12,000 feet over a series of severe switchbacks. Carole was the local champion. Jacquie was a visitor, but her reputation had preceded her.

"I was going down to the lower loop—a single-track trail, so it was difficult to pass in there," remembers Carole. "I'm buzzing along, and this chick comes streaming past me. I went, 'Whoa, what was that!' " Carole got closer to Jacquie on the grueling uphill switchbacks, but couldn't catch her. "Then I knew she'd beat me on the downhill, because she's a maniac and I'm a real chicken."

After the race, "she wanted to come over and see who I was," Carole remembers. "It was funny. She really encouraged me to beat her. It was great. She was saying, 'Don't give up, you came in second and it was really close.' Which made me feel great."

Eventually someone did beat Jacquie. Cindy Whitehead, a woman who once rode 49 miles of a 50-mile race without a seat, beat her at the NORBA championship in 1986, after Jacquie had gone undefeated for more than three years. "I was quite happy to have her beat me," says Jacquie. "When she came past me, I said, 'Go, Cindy.' Part of me wants to be gracious like a real queen and know when to get off the throne. I study people who are shitty losers. I thought, I'm not going to be like that, I'm going to hug Cindy when she wins."

Why did she say, "Go, Cindy"?

"I've never not said 'Go' to anybody. As I'd come blazing by, I'd say, 'Come on, just because I'm passing you doesn't mean you can't keep riding as hard as you can,' or, 'Even though I'm lapping you, you're winning your division,' or whatever. So I could still do it to Cindy."

But when asked if she has any regrets, she acknowledges, "Part of me feels like I gave it away, I expired breath, I gave [Cindy] some power, I handed it to her. Well, maybe I did." She shrugs. "I wish I hadn't said it. If she had thanked me, I would have been happy to have done it. But she didn't thank me. She was too busy racing. I should have been busier racing myself."

Jacquie has not yet perfected the partnership model, but she's working on it, experimenting with ways to be helpful and compassionate and also competitive. As Cheryl Cole says, there is no road map, and at times Jacquie feels as lost as a midnight cyclist on a dense mountain trail.

She keeps riding, though, keeps racing, and keeps recruiting women. She conducts camps and clinics for women in several states and Canada; she invites women to join her on moonlight rides; she populates the mountains with women.

Lately Jacquie finds herself thinking about road racing again, maybe in the annual Ore-Ida Women's Challenge. Last time she tried road racing, she says, she developed tendinitis in her knees but was too afraid to tell her teammates anything was wrong. Maybe now, hundred of hours of therapy later, she's more self-confident. Wouldn't it be fun, she thinks, an all-women's race? There still aren't any such races in mountain biking.

Meanwhile, to create for herself and other women a friendship network free from the come-ons and clashes of men's cycling groups, she has founded the WOMBATS, the Women's Mountain Bike and Tea Society. Characteristically, inclusion is a high priority. She says: "If I'm going to have a club for women I want to have a good time and have the best things of those fifties clubs: decoder rings and secret handshakes and all [those things] that we never got to have. Mostly, include everybody. I even include guys in it—I don't want to deny them being supporting members and coming on rides."

She particularly enjoys the company of women. "Some of the stuff about being a woman is just a gas—the idea of cackling instead of laughing, calling [WOMBAT parties] hen parties. Women speak a different language than men, and it's music to my ears."

The WOMBATS now boasts four chapters and four hundred members in California and Montana, with chapters planned in Colorado Springs; Amherst, Massachusetts; and Fresno. Members receive WOMBATS T-shirts and issues of the quarterly *WOMBAT News,* and become instant members of a circle of cycling pals who also volunteer for ecologically minded chores such as maintaining mountain trails.[7]

But the groups are not always the idyllic islands of athletic harmony Jacquie envisioned. "Some women in one chapter [feel] threatened by the fact that many of the women in a nearby chapter are gay, and they don't want to be associated with [them] because it might hurt their chances of finding a man," she says, rolling her eyes. Jacquie jokingly talks of creating the GLOMBATS—"for singles who want to glom onto somebody."

At the Mountain Bike Hall of Fame ceremony, it's clear that despite her conflicts, Jacquie remains enormously popular among the still mostly male mountain bike set. She was, after all, selected for this first Hall of Fame induction, along with stars Charlie Cunningham; Gary Fisher, who coined the term "mountain bike" and makes the popular Fisher bikes; Tom Ritchey, founder of Ritchey, the manufacturer of the first widely distributed mountain bike; Mike Sinyard, founder of Specialized Bicycle Imports ($50 million in annual sales); and five other male pioneers.

The ceremony takes place on a Thursday night during Fat Tire Bike Week, a kooky autumn festival that includes a bicycle rodeo, the World Official Bicycle Polo Championships, and an all-downhill chainless race. Jacquie, recovering from an illness, has not participated in the races, rides, and games. Sara Ballantyne, a strong, tiny twenty-eight-year-old, wins consistently in the women's division. Although Jacquie retains a third-place ranking nationwide, Ballantyne has replaced her as queen of the dirt.

In the parking lot of Crested Butte's Center for the Arts, the few cars and trucks are nearly buried by hundreds of bicycles, none of them locked. Some of the Ritcheys and Fishers and Specializeds and Cunninghams cost as much as $6,000, but they lie cast about as casually as children's bikes; theft is unheard of in this tiny mountain town.

Inside, the stage is similarly strewn with bikes of all incarnations. Charlie Kelly, a founding member of NORBA and founder of the first mountain bike periodical, *Fat Tire Flyer*, is master of ceremonies; he is also one of the ten inductees. He begins with music and slides of cyclists grinning from various bike perches high in the colorful Colorado mountains. The audience of about four hundred includes some noncompeting locals and some women still muddy from the day's festivities, but it consists mainly of rowdy men: athletes who have devised a way to make their adulthood as adventurous and scraped up as their boyhood.

They cheer identifiable riders in the slide show, the most enthusiastic response going to Carole Bauer, the local hero and an organizer of the Hall of Fame. A slide of her astride a bike, wearing only brief strips of colorful Lycra, beams down at the eager audience. Whistles, hoots, and cheers fill the hall. ("I was whistling too," Jacquie explains afterward. "She looked great. Everyone loves her.")

Charlie Kelly then introduces the inductees with long, humorous stories about mountain biking in snowstorms, mountain biking drunk, and mountain biking on the heavy relics now enshrined in Crested Butte's Mountain Bike Museum.

Jacquie has worn an unusually conservative outfit for the occasion: olive corduroy jeans and a brown sweater; a few strands of her hair, shoulder-length now, are in a small braid on one side. Kelly recalls his early meetings with her—"This woman shows up on a [five-speed], with a basket, and flowers in the basket"—and notes that she often placed very well in an all-men's field. The audience reacts with approval, even idolatry.

There is an air of anticipation in the room as Jacquie, never one to disappoint, climbs onstage for her acceptance speech. She has decided, she explains later, to address the accusations of promiscuity head-on, with humor. "Gary Fisher introduced me to my husband, Charlie Cunningham," she says slowly into the microphone. "Fisher and I are long-standing exes. Which means I've slept with twenty percent of the inductees."

The audience explodes with laughter.

"Thirty," she adds, "if you count . . ."

More uproarious laughter.

". . . myself . . ."

She closes with her rallying cry, "Ladies, don't stay home!"

The success of women's sports will be measured neither in win-loss columns nor, let's hope, in dollar amounts. It's not a question of, Should sports be coed? Or, Are women as capable as men?

The partnership model points away from such either/or, yes/no thinking. What Jacquie Phelan is trying to do is both/and. She's playing with the men *and* creating a sports structure by and for women that, in a true show of partnership, does not exclude men. The WOMBATS—and her racing style—are competitive *and* cooperative. They are straight *and* gay. They search for personal excellence *and* are supportive of others.

Women need to compete with men on an equal footing *and* in certain sports under certain conditions they need special considerations, handicaps to compensate for lack of speed, upper body strength, or mere experience. We must encourage fitness trainers to stop assuming women don't want to "bulk up," *and* at the same time we must watch out that bodybuilding doesn't become yet another beauty trap.

We need to expand and develop the partnership model, the perception of sports as an opportunity for everyone, not just half of the players, to be victorious. We need rules that are inclusive, and we also need the right to go ahead and play by the traditional rules. We need money and fame and glory and the opportunities elite men have, including heroes—female heroes. And we need not only heroes who are prim and palatable; we should make room for the rebels and the radicals.

Can women enter the men's sports world not as cheerleaders but as leaders? Can both women and men search for saner, safer, more ethical methods of playing sports, beyond the ritualized violence of the military model?

We live in a heterogeneous world, and the integration of genders, races, and cultures potentially enriches all groups. Ideally, assimilated people don't just fit in but also transform the dominant culture by contributing their unique cultural wisdom and tradition. Professional football—the most visible illustration of the military model—shows no signs of partnership influence. But few athletes are pro football players. At the grass-roots level, men like Charlie Cunningham and tennis player Mark Otto have clearly recognized "the advantage to masculine character of comradeship with women who [are] as skilled and ingenious . . . as they." Bob Kersee, like other male coaches, is learning from women as well as teaching them.

Women's presence in weight rooms and gyms, like women's presence in boardrooms and bars, is subtly and insistently challenging men to see women as peers, and to adapt their playing style to what women want and need. By playing sports, women are challenged to see themselves not as the same as men but as equally entitled to define the nature of the games and the relationships between and among players.

After all, men change rules annually. Designated hitters, three-point field goals, and twelve-point tiebreakers are just a few of the ways baseball, basketball, and tennis have changed to suit the needs of players and fans. There's no reason sports—not just women's sports but all sports—shouldn't continue to evolve to suit the needs and desires of women.

There are times when it may make sense for women to retreat from the dominant culture in order to gain strength and confidence, learn leadership skills, and enjoy each other's company. Women still need organizations and events that address the specific concerns of women. But they must also compete—and cooperate—in the larger, public domain.

How they do this is the basic question. How do women play? Some mimic the military model, battling their way through competitions. Many women are good sports to a self-destructive degree, "good girls" who are too ready to be obediently beautiful, obediently silent, obediently skinny— whatever it takes to keep the recognition and opportunity coming. Some women do follow in men's sneakersteps, sacrificing personal and bodily integrity in exchange for sports rewards.

But despite the "female apologetic," most women do not seem corrupted by their integration into the male sports arena. Even when money and prestige are at stake, Jackie Joyner-Kersee, Susan Butcher, Vivian Stringer, and many other top female athletes and coaches view opponents not as barricades to success but as fellow travelers on the same journey. Like the cyclists of a century ago, Kitty Porterfield, Sydney Jacobs, Barbara Logan, Andra Chamberlin, and other recreational athletes embrace sports with the wisdom of outcasts and the gusto of beginners.

Perhaps because women know the experience of exclusion, they become sensitive to the exclusion of others. Perhaps because women have stood on the sidelines of the military model, they have seen most clearly its fallacy. Perhaps because women are acutely aware of their own vulnerability, the idea of tackling and potentially injuring others in the name of sports just doesn't have much appeal. Surely too, good sportswomanship is traceable to socialization: women are raised to think of others. There may be a biological component, but the fact that many male athletes do not subscribe to the military model is a reminder that biology, even if relevant, is not destiny.

Most women aren't choosing between coed and single-sex sports, or between ladylike and manlike behavior; instead, they're developing a sporting ethic that includes competition—"seeking together"—and making room for "wimps." It takes courage, but not the sacrificial, military sort. By taking their sports equipment and their sports ethics into the public sphere, women are sometimes changing the sports themselves and often the nature of the relationship between "opponents." In Vivian Stringer's words: *The playing of a game has to do with your feelings, your emotions, how you care about the people you're involved with.*

Sometimes women fail: they become greedy, break rules, recklessly injure themselves and others, and forget the spirit of the game. But often they succeed. They're joining the larger sports world without losing sight of their own values. Along the way they're making the ordinary athletic field a more caring, more sporting place to be.

We don't need to ask men to move over, says Susan Butcher. *We're just there. We just have to do it now.*

Says Jacquie Phelan: *Ladies, don't stay home.*

Notes

Playing with the Boys: An Introduction

1. *National Federation of State High School Associations 1989–1990 Handbook* (Kansas City, MO: National Federation of State High School Associations, 1989), p. 72.

2. R. Vivian Acosta and Linda Carpenter, "Women in Intercollegiate Sport: A Longitudinal Study—Thirteen Year Update 1977–1990." Unpublished paper. For more information, contact the authors at the Department of Physical Education, Brooklyn College, Brooklyn, NY 11210.

3. Anne Flannery, "Survey Shows Women Missing on Some Olympic Sports Boards," *Headway: Women's Sports Foundation Newsletter* (Summer 1989).

4. Estimate provided by the Association for Women in Sports Media, P.O. Box 355, Alameda, CA 94501.

5. Acosta and Carpenter.

6. Carole Oglesby, "Athleticism and Sex Role," a paper presented at the "New Agenda: A Blueprint for the Future of Women's Sports" conference (Washington, DC, Nov. 3–6, 1983); Carole Oglesby, "Women and Sport," in Jeffrey H. Goldstein, ed., *Sports, Games and Play* (Hillsdale, NJ: Lawrence Erlbaum Associates, 1989), p. 143.

7. Pete Axthelm with Pamela Abramson, "A Star Blazes in the Fast Lane," *Newsweek* (Sept. 19, 1988), p. 55.

8. For this phrase I am indebted to Riane Eisler, who in *The Chalice and the Blade: Our History, Our Future* (San Francisco: Harper & Row, 1987) uses "dominator model" (the ranking of one

half of humanity over the other) and "partnership model" ("the principle of linking, rather than ranking, [so] diversity is not equated with either inferiority or superiority") to characterize social organizations throughout history.

Others have used the phrases a "win-win" situation, "feminist sport," and "the feminization of sport" to describe the concept. But "win-win" reinforces the notion that winning is of paramount importance. "Feminist sport" and "the feminization of sport" can be misleading since some feminists ("liberal feminists") only want equal access to male-established sports, while others ("radical feminists") seek a new approach to those sports. Since a few men have helped create this alternative sports model and since many men would benefit from adopting it, I prefer a label that does not allude to gender.

9. Numerous writers have documented and discussed the abuses inherent in the military model. See Donald F. Sabo, Jr., and Ross Runfola, *Jock: Sports and Male Identity* (Englewood Cliffs, NJ: Prentice-Hall, 1980); Bruce Ogilvie and Thomas Tutko, "Sport: If You Want to Build Character, Try Something Else," *Psychology Today* (Oct. 1971); Mike Messner, "Sport, Men, and Masculinity," *Arena Review* 9, no. 2 (Nov. 1985); Rick Telander, *The Hundred Yard Lie* (New York: Simon & Schuster, 1989); and Alexander Wolff and Armen Keteyian, *Raw Recruits* (New York: Simon & Schuster, 1990).

10. Art Plotnik, "Hey Guys, Let's Keep Bowling Low-Tech," *The New York Times* (Jan. 21, 1989), p. 27.

11. Several feminist writers have made this distinction, among them Birgit Brock-Utne, *Feminist Perspectives on Peace and Peace Education* (New York: Pergamon Press, 1989), p. 145.

12. Carole Oglesby, "Women and Sport," in Jeffrey H. Goldstein, ed., *Sports, Games, and Play: Social and Psychological Viewpoints* (Hillsdale, NJ: Lawrence Erlbaum Associates, 1989), pp. 132–133.

13. Mike Plant, "The Swift Ascension of Kirsten Hanssen," *Outside* (Oct. 1988), p. 81.

14. Thanks to Carolyn Heilbrun for inspiring my thinking about the importance of women athletes playing sports in "the public domain." She wrote: "[Myra] Jehlen understands the hardest fact of all for women to admit and defend: that woman's selfhood, the right to her own story, depends upon her 'ability to act in the public

domain.' " Carolyn G. Heilbrun, *Writing a Woman's Life* (New York: Ballantine Books, 1988), p. 17, citing Myra Jehlen, "Archimedes and the Paradox of Feminist Criticism," *Signs* 6, no. 4 (1984), pp. 575–601.

Alone at First

1. Billie Jean King with Frank Deford, *Billie Jean* (New York: Viking, 1982), p. 12.

2. Julie Croteau was the first woman to play a full season of college baseball; another woman, reportedly, played a few innings.

3. Craig Neff, ed., "Diamond Pioneer," *Sports Illustrated,* March 27, 1989, p. 17.

4. Sylvia Pressler, hearing officer, ruling on the integration of Little League baseball, Hoboken, NJ, Nov. 7, 1973, cited in Suzanne Levine and Harriet Lyons, eds., *The Decade of Women: A* Ms. *History of the Seventies in Words and Pictures* (New York: Paragon, 1980), p. 65.

5. Helen Dewar, "Quenching the Senate's Endless Simmer on Nicaragua," *The Washington Post,* March 2, 1990, p. A16.

6. Amy Feldman, "Wrestling for Her Rights," *GO!,* Summer 1988, p. 7.

7. Sarah Lyall, "Truth Is, Says Team, She Scares You Guys," *The New York Times,* Nov. 11, 1988, p. B1.

8. Felicia E. Halpert, "Tempest in a Teacup," *Special Report on Sports,* Aug.–Oct. 1989, p. 21.

9. Beth Balsley with Patricia Freeman, "Believe It or Not—Beth's Back for More," *Women's Sports and Fitness,* Sept. 1986, p. 86.

10. Jack Murray, "Female Right Wing Hit Liberally," *USA Today,* Dec. 20, 1988, p. 2C.

11. Michelle Brooks, "Boy Meets Girl, Girl Meets Boy, Helmet Meets Helmet," *The Washington Post,* Aug. 31, 1989, p. C3.

12. David Streitfeld, "Girls in Sports: No Contest," *The Washington Post,* April 8, 1988, p. D5.

13. Gary Smith, "She Who Laughs Last," *Sports Illustrated,* May 22, 1989, p. 89.

14. According to the new MPBA, the name change was due to its move to Akron, Ohio, where it would have been confused with the Professional Bowlers Association.

15. *National Federation of State High School Associations 1989–1990 Handbook* (Kansas City, MO: National Federation of State High School Associations, 1989), pp. 72, 83.

Staggered Starts

1. Adrianne Blue, *Faster, Higher, Further: Women's Triumphs and Disasters at the Olympics* (London: Virago, 1988), p. 139.
2. Harvey Lauer, *1988 American Sports Analysis Study* (conducted by American Sports Data, Hartsdale, NY, 1988).
3. Roberta S. Bennett, K. Gail Whitaker, Nina Jo Woolley Smith, and Anne Sablove, "Changing the Rules of the Game: Reflections Toward a Feminist Analysis of Sport," *Women's Studies International Forum* 10, no. 4 (1987), pp. 369–379.
4. *National Federation of State High School Associations 1989–1990 Handbook* (Kansas City, MO: National Federation of State High School Associations, 1989), p. 72.
5. Iris Marion Young, "Throwing Like a Girl: A Phenomenology of Feminine Body Comportment, Mobility and Spatiality," *Human Studies* 3 (1980), p. 143.
6. Some women have told me that since becoming mothers, they find themselves more cautious in their play, aware of their responsibility to their children and no longer willing to risk life or limb for the sake of sport. I'd be interested to see this matter explored further.
7. Young, p. 144.
8. Linda Bunker, "Physiological Factors Affecting Girls in Sports." Paper presented at the annual meeting of the Women's Sports Foundation (San Francisco, Jan. 1989).
9. Ibid.
10. Ibid.
11. John Crothers Pollock, *The Miller Lite Report on Women in Sports* (conducted for the Women's Sports Foundation by New World Decisions, Iselin, NJ, 1985).
12. Elizabeth A. Garfield, *The Wilson Report: Moms, Dads, Daughters and Sports* (conducted for the Women's Sports Foundation by Diagnostic Research, Los Angeles, 1988).
13. Bennett et al., p. 376.

14. Lauer.

15. Bennett et al., p. 376.

I Never Thought a Woman Could Go This Fast

1. Diane Ackerman, *On Extended Wings* (New York: Atheneum, 1985), pp. 54–55.

2. Donna de Varona, *McDonald's Sportswomen of the Year*, ESPN, Oct. 21, 1988.

3. Ruth M. Sparhawk, Mary E. Leslie, Phyllis V. Turbow, and Zina R. Rose, *American Women in Sport, 1887–1987: A 100-Year Chronology* (Metuchen, NJ: Scarecrow, 1989), p. 14.

4. De Varona.

5. Helen Lenskyj, *Out of Bounds: Women, Sport, & Sexuality* (Toronto: Women's Press, 1986), p. 144.

6. Sharron Hannon, "Women in Sports," *The Main Event*, Aug. 1988, p. 60.

7. John Skow, "The Long and Short of It," *Time*, Sept. 19, 1988, p. 58.

8. C. J. Olivares, Jr., "From the Editors," *Triathlete*, Jan. 1989, p. 4.

We Are the Best

1. The race alternates between a northern and southern route, each more than 1,000 miles. According to Nicki J. Nielsen in *The Iditarod: Women on the Trail* (Anchorage, AK: Wolfdog, 1986), it is billed as a 1,049-mile race to indicate the approximate distance and to represent Alaska, the forty-ninth state. Legend has it that the town of Iditarod was named by gold prospectors who, proud of having dug sixteen feet—a rod—in a day, would proclaim, "I did a rod."

2. Doug Smith, "Celebrated Capriati, 13, Debuts Today," *USA Today*, March 6, 1990, p. 2C.

3. Donna de Varona, *McDonald's Sportswomen of the Year*, ESPN, Oct. 21, 1988.

4. Adrianne Blue, *Grace Under Pressure: The Emergence of Women in Sport* (London: Sidgwick & Jackson, 1987), pp. 90–91.

5. Ibid., p. 91.

6. Ibid.

7. Susan Trausch, "Call of the Wild," *The Boston Globe Magazine*, Oct. 18, 1987, p. 48.

8. Gary Smith, "She Who Laughs," *Sports Illustrated*, March 23, 1989, p. 88.

9. Chris Evert, as told to Curry Kirkpatrick, *Sports Illustrated*, Aug. 28, 1989.

10. Robert F. Jones, "Man's Best Friends," *Sports Illustrated*, March 23, 1989, pp. 40–47.

Different Strokes

1. Marilyn French, *Beyond Power: On Women, Men, and Morals* (London: Abacus, 1986), pp. 479–480.

2. Riane Eisler's *The Chalice and the Blade: Our History, Our Future* (San Francisco: Harper & Row, 1987) presents compelling evidence for the existence of an ancient era neither patriarchal nor matriarchal, when women and their life-giving abilities were revered.

3. Jaquetta Hawkes, *Dawn of the Gods: Minoan and Mycenaean Origins of Greece* (New York: Random House, 1968), p. 124.

4. Lee Green, *Sportswit* (New York: Harper & Row, 1984), p. 241.

5. Don Sabo, "Sport, Patriarchy, and Male Identity: New Questions About Men and Sport," *Arena Review* 9, no. 2 (Nov. 1985), p. 23.

6. John Crothers Pollock, *The Miller Lite Report on Women in Sports* (conducted for the Women's Sports Foundation by New World Decisions, Iselin, NJ, 1985).

7. Ibid.

8. Betty Hicks, "How to Play with Men," *womenSports*, June 1976, p. 23.

9. Susan Birrell, "Separatism as an Issue in Women's Sport." Presentation at the "Feminism and Sport: Continuity and Change" workshop of the "Women as Leaders in Physical Education" conference (Iowa City, University of Iowa, 1983).

10. Pollock.

11. Susan Okie, "Prize in Playing Not to Win," *The Washington Post*, April 3, 1989, p. A2.

12. Ibid.

You Can't Just Be Muscular

1. Scott Bradfield, *The History of Luminous Motion* (New York: Knopf, 1989), p. 88.

2. Jan Felshin, "The Triple Option for Women in Sport," *Quest* 21 (1974), p. 36.

3. Patricia Del Rey, "The Apologetic and Women in Sport," in Carole A. Oglesby, ed., *Women and Sport: from Myth to Reality* (Philadelphia: Lea & Febiger, 1978), pp. 107–111.

4. Charles Gaines and George Butler, *Pumping Iron II: The Unprecedented Woman* (New York: Simon & Schuster, 1984).

5. Laura Dayton, "What Price Glory?," *Women's Sports and Fitness*, March 1990, p. 53.

Running Scared

1. Bureau of Justice Statistics, *Lifetime Likelihood of Victimization* (Washington, DC: Government Printing Office, March 1987).

2. David Gelman with Peter McKillop, "Going 'Wilding' in the City," *Newsweek*, May 8, 1989, p. 65.

3. Letty Cottin Pogrebin, "Boys Will Be Boys?," *Ms.*, Sept. 1989, p. 24.

4. Phoebe Jones, "Resources for Women's Fitness and Sports." Paper presented at the "New Agenda: A Blueprint for the Future of Women's Sports" conference (Washington, DC, Nov. 3–6, 1983).

5. Ibid.

6. Barbara Logan and I met in first grade and have been friends ever since.

7. Pete Shields, *Guns Don't Die, People Do* (New York: Arbor House, 1981).

8. Copies of "Women Running Smart" or information about the videotape of the Women's Safety Summit can be obtained by sending a stamped, self-addressed envelope to the RRCA national office, 629 South Washington Street, Alexandria, VA 22314.

9. William Dunnett, "The Rape Threat," *Runner's World*, June 1981, p. 55.

10. For more information, send a stamped, self-addressed envelope to Project Safe Run, 2226 Fairmount Boulevard, Eugene, OR 97403.

11. Catharine A. MacKinnon, *Feminism Unmodified: Discourses on Life and Law* (Cambridge, MA: Harvard University Press, 1987), p. 118.

12. *The Sourcebook of Criminal Justice Statistics* (Washington, DC: Government Printing Office, U.S. Department of Justice, Bureau of Justice Statistics, 1987).

13. Nancy M. Henley, *Body Politics* (Englewood Cliffs, NJ: Prentice-Hall, 1977), p. 149.

14. Susan Brownmiller, *Femininity* (New York: Linden/Simon & Schuster, 1984), p. 201.

15. For more on this topic, see Donald F. Sabo, Jr., and Ross Runfola, *Jock: Sports and Male Identity* (Englewood Cliffs, NJ: Prentice-Hall, 1980), pp. 113–157; and Don Sabo, "Pigskin, Patriarchy and Pain," *Changing Men,* Summer 1986, pp. 24–25.

16. Raleigh Mayer, "Dead Women Don't Run," *New York Running News,* Dec. 1988/Jan. 1989, p. 8.

17. Jerry Kirshenbaum, "An American Disgrace," *Sports Illustrated,* Feb. 27, 1989, p. 17.

18. Harvey Lauer, *1988 American Sports Analysis Study* (conducted by American Sports Data, Hartsdale, NY, 1988).

A Silence So Loud It Screams

1. Billie Jean King with Frank Deford, *Billie Jean* (New York: Viking, 1982), p. 26.

2. John Crothers Pollock, *The Miller Lite Report on Women in Sports* (conducted for the Women's Sports Foundation by New World Decisions, Iselin, NJ, 1985).

3. Dwight Chapin, "Bias Lingers in Sports," *San Francisco Examiner,* June 24, 1989 (Special Report: Gay in America), p. 57.

4. Pat Griffin, "How Can a Female Sports Performer Avoid, Diminish, or Disarm Threats to Her Own Sense of Femininity?" Paper presented at the "New Agenda: A Blueprint for the Future of Women's Sports" conference (Washington, DC, Nov. 3–6, 1983).

5. Frank Deford, *Big Bill Tilden: The Triumphs and the Tragedy* (New York: Simon & Schuster, 1975), pp. 218–219.

6. Elizabeth A. Garfield, *The Wilson Report: Moms, Dads, Daughters and Sports* (conducted for the Women's Sports Foundation by Diagnostic Research, Los Angeles, 1988).

7. Thanks to Doris Corbett, Howard University professor and president of the American Alliance for Health, Physical Education, Recreation, and Dance, for this example.

8. JoAnn Loulan with Mariah Burton Nelson, *Lesbian Passion* (San Francisco: Spinsters/Aunt Lute, 1987), p. 35.

9. Chapin, p. 57.

10. Michele Kort, "Ms. Conversation," *Ms.*, Feb. 1988, pp. 61–62.

11. Anonymous, "Admissions of Mortality: The Pleasures and Problems of Lesbian Athletes," in Marcy Adelman, ed., *Long Time Passing: The Lives of Older Lesbians* (Boston: Alyson, 1986), p. 69.

12. Brenda G. Pitts, "Leagues of Their Own: Organized Responses to Sport Homophobia." Paper presented at the American Alliance for Health, Physical Education, Recreation and Dance Annual Convention (Boston, April 19–23, 1989).

13. Yvonne Zipter, *Diamonds Are a Dyke's Best Friend* (Ithaca, NY: Firebrand, 1988), p. 13.

Who's Running the Show?

1. Merrie A. Fidler, "The All-American Girls' Baseball League, 1943–1954," in Reet Howell, ed., *Her Story in Sport: A Historical Anthology of Women in Sports* (West Point, NY: Leisure, 1982), pp. 595–598.

2. R. Vivian Acosta and Linda Carpenter, "Women in Intercollegiate Sport: A Longitudinal Study—Thirteen Year Update 1977–1990." Unpublished paper. For more information, contact the authors at the Department of Physical Education, Brooklyn College, Brooklyn, NY 11210.

3. Ibid.

4. Ibid.

5. Anita DeFrantz, "The Sky Is the Limit," *Headway: Women's Sports Foundation Newsletter*, Summer 1989.

6. B. L. Parkhouse and J. M. Williams, "Differential Effects of Sex and Status on Evaluation of Coaching Ability," *Research Quarterly for Exercise and Sport* 57 (1986), pp. 53–59.

7. Jay J. Coakley and Patricia L. Pacey, "How Female Athletes Perceive Coaches," *Journal of Physical Education, Recreation, and Dance,* Feb. 1982, pp. 54–56.

8. Susan Molstad and Gail Whitaker, "Perceptions of Female Basketball Players Regarding Coaching Qualities of Males and Females," *Journal of Applied Research in Coaching and Athletics,* Jan. 1987, pp. 57–71.

9. Beverly A. Forbes, "Why It's Women's Leadership That Best Fits the 1990s." Paper presented at the "Leadership Washington" conference (Seattle University, Sept. 13, 1989).

10. Charol Shakeshaft, "A Gender at Risk," *Women in Education,* March 1986, p. 503.

11. For more information about the American Coaching Effectiveness Program, call (800) 747-4457 or write ACEP, PO Box 5076, Champaign, IL 61820.

12. Acosta and Carpenter.

13. Annelies Knoppers, Barbara Bedker Meyer, Marty Ewing, and Linda Forrest, "The Structure of Athletic Obstacles to Women's Involvement in Coaching." Paper presented at the annual forum of the Council of Collegiate Women Athletic Administrators (Washington, DC, Sept. 17–19, 1989).

14. Ibid.

15. Ibid.

16. Nina Killham, "A Washington Life," *The Washington Post Magazine,* Jan. 14, 1990, pp. 24–27.

New Wave: Partnership in Action

1. Susan Birrell and Diana M. Richter, "Is a Diamond Forever? Feminist Transformations of Sport," *Women's Studies International Forum* 10, no. 4 (1987), p. 407.

2. Phoebe Jones, "Resources for Women's Fitness and Sports." Paper presented at the "New Agenda: A Blueprint for the Future of Women's Sports" conference (Washington, DC, Nov. 3–6, 1983).

3. Steve Wieberg, "Knee Deep in Injuries, Women Ask Why," *USA Today,* Feb. 3, 1988, p. 4C.

4. Robert Gardner, *The Art of Body Surfing* (Philadelphia: Chilton, 1972), p. 1.

5. James A. Michener, *Sports in America* (New York: Ballantine, 1976), p. 533.

6. Birrell and Richter, p. 403.

7. Martina Navratilova with George Vecsey, *Martina* (New York: Knopf, 1985), p. 270.

Together at Last

1. Stephanie Twin, *Out of the Bleachers: Writings on Women and Sport* (Old Westbury, NY: The Feminist Press, 1979), p. 104.

2. Sidney H. Aronson, "The Sociology of the Bicycle," in Marcello Truzzi, ed., *Sociology and Everyday Life* (Englewood Cliffs, NJ: Prentice-Hall, 1968), pp. 293–303.

3. Barbara J. Mitchell, "When the Wheels Began to Turn," *Women's Sports and Fitness*, March 1987, p. 14.

4. Aronson, pp. 294–296.

5. Ibid., p. 296.

6. Hugh J. Delehanty, "The Blooming of Bicycling," *Women's Sports and Fitness*, Aug. 1981, p. 14.

7. For more information about the WOMBATS, send a stamped, self-addressed envelope to Jacquie Phelan, 121 Wood Lane, Fairfax, CA 94930.

Index

About the Author

MARIAH BURTON NELSON was raised in Blue Bell, Pennsylvania, graduated from Stanford University, and has a master's in public health from San Jose State University. She played basketball (center) for Stanford, for a French professional team, and for the New Jersey Gems of the Women's Pro Basketball League. Nelson has been a columnist for *The Washington Post* and an editor for *Women's Sports and Fitness* magazine. Her work has also appeared in the *Los Angeles Times, Ms., Vogue, Working Woman, Golf Illustrated,* and several other magazines and newspapers. Her play *Out of Bounds* was published in *Places Please* and has been produced in eight cities in the United States and Canada. In 1988, Nelson won the Miller Lite Women's Sports Journalism Award. She lives in Arlington, Virginia.